"As a highly experienced and capable leader, Brad has captured both the essence of and the challenges associated with principalship. *From Burnout to Breakthrough* is a powerful, heartfelt guide that transforms personal struggle into a practical framework for sustainable leadership. Brad blends lived experience, neuroscience, and comprehensive strategies to help leaders move from exhaustion to professional growth. His RESET model provides a clear pathway for personal and professional growth and self-care.

When all the evidence we have suggests principalship is more challenging than ever before, this book is both timely and highly relevant. It is honest, insightful, and deeply validating - a must-read for anyone ready to lead with resilience, compassion, and heart."

Phil Schultz, President, Australian Catholic Primary Principals Association

"Brad's book is a rare and courageous look at leadership burnout, its warning signs, its impact, and the path back to joy. With honesty, practical strategies, and thought-provoking questions, he reminds us burnout is not a personal failure but an organisational issue. This is essential reading for leaders who want to thrive, not just survive."

Angelka Falkenberg, President, Australian Primary Principals Association

"*From Burnout to Breakthrough* is a thoughtful contribution by Brad as both a former principal and advocate, offering a practical, research-informed guide drawn from real-world leadership. In an era where education leaders face intensifying psychosocial demands, his work stands as a hopeful, user-friendly resource, not just for those under strain, but for those already thriving, reminding us all that self-preservation is a noble discipline in service to others. With universal value that extends beyond schools into all enterprises, Brad's reflections are both timely and timeless."

Toby Ford, Founder, Ford Health

"*From Burnout to Breakthrough: The Leadership Reset* by Brad Gaynor is an essential guide for leaders seeking to overcome burnout and restore effective leadership. Grounded in neuroscience, emotional intelligence, and practical strategies, Gaynor's framework - Recognition, Reflection, Realignment, and Reinvention - provides a clear path to recovery. This book is honest, accessible, and a must-read for those dedicated to leading with renewed purpose and balance."

Michael Boots, Educational Leader

"*From Burnout to Breakthrough* is an inspiring and practical guide for today's educational leaders who want to transform challenge into opportunity. With clarity, compassion, and unflinching honesty, it offers a roadmap from exhaustion to genuine renewal. This is more than a book - it's a call to action to prioritise our wellbeing so we can lead with purpose, hope, and resilience. Engaging, insightful, and deeply encouraging, it empowers leaders to reimagine their role, nurture themselves, and create a thriving, future-focused culture in their schools."

Michael Gray, President, Victorian Association of Catholic Primary Principals (VACPSP)

"Brad has woven personal insight with evidence-based tools and strategies, making it accessible, actionable, and full of heart. His framework provides a roadmap for leaders who want to sustain their performance and their wellbeing. As someone passionate about positive psychology, emotional intelligence, and creating thriving workplaces, I believe in the science behind this book. It is a valuable reminder that leadership is about leading with balance, empathy, and resilience. Brad offers leaders hope, clarity, and a path to thrive."

Sue Langley, CEO and Founder, Langley Group

"This book cuts through the noise with a brutally honest account of leadership burnout, recovery, and proactive prevention. Brad Gaynor courageously shares his lived experiences, while weaving in research on emotional intelligence and organisational change that every leader needs to hear. This book doesn't just name the problem, it sets a clear course for leaders to reset and lead with clarity, courage, and care."

Nathaniel Swain, Instructional Coach

FROM BURNOUT TO BREAKTHROUGH

From Burnout to Breakthrough is the ultimate guide for leaders striving to balance personal wellbeing with professional success in today's demanding world.

As leadership roles grow more complex and relentless, the toll on mental health, emotional resilience, and organisational effectiveness is undeniable. This groundbreaking book offers a fresh, practical approach to overcoming burnout, fostering resilience, and redefining leadership through a wellbeing-centred lens. Written by an experienced leader who has faced burnout firsthand, this book goes beyond theory to deliver actionable insights, tools, and strategies that leaders can implement immediately. You'll learn how to recognise the early warning signs of burnout, harness emotional intelligence, integrate life-first leadership practices, and create a supportive organisational culture that prioritises wellbeing without compromising results. Each phase of the leadership reset is accompanied by complementary worksheets, templates, trackers, and exercises.

With engaging case studies from leading companies, cutting-edge neuroscience, and the step-by-step Leadership Reset Framework, From Burnout to Breakthrough equips readers with the knowledge and confidence to transform leadership fatigue into sustainable growth and impact.

Brad Gaynor is a seasoned educational leader with over 35 years of experience, including 25 in school leadership. As a school performance and development leader, he champions leadership development, evidence-based practices, and school improvement. An award-winning principal and accredited coach, Brad advocates for resilient, adaptive leadership, and transformative education.

FROM BURNOUT TO BREAKTHROUGH

The Leadership Reset

Brad Gaynor

Designed cover image: Getty Images

First published 2026
by Routledge
4 Park Square, Milton Park, Abingdon, Oxon OX14 4RN

and by Routledge
605 Third Avenue, New York, NY 10158

Routledge is an imprint of the Taylor & Francis Group, an informa business

© 2026 Brad Gaynor

The right of Brad Gaynor to be identified as author of this work has been asserted in accordance with sections 77 and 78 of the Copyright, Designs and Patents Act 1988.

All rights reserved. No part of this book may be reprinted or reproduced or utilised in any form or by any electronic, mechanical, or other means, now known or hereafter invented, including photocopying and recording, or in any information storage or retrieval system, without permission in writing from the publishers.

For Product Safety Concerns and Information please contact our EU representative GPSR@taylorandfrancis.com. Taylor & Francis Verlag GmbH, Kaufingerstraße 24, 80331 München, Germany.

Trademark notice: Product or corporate names may be trademarks or registered trademarks, and are used only for identification and explanation without intent to infringe.

British Library Cataloguing-in-Publication Data
A catalogue record for this book is available from the British Library

Library of Congress Cataloging-in-Publication Data
Names: Gaynor, Brad author
Title: From burnout to breakthrough : the leadership reset / Brad Gaynor.
Description: Abingdon, Oxon ; New York, NY : Routledge, 2026. | Includes bibliographical references and index.
Identifiers: LCCN 2025029429 (print) | LCCN 2025029430 (ebook) | ISBN 9781041132073 hardback | ISBN 9781041132066 paperback | ISBN 9781003668626 ebook
Subjects: LCSH: Burn out (Psychology) | Work-life balance | Leadership
Classification: LCC BF481 .G335 2026 (print) | LCC BF481 (ebook)
LC record available at https://lccn.loc.gov/2025029429
LC ebook record available at https://lccn.loc.gov/2025029430

ISBN: 9781041132073 (hbk)
ISBN: 9781041132066 (pbk)
ISBN: 9781003668626 (ebk)

DOI: 10.4324/9781003668626

Typeset in Joanna
by codeMantra

CONTENTS

About the Author ix
Foreword x
Toby Ford
Preface xii
Author's Note xv

Introduction: Why Leadership Burnout Matters 1

Part 1: Understanding the Challenge 5

1 What Is Leadership Burnout? Understanding the Warning Signs 7

2 Types of Burnout in Leadership 27

3 Life Before Work: The Foundation of Sustainable Leadership 44

4 The Neuroscience of Leadership Burnout: How the Brain Reacts to Stress 60

5 The Cost of Leadership Burnout: Impact on Organisational Success and Financial Stability 73

Part 2: The Leadership Reset Framework — 85

6 Introduction to the Leadership Reset Framework — 87

7 Phase 1 – Recognition: Recognising the Breaking Point — 102

8 Phase 2 – Reflection: Gaining Clarity Through Self Awareness — 115

9 Phase 3 – Realignment: Setting Clear Boundaries and Priorities — 127

10 Phase 4 – Reinvention: Adopting a New Leadership Approach — 136

Part 3: Organisation Solutions — 149

11 Organisational Solutions: How Organisations Can Prevent Leadership Burnout — 151

12 Leadership Burnout in Hybrid and Remote Work Environments — 166

13 Building Resilient Leadership Teams: Peer Support and Shared Leadership Models — 180

14 Building a Resilient Leadership Pipeline: Preventing Burnout in Future Leaders — 196

Conclusion: Embracing a Wellbeing First Approach to Leadership — 211

Epilogue: I Didn't Set Out to Write a Book — 217
References — 219
Tools and Templates — 228
Index — 277

ABOUT THE AUTHOR

Brad Gaynor is an accomplished leadership coach, performance and development leader, and former school principal with a passion for transforming leadership practices. With decades of experience leading multiple schools and mentoring fellow leaders, Brad brings a wealth of insight into the complexities and demands of high pressure leadership roles. His personal journey through burnout and recovery has shaped his mission to redefine leadership success by prioritising resilience, emotional intelligence, and wellbeing.

Brad combines evidence-based strategies with personal experience to empower leaders to thrive sustainably, avoiding the pitfalls of chronic stress and emotional exhaustion. He is committed to fostering leadership models that prioritise balance, wellbeing, and long term impact. Through his coaching, writing, and speaking, Brad continues to inspire leaders at all levels to embrace a healthier, more fulfilling approach to leadership.

FOREWORD

I first met Brad in his role as an advocate for principals in education. I quickly learnt of his passion and deep interest in representing colleagues to ensure their voices were heard. At the time, we at Ford Health were a small enterprise embarking on our own journey to understand and support the incredible work that education leaders set out to do each day, actively balancing the needs of all, while privately shouldering the anxieties that come with knowing you can't help everyone, and that compromise is inevitable.

How that compromise is managed, internally, privately, and effectively, has been the subject of many old and new books, each offering a twist of something unique and special.

Through the countless dialogue exchanges our team has had with education leaders, it became clear that a new wave of demands has emerged, particularly since COVID, with all its influences over psychosocial threats to daily living standards. Leaders are now asked to oversee and adjudicate the rights of individuals in ways that can, at times, overshadow the benefits of the collective. This is where relationship friction becomes daily tinder – quick to flare and exhausting to manage.

I've often been asked how to offer simple, effective interventions to address burnout. From our work, we know that leaders in any enterprise who operate within a *harmonious passion* framework tend to cope better.

Meanwhile, those with a razor-sharp, obsessive focus on delivering their role — at the expense of family, connection, and wellbeing — suffer the greatest burnout.

And yet, there is cause for optimism. We can recognise a message of hope: not all education leaders are falling like flies. In fact, a significant proportion are doing very well. Their "Ford Health Wellbeing Index", as we call it, is strong. And yet even these leaders can read Brad's reflections and still benefit from it. This is because his message is not just about rescue; it's about reinforcement. Reinforcing the systems and habits that keep people well.

With thoughtful caution, Brad has set out to convey in practical terms lessons from his own experience, underpinned by solid research recognised by others. It is delivered with a touch of old-school principal discipline. The result is a user-friendly playbook that I believe not only education leaders should take time to read, but also leaders across all enterprises. Perhaps it's best approached with a quiet moment, a cup of something warm, and without the invasion of electronic gadgetry, allowing the back half of the brain to digest and incorporate these ideas into daily practice.

Good luck — I hope you enjoy this read as much as I have.

Dr Toby Ford, Founder, Ford Health

PREFACE

Leadership has always been demanding, but I never fully understood the personal cost until I experienced it firsthand. Like many leaders, I believed that pushing through stress was simply part of the job. The warning signs were there, irritability, disrupted sleep, growing cynicism, difficulty concentrating, but I chose to ignore them. Every day, I put on a mask and pushed through, determined to keep going.

It would take me a few more incidents, ones that I'll detail in the book, to realise that I was dealing with burnout and it wasn't something I could simply power through.

When I learnt about burnout and did more research into it, I felt like I finally understood what was happening to me. The reality hit home completely during a routine check-up with my GP. When I asked what "MDD" meant – a term he'd used repeatedly during a prescription call – his response left me speechless: major depressive disorder.

Hearing a clinical diagnosis, one that suggested a profound psychological impact rather than simply being overworked, forced me to confront the gravity of what had happened. I wasn't just tired; my mental health had been fundamentally affected.

This diagnosis was not just a label; it was validation. It confirmed that what I had experienced was not a personal failing or a lack of resilience, but a legitimate medical condition. More importantly, it meant there was a pathway forward, one based on understanding rather than denial.

The clarity shifted everything. I began to understand that burnout had not only eroded my health, but had also blurred my ability to see what was happening to me. I realised I was not alone, that many leaders are walking the same path, mistaking burnout for ordinary pressure until it is too late.

That understanding eventually led me to write this book. It became clear that burnout was not just a personal struggle, but a leadership crisis, one that many face without fully recognising its implications. From Burnout to Breakthrough: The Leadership Reset was born from both personal experience and a desire to help others avoid the same fate. I want to share the practical tools and strategies I have gathered along the way to help leaders recognise burnout before it spirals out of control.

The pages that follow will explore the key symptoms of burnout – physical exhaustion, emotional detachment, reduced performance – and offer concrete steps to address them. This book is about resetting leadership to foster resilience, wellbeing, and sustainability. It challenges the traditional notion that leadership is about pushing through stress at all costs. Instead, I believe it's about developing a leadership model that balances high performance with personal wellbeing. Leadership that prioritises empathy, emotional intelligence, and mental health is not only more effective but also more sustainable.

While my own experience of burnout became severe enough to be diagnosed as major depressive disorder, this book does not aim to explore mental illness from a clinical perspective. My focus is on burnout, what it looks like in leadership, why we often miss it, and how we can recover and reset before the consequences become unmanageable.

If you're feeling overwhelmed, exhausted, or unsure how to maintain balance in your leadership role, this book is for you. It's a reminder that burnout doesn't have to be inevitable, and it certainly doesn't have to define your leadership journey. By recognising the signs early and taking proactive steps, you can reset your approach and lead with renewed energy, focus, and purpose.

As you read, I hope you find inspiration and practical advice to guide your own leadership reset. Whether you're a seasoned leader or just beginning your journey, the insights and strategies in this book can help you redefine leadership into something fulfilling, sustainable, and impactful.

This book is intentionally practical and concise. I know from experience that when you're deep in stress or nearing burnout, you don't have the time or headspace for long theory. You need clarity, compassion, and something you can use. Each chapter is designed to be accessible, grounded in research, and immediately useful whether you're reading with a pen in hand or catching a moment between meetings.

Together, we can move beyond burnout and towards a new model of leadership – one that enables us to thrive, rather than just survive.

AUTHOR'S NOTE

This book represents my personal views and opinions of wellbeing, and does not necessarily reflect the positions or opinions of any organisation, institution, or individual with which I am affiliated.

Additionally, while this book provides educational information about leadership burnout, it is not intended as medical or psychological advice. If you are experiencing persistent symptoms described in this chapter, particularly depression, anxiety, or thoughts of self harm, please consult with qualified healthcare professionals. The assessment tools and strategies presented are for general guidance only and do not replace professional diagnosis or treatment.

INTRODUCTION

WHY LEADERSHIP BURNOUT MATTERS

Leadership is often associated with power, influence, and success. It's easy to imagine that those in leadership roles have everything under control – that they are driving innovation, making crucial decisions, and leading their organisations towards growth. But what we often fail to acknowledge is the hidden cost of leadership: burnout.

In today's rapidly evolving world, the demands on leaders have grown exponentially. Leaders are expected to navigate constant change, manage complex teams, and deliver results, all while maintaining emotional intelligence, resilience, and a sense of personal balance. For many, this combination of pressures leads to one outcome – burnout.

Leadership burnout is not just about feeling tired or overworked. It is a state of emotional, physical, and mental exhaustion caused by prolonged stress. When burnout takes hold, it robs leaders of their energy, creativity, and purpose, eroding decision making abilities, diminishing emotional resilience, and ultimately compromising both personal wellbeing and organisational success.

The COVID-19 pandemic further intensified these pressures, acting as a global stress test for leadership. Leaders were often expected to be constantly available, emotionally stable, and digitally connected, all while navigating crisis-level decision making without access to their usual support systems. Now, in a post-pandemic context, leadership requires recalibration. This new reality demands a more human centred model – one that places sustainability, reflection, and personal wellbeing at the forefront of effective leadership design (Spataro, 2022a).

Why does this matter? Because when leaders burn out, it doesn't just affect them – it impacts their families, teams, their organisations, and the broader communities they serve. A burnt out leader is less able to inspire or guide their team effectively, leading to disengaged employees, decreased productivity, and a workplace culture that values output over wellbeing.

The real danger is that burnout often goes unnoticed or is accepted as part of the leadership experience. Many leaders see it as a badge of honour, proof of their dedication. But burnout is not a sign of strength; it's a signal that something has gone wrong.

This book offers a roadmap for that reset. Through the Leadership Reset Framework, we will explore steps to recognise burnout's early signs, reflect on values, realign actions, and reinvent leadership in a way that supports both personal wellbeing and professional success.

I've designed this journey around what I call the RESET approach – not just a roadmap for recovering from burnout, but a foundation for reimagining leadership itself. RESET captures the full arc of meaningful change:

Recognise the signs and cost of burnout
Explore what matters most through self awareness and reflection
Shift your leadership habits and priorities
Embed new ways of leading
Thrive as both a leader and human being

While RESET is introduced here as a response to burnout, it has the potential to become something more: a universal blueprint for any leader seeking to reset, realign, and lead with greater purpose, balance, and impact. The four phases of this book are grounded in this framework – **Recognition**,

Reflection, **Realignment**, and **Reinvention** – and we will explore them throughout the book.

By understanding why burnout matters, we open the door to a new kind of leadership – one that embraces emotional intelligence, resilience, and life work integration. Whether you are already experiencing burnout or seeking ways to avoid it, this book will provide tools and strategies to lead with renewed energy, focus, and purpose. Burnout may be a challenge, but it is also an opportunity for growth and transformation. Together, let's move from burnout to breakthrough.

Part 1

UNDERSTANDING THE CHALLENGE

1

WHAT IS LEADERSHIP BURNOUT?

UNDERSTANDING THE WARNING SIGNS

Overview

Leadership burnout has emerged as a pervasive issue across industries – corporate environments, education, healthcare, and technology. For years, the demands of leadership have been equated with resilience and unrelenting dedication, yet this mindset often pushes leaders to their breaking points.

I didn't realise I was burning out until it was too late. Like many leaders, I chalked up the exhaustion, irritability, and sleepless nights to the pressures of the role. What I failed to see were the warning signs that my body and mind were overwhelmed by chronic stress. My experience was not unique, as research increasingly shows that leaders face disproportionate rates of burnout, often leaving them emotionally depleted and physically unwell.

This chapter explores the nature of leadership burnout, the differences between burnout and ordinary stress, its wide ranging symptoms, and the organisational and neurological factors that contribute to it. By recognising the signs early, leaders can take proactive steps to prevent burnout and protect their wellbeing.

DOI: 10.4324/9781003668626-3

Recognising the Symptoms: My Personal Experience

Most people would have had no idea this was going on. Outwardly, I was still showing up, still performing, still doing the work. But behind the scenes, burnout was slowly touching every part of my life.

Burnout does not announce itself loudly. It creeps in gradually, disguised as the natural demands of leadership, until it becomes impossible to tell where the role ends and the suffering begins. Looking back, I can now see how it unfolded across every part of my life, creating a slow, silent collapse I did not recognise at the time.

My body started sending signals long before I listened. I was constantly exhausted, no matter how much rest I tried to get. Sleep became elusive. I would lie awake with racing thoughts, then wake more tired than when I had gone to bed. Tension headaches became regular companions. At the time, I convinced myself it was just part of the job.

Then came the mental fog. My decision making dulled. Tasks that once came easily started feeling overwhelming. I would read the same sentence repeatedly and still not take it in. Conversations slipped out of memory halfway through. Creative thinking, which had always been a strength, felt out of reach. And the more I felt my performance was slipping, the more pressure I felt – which only made things worse.

The most difficult part to admit was the shift in how I felt. That familiar sense of purpose started to fade. I no longer registered the wins. Minor setbacks felt enormous. I became more cynical and started questioning work I had once felt passionate about. I was irritable, reactive, and eventually numb. It felt like I was watching my motivation and joy dissolve in slow motion.

I began to withdraw. I avoided conversations that might expose how much I was struggling. Meetings that used to energise me became just another thing to get through. I found myself less present, less patient, less able to truly listen. I reached for unhealthy coping strategies – a drink became a nightly habit, not for pleasure but to quiet my mind. I abandoned exercise and stopped paying attention to what I was eating. I was just trying to get through the day.

At work, it still looked like I was coping. I kept showing up, kept delivering, kept meeting expectations. From the outside, there were no obvious signs. But on the inside, something had shifted. The projects that once energised me now felt heavy. I was no longer leading with vision or creativity – I was just surviving. I could feel the difference, even if no one else could. My leadership no longer felt like it came from strength. It felt like effort layered on effort.

At home, I was present but disconnected. Conversations felt like a drain rather than a comfort. The things I once enjoyed started to feel like burdens. I withdrew even from the people I loved most. And because I did not really understand what was happening, I could not explain it to anyone.

Burnout is not just stress. It is a breakdown that seeps into every part of your life – physical, emotional, mental, relational, and professional. In hindsight, the pattern is obvious. But when you are inside it, it feels like personal failure. Naming it helped. It allowed me to see that what I was going through was not weakness or poor resilience. It was burnout. And naming it gave me the first foothold towards recovery.

Burnout Defined: More Than Stress

Burnout is not just about being tired or overwhelmed – it is a profound, chronic condition that gradually erodes a leader's energy, engagement, and sense of purpose.

The International Classification of Diseases defines burnout as "a syndrome resulting from chronic workplace stress that has not been successfully managed." According to the World Health Organization (2019), burnout is an "occupational phenomenon," not a medical diagnosis, defined by three key dimensions:

- Feelings of energy depletion or exhaustion
- Increased mental distance or cynicism related to one's job
- Reduced professional efficacy

Unlike ordinary stress, which might ease after a weekend or a good night's sleep, burnout lingers and compounds. It is the slow unravelling of your inner drive.

During my own experience with burnout, I felt like I was fading from the inside out. Cynicism crept in where passion used to live. The projects I once led with energy became emotionally heavy, not because I didn't care, but because I cared too much for too long without recovery. I wasn't just tired – I was disconnected from the leader I wanted to be.

Burnout leads to more than physical fatigue; it chips away at your identity, your confidence, and your capacity to show up fully – for your team, your mission, and yourself. Recent Australian data reveals the severity of this issue, with 61% of workers reporting burnout, significantly higher than the global average of 48%, and burnout now being attributed to 40% of employee resignations (Foremind, 2024).

> **BURNOUT BY NUMBERS: THE LEADERSHIP CRISIS**
>
> - 76% of employees experience burnout (Gallup, 2020)
> - Nearly 60% of leaders feel "used up" at day's end (Harvard Business Review, 2023)
> - 61% of Australian workers report burnout vs. 48% global average (Foremind, 2024)
> - 42.6% of Australian school principals trigger "red flag" wellbeing alerts (Australian Catholic University, 2024)
> - More than 50% of Australian principals intend to quit or retire early (Australian Catholic University, 2024)
> - 40% of employee resignations now attributed to burnout (Foremind, 2024)

The Identity Crisis of Burnout

One of the least discussed aspects of leadership burnout is how it disrupts identity. For high performing leaders, the role often becomes so closely tied to their sense of self that burnout is not just a matter of exhaustion, it is a collapse of identity.

When I burned out, I did not just lose energy. I lost myself. Leadership had become so entangled with my worth that when it cracked, I did not know who I was without it. The questions that surfaced were not just "How do I work differently?" but "Who am I if I am not constantly achieving? What is my value beyond what I produce?"

A growing body of research shows that social identity and a sense of shared purpose can play a protective role against burnout. Leaders who foster strong group identification are less likely to experience identity fragmentation when under pressure (Steffens et al., 2017). This suggests that burnout recovery must involve more than rest; it requires rebuilding a sense of self rooted in values, relationships, and intrinsic worth, not just productivity.

The Leadership Pressure Cooker: Why Leaders Are Vulnerable to Burnout

Leadership positions create a unique set of pressures that make burnout almost inevitable without intentional prevention. My experience has shown that several key factors significantly increase a leader's vulnerability to burnout.

The sheer volume of decision making in leadership creates a cognitive burden that accumulates over time. As a leader, I made dozens of consequential decisions daily – from budget allocations to staffing issues to strategic planning – each carrying significant implications. This constant decision fatigue gradually eroded my mental sharpness and emotional resilience.

Leadership isolation compounds this stress. Without peers in my immediate environment to openly discuss challenges, I carried burdens silently. This "lonely at the top" phenomenon created significant emotional strain as I maintained a composed exterior while navigating internal doubts.

Competing stakeholder expectations pulled me in contradictory directions. Staff, students, parents, and the system all had legitimate needs, yet it was impossible to satisfy all simultaneously. This tension created constant underlying anxiety about disappointing people I cared about, regardless of my choices.

The blurring of work life boundaries further accelerated burnout. The psychological separation between professional and personal life became increasingly difficult as I checked emails at dinner, took calls on weekends, and mentally problem solved during family time. This constant connectivity prevented essential recovery.

Cultures that celebrate the "always available" leader intensify these pressures. The implicit expectation that good leaders are perpetually accessible reinforces unhealthy patterns. I felt compelled to demonstrate commitment through constant availability, even when I desperately needed rest.

The emotional labour required in leadership roles is perhaps most taxing. I spent countless hours managing others' anxieties, mediating conflicts and providing reassurance, all while suppressing my own emotions. This constant emotional regulation, showing confidence despite feeling uncertain, remaining calm during crises, extracted a heavy psychological toll.

Understanding these structural challenges helps explain why burnout is so prevalent among leaders. The leadership pressure cooker creates conditions where burnout becomes a predictable outcome unless intentionally countered with systematic support and personal boundaries.

Burnout vs. Workplace Fatigue

Reflecting on my own leadership journey, I can now distinguish between ordinary workplace fatigue and burnout:

- **Fatigue:** A temporary state resolved with rest or a change of pace.
- **Burnout:** A prolonged condition of emotional, mental, and physical exhaustion that persists even after rest.

Emerging research suggests that leadership burnout often stems from universal issues within organisations, such as lack of support, overwhelming demands, and a culture focused on productivity over wellbeing (Maslach & Leiter, 2016). Leaders face unique challenges, including high stakes decision making, managing diverse teams, and the pressure to maintain performance, making them particularly vulnerable to burnout.

Recent neurological studies show that chronic stress can alter the structure and function of the brain, particularly in areas like the prefrontal cortex, which controls decision making and emotional regulation (Schaufeli & Taris, 2014). These changes can impair leaders' abilities to make clear decisions and manage their emotional wellbeing.

Burnout or Just Tired? A Quick Self Check

Leadership fatigue is real, but it doesn't always mean burnout. Table 1.1 is designed to help you distinguish between everyday tiredness and something deeper. Reflect honestly. What patterns are showing up for you?

Quick Reflection: If most of your answers lean into the Burnout column, it's a signal worth listening to. You may be in the early stages of burnout – or already there. The good news? You're not alone. This book is here to help you press reset.

Table 1.1 Self Check: Differentiating Between Symptoms of Fatigue and Burnout

Symptom	Fatigue	Burnout
Energy Levels	Tired but recharged after rest or a break	Exhausted no matter how much rest you get
Sleep	May feel tired but can fall and stay asleep	Struggles with insomnia, racing thoughts, or unrestful sleep
Focus	Distracted, but can regain attention with effort	Constant brain fog, forgetfulness, or indecision
Mood	Occasionally low or irritable under pressure	Ongoing cynicism, numbness, or emotional volatility
Motivation	Motivation dips during busy or stressful periods	Deep disconnection from purpose or passion
Physical Health	Headaches or muscle tension that ease with time off	Frequent illness, gut issues, or chronic pain
Recovery	Bounces back after a break or good weekend	Struggles to feel "normal" again, even with time off
Work Engagement	May feel disinterested occasionally, but still cares	Feels detached, resentful, or indifferent towards work
Outlook	Sees pressure as temporary or manageable	Feels hopeless, stuck, or that things won't get better
Relationships	May be more withdrawn temporarily	Avoids people, disconnects emotionally, or reacts with frustration

Symptoms of Leadership Burnout

Leadership burnout manifests in interconnected ways – affecting the physical, emotional, cognitive, behavioural, psychological, and relational dimensions of a leader's life. My story provides a window into how these symptoms can compound over time.

1. **Physical Symptoms**

Burnout often first presents through physical symptoms, which can worsen over time if ignored.

- **Chronic Fatigue:** Leaders may feel exhausted even after a full night's rest or a weekend break. This persistent fatigue does not improve with rest.

- **Frequent Headaches and Muscle Tension:** Stress induced tension often leads to headaches, neck pain, and tightness in the back and shoulders.
- **Weakened Immune System:** Prolonged stress weakens the immune system, making leaders more susceptible to illnesses.
- **Sleep Disturbances:** Many leaders experience insomnia or poor quality sleep due to stress, with their minds racing even when they try to rest.

2. **Emotional Symptoms**

The emotional toll of burnout can be especially debilitating for leaders, whose roles require emotional engagement and decision making.

- **Emotional Exhaustion:** A deep sense of depletion where leaders feel like they have nothing left to give.
- **Cynicism and Detachment:** Leaders may become disengaged from their work, losing passion and interest in projects they once cared about.
- **Irritability and Mood Swings:** The emotional strain of leadership burnout can lead to increased irritability and emotional instability.

3. **Cognitive Symptoms**

Burnout also impairs cognitive function, making it difficult for leaders to manage their responsibilities effectively.

- **Difficulty Concentrating:** Leaders may struggle with mental clarity, resulting in procrastination, mistakes, and difficulty focusing.
- **Forgetfulness:** Memory lapses become more common, and leaders may forget important details or deadlines.
- **Reduced Decision Making Ability:** Leaders may become indecisive or make hasty decisions without the careful thought they usually apply to important matters.

4. **Behavioural Symptoms**

Burnout often leads to changes in behaviour, impacting how leaders interact with others and handle their workload.

- **Withdrawal from Social Interactions:** Leaders may isolate themselves, avoiding meetings or casual conversations with colleagues.

- **Increased Reliance on Unhealthy Coping Mechanisms:** Some leaders may turn to alcohol, overeating, or excessive screen time as a way to cope with stress.
- **Procrastination and Decreased Productivity:** Burnout leads to feelings of overwhelm, making it difficult for leaders to take action or meet deadlines.

5. Psychological Symptoms

Burnout significantly impacts psychological wellbeing, often resulting in internal struggles.

- **Imposter Syndrome:** Leaders may doubt their abilities, feeling inadequate or unworthy of their roles despite their successes.
- **Feelings of Hopelessness or Helplessness:** As burnout intensifies, leaders may feel trapped, seeing no clear solutions to their problems.
- **Depression and Anxiety:** Burnout can trigger or worsen depression and anxiety, leaving leaders feeling overwhelmed and incapable of managing their responsibilities.

6. Relational Symptoms

Burnout can damage relationships both at work and at home.

- **Breakdown in Communication:** Leaders may avoid difficult conversations or become short tempered in their interactions.
- **Strained Personal Relationships:** The emotional toll of burnout often spills over into personal relationships, causing tension with family members or friends.
- **Reduced Empathy:** Leaders may become less empathetic towards the challenges and concerns of their teams, unable to provide emotional support when they are struggling themselves.

Personal Reflection: The Mask

Nothing about my professional role gave this away. I was still leading, still speaking at events, still ticking the boxes. But all the while, I was hiding in plain sight.
The mask I had worn for years had become too heavy to carry.

Leadership can become a performance. We put on a version of ourselves that looks composed, capable, in control – even when we are quietly falling apart. I did not realise how much this performance was costing me until I could no longer keep it going.

Over the years, I had created a version of myself that appeared steady. In meetings, I projected calm. In crisis, I looked collected. When others were anxious, I reassured them – even though I was feeling the same fear inside. I was not trying to be dishonest. I genuinely believed that strong leadership meant appearing strong at all times.

Over time, this mask became more and more refined. I had familiar expressions, go to phrases, a certain tone of voice that signalled everything was under control. People would often compliment me on how composed I was. They had no idea that inside, my thoughts were racing, my chest was tight, and I was struggling to keep it together. I was not coping. I was performing.

And performing takes a toll. Every morning, I would gather what energy I had to get through the day looking functional. By evening, I was drained. The performance did not stop when I left work. Social events, casual conversations – all of it became part of the same show. I was always on. And it was exhausting.

Psychologists call this emotional labour – the effort of showing one thing while feeling another. That constant mismatch between my internal state and outward behaviour eroded my energy. It also distorted my own awareness. How could I be burning out when I still looked like I was doing fine?

The worst part was the isolation. Because I appeared fine, no one asked if I was struggling. And even if they had, I would not have admitted it. "I'm fine" became my default line. It was a script I repeated so often I started to believe it myself. There was no space for vulnerability, no chance to say, "Actually, I am not okay."

Eventually, I could not take the mask off even at home. I had been wearing it so long, I forgot what it felt like not to. My family did not know how far I had fallen until I hit the wall completely.

It happened on an ordinary drive along Military Road. My chest tightened. My vision blurred. My hands started shaking. I had to pull over, sobbing uncontrollably. That panic attack was not a one off. It was the pressure that had built up behind the mask, finally breaking through.

Psychologists sometimes call this dissonance collapse – when the gap between your internal world and external presentation becomes too wide to maintain. When the mask finally cracked, I felt both relief and shame. I had built my identity around being strong. Admitting I was not felt like failure.

But that breaking point also led me to help. I spoke to my GP. Later, I saw a psychologist. I started to understand that vulnerability is not weakness. It is strength of a different kind. I had to unlearn the belief that leadership meant hiding struggle. What I found instead was a more grounded, human way to lead.

This did not mean abandoning boundaries or oversharing every emotion. It meant finding alignment between what I felt, what I valued, and how I showed up. It meant learning to lead without disconnecting from myself.

Even now, I sometimes catch myself slipping back into performance mode. But I recognise it. I pause. I ask myself who I am protecting, and whether it is helping.

The mask is not always the enemy. Sometimes we need it. But when it becomes permanent, when we start believing it can never slip – that is when it becomes dangerous.

Leadership does not require perfection. It requires presence. And presence means showing up as a whole person, not just a curated one.

Global Leadership Burnout: The Evidence Base

I was amazed when I started to research the topic of burnout. Burnout is a widespread issue affecting leaders across the globe, from tech companies to healthcare institutions and schools. As leaders are expected to perform at consistently high levels while managing crises and motivating teams, the rate of burnout continues to climb.

Leadership Burnout: Global Trends

The data reveals a concerning picture of leadership burnout worldwide:

- More than 50% of managers report experiencing burnout, slightly higher than the general employee population (Harvard Business Review, 2023).
- A quarter of leaders feel burned out often or always, and two thirds experience it at least sometimes (Gallup, cited in Leaders Edge Inc., 2024).

- In the UK, burnout among leaders increased by 20% from 2021 to 2022, driven by post-pandemic work adjustment pressures (Gallup, 2021a).
- 77% of corporate leaders rank employee wellbeing as a top challenge, yet over half have experienced burnout themselves within the past year (Deloitte *Global Human Capital Trends Report*, cited in McKinsey & Company, 2022).
- In the tech industry, 79% of leaders report feeling constant pressure to be "on," contributing to higher burnout rates (McKinsey & Company, 2022).

Industry Specific Leadership Burnout

Education Leadership

- 42.6% of Australian school principals are triggering "red flag" alerts indicating risk of self harm or serious impact on quality of life (Australian Catholic University, 2024).
- More than half of Australian school principals intend to quit or retire early, with experienced leaders (15+ years) leading this concerning trend (Australian Catholic University, 2024).
- School principals face increasing violence, with 48.2% reporting incidents of physical violence, up from 44.0% previously (Australian Catholic University, 2024).

Healthcare Leadership

- Physician burnout rates have shown improvement, decreasing from 56% in 2021 to approximately 45% in early 2024 (American Medical Association, 2024).
- Despite this improvement, only 23% of physicians believe their employers recognise burnout issues (Augnito, 2024).

Broader Workforce Burnout Context

Regional Variations

- 61% of Australian workers reported experiencing burnout in 2024, significantly higher than the global average of 48% (Foremind, 2024).

- Stress related absenteeism costs the Australian economy an estimated $14 billion annually (Foremind, 2024).
- Australia ranks among the top three countries globally for workplace burnout prevalence, alongside the US and UK (Spill, 2024).
- 63% of Australian professionals say they work more than their contracted hours every week, contributing to elevated burnout levels (Spill, 2024).
- Only 24% of Australian workers feel comfortable taking a mental health day when experiencing burnout symptoms (Spill, 2024).

Industry Specific Patterns

- Education: K-12 workers have the highest burnout rate in the US at 44%, compared with 30% of all other workers (Gallup, 2022).
- Legal: 73% of lawyers report experiencing burnout, with 27% feeling burned out daily (Spill, 2024).
- Finance: The finance and insurance sector has one of the highest burnout rates at 82.5% (Burnout Nutrition, 2024).
- Sales: 62.2% of salespeople experience burnout due to insufficient time for focused work (CreateAndGrow, 2024).
- Technology: 42% of tech workers are considering leaving their jobs in the next six months due to burnout (FitSmallBusiness, 2024).

The healthcare sector faces some of the highest burnout rates globally, with 82% of healthcare workers reporting burnout symptoms. This matches the services, tourism, and restaurants sector (82%), while construction and real estate (77%) follow closely behind (Spill, 2024). For leaders in these high pressure industries, understanding the specific stressors within their sector is crucial for developing targeted prevention strategies.

Organisational Response and Economic Impact

- Employees who believe their employer cares about their wellbeing are three times more engaged and 71% less likely to report burnout (Hubstaff, 2024).
- 74% of organisations recognise the importance of measuring worker performance beyond traditional productivity metrics (Deloitte, 2024).

- The World Health Organization estimates mental health challenges cost the global economy approximately $1 trillion in lost productivity (ClickUp, 2024).
- The financial burden of burnout is increasingly significant for organisations worldwide. In the UK alone, burnout costs businesses over £700 million annually due to employees calling in sick with stress and exhaustion symptoms (Spill, 2024).
- At the individual level, burnt out employees cost approximately $3,400 out of every $10,000 in salary through combined effects of reduced productivity and higher turnover (Spill, 2024), representing a substantial hidden tax on organisational performance.
- Burnout drives $125–190 billion in healthcare costs annually (ClickUp, 2024).

Psychological Safety and Workplace Culture

Burnout is not just a result of overwork – it often stems from deeper cultural issues within organisations.

- 46% of employees report that a lack of psychological safety is a major driver of burnout in their current workplace (Spill, 2024).
- Only 1 in 3 workers feel comfortable discussing stress or burnout with their manager, creating a culture of silence that prevents early intervention (Spill, 2024). This silence is particularly damaging for leadership development, as it prevents organisations from identifying potential burnout risks before they escalate into serious problems.
- Employees in companies that invest in mental health resources are 32% less likely to experience burnout (Spill, 2024).

The Uneven Impact: Gender and Diversity Dimensions of Burnout

Burnout does not affect all leaders equally. Recent research reveals significant disparities in how different groups experience and manage leadership stress. Most notably, women's burnout rates have increased to 42% (from 38% in 2023), while men's rates have decreased to 30% during the same period (American Psychological Association, 2022). This widening gender gap reflects the complex interplay of professional pressures and societal expectations.

The gender disparity in leadership burnout is particularly stark. According to Spill (2024), more than 50% of women in leadership positions feel constantly burned out. Women are also more likely than men (54% compared to 35%) to call in sick due to burnout symptoms. This gender gap in leadership burnout reflects not only workplace pressures but also societal expectations that often place additional burdens on women leaders.

Several factors contribute to these disparities. Research from the World Economic Forum (2022) highlights that women leaders often navigate "compounding pressures" facing higher performance scrutiny while simultaneously managing disproportionate domestic responsibilities. Additionally, leaders from underrepresented groups frequently experience "cultural taxation," where they shoulder additional unrecognised work supporting diversity efforts or serving as cultural bridges, further depleting their emotional resources. For people of colour, the burden of "code-switching" as a means of professional survival to fit into workplace norms often leads to emotional exhaustion and burnout (Spill, 2024). This invisible emotional labour represents an additional tax on diverse leaders that is rarely acknowledged in traditional leadership development programs.

These findings underscore the importance of addressing burnout through an inclusive lens. Organisations committed to leadership sustainability must consider how social dynamics and expectations create different burnout risks for various demographic groups. Recognition of these differences enables more tailored preventative approaches and ensures that resilience strategies address the specific challenges faced by different leaders.

Identity Based Leadership Burnout

Beyond gender disparities, leaders from historically marginalised groups often carry invisible burdens that compound burnout. The daily experience of code switching, cultural taxation, identity suppression, and expectations to represent their entire community creates what might be termed "identity based burnout."

First Nations leaders offer a compelling example of these additional pressures. Many navigate intergenerational trauma, cultural obligations, and systemic inequities while leading in spaces not designed with their identities in mind. Australian research from the Australian Indigenous Leadership Centre highlights how Aboriginal and Torres Strait Islander leaders often practice "both ways leadership" – simultaneously meeting Western organisational expectations while fulfilling cultural responsibilities to community and country.

This understanding demands a more nuanced approach to leadership wellbeing. Diversity must not just be represented in leadership; it must be protected, respected, and supported. Culturally responsive wellbeing strategies and safe spaces to lead authentically are not optional extras. They are essential components of truly inclusive leadership development.

Insights on Leadership Burnout

Research into leadership burnout reveals that it often stems from organisational issues rather than individual shortcomings. High pressure work environments, unrealistic expectations, and a focus on productivity at the expense of wellbeing contribute to a culture of burnout. Organisational solutions, including better leadership support, a balanced workload, and an emphasis on emotional resilience, are essential to addressing the root causes of burnout.

It's also important to recognise that burnout affects different groups of leaders in varying ways. The Women @ Work 2023 report by Deloitte reveals that, although the percentage of women feeling burned out decreased from 46% in 2022 to 28% in 2023, many still grapple with challenges such as an "always on" culture, lack of flexibility, and disproportionate caregiving responsibilities. These factors continue to contribute to stress and burnout among women in leadership roles. Addressing these disparities through flexible policies, shared caregiving responsibilities, and gender conscious wellbeing initiatives is essential for retaining and empowering female leaders.

Additionally, emerging technologies like biofeedback and wearable devices (e.g., heart rate variability trackers) provide leaders with real time data on their stress levels, offering a new way to prevent burnout. These tools enable leaders to monitor their physical responses to stress and take proactive measures – such as practicing mindfulness or taking breaks – before burnout escalates.

Practical Application: Recognising Your Burnout Signals

To identify your personal burnout warning signs:

1. **Track physical symptoms:** Note recurring physical signals like headaches, disturbed sleep, or persistent fatigue. Keep a simple log for one week to identify patterns rather than isolated incidents.
2. **Monitor emotional changes:** Pay attention to shifts in your emotional state, particularly increased irritability, emotional detachment, or anxiety. Ask a trusted colleague or partner to share observations about changes they notice.
3. **Assess cognitive impacts:** Evaluate changes in your thinking processes: difficulty concentrating, indecisiveness, or memory lapses. Consider whether these occur more frequently during specific situations or times.
4. **Observe behavioural shifts:** Notice changes in your actions: withdrawing from social interaction, procrastinating on important tasks, or relying more heavily on coping mechanisms.
5. **Compare with baseline:** Contrast your current state with periods when you felt energised and engaged. This comparison often reveals subtle changes that might otherwise go unnoticed.

The **Burnout Symptom Tracker** in the Tools and Templates section provides a comprehensive daily tracking system to help you identify your most significant warning signs and trigger patterns.

The Grief Dimension of Burnout

Perhaps the most profound aspect of burnout that often goes unnamed is grief. Leadership burnout frequently involves mourning lost ideals, unmet expectations and the gap between the leader we aspired to be and the reality we face.

Burnout felt like grief. I was mourning the version of leadership I believed in, and the version of me who thought I could do it all. This grief dimension explains the deep sadness that often accompanies burnout, beyond mere exhaustion. Like all grief, it requires acknowledgement, expression, and integration rather than simply pushing through.

Research confirms this connection between burnout and grief reactions, particularly among professionals with strong vocational identities (Thompson et al., 2022). Recognising burnout as a form of grief opens pathways to healing that go beyond traditional stress management. It invites leaders to honour what has been lost, to let go of unsustainable expectations and to rebuild a leadership vision grounded in current reality rather than idealised notions of what leadership should be.

Final Thoughts

Recognising the signs of burnout was only the beginning. The real change came when I made the decision to prioritise my own wellbeing. That wasn't easy, I had spent years believing that leadership meant pushing through, no matter the cost. But I came to realise that effective, sustainable leadership starts with taking care of yourself.

This isn't just about survival; it's about learning to thrive and bringing your best self to both your work and your life. Burnout taught me that leadership isn't about being unbreakable, it's about being self aware, adaptable, and willing to confront both personal challenges and the systems that contribute to them. True resilience comes not from endurance alone, but from knowing when to step back and reset.

In this chapter, I've shared how I came to understand burnout and recognise its causes. In the chapters ahead, I'll offer the practical strategies that helped me reset – strategies I hope will support you not only to withstand the pressures of leadership, but to rediscover purpose, energy, and joy in the way you lead.

In the Next Chapter

Before we can address burnout, we need to understand its shape – and the many ways it shows up in leadership. In Chapter 2, we'll unpack the different types of burnout leaders experience, from emotional and physical exhaustion to decision fatigue, relational strain, and even cultural and organisational burnout. Recognising your own pattern is key to recovery – because one-size-fits-all solutions rarely work when burnout wears so many faces.

Reflection Questions

Personal Reflection Questions

1. Which early warning signs of burnout have you personally experienced but perhaps dismissed? How might acknowledging these signals earlier have changed your leadership journey?
2. How do you currently distinguish between normal work pressure and the onset of burnout in your own experience? What subtle indicators suggest you need deeper intervention?
3. In what specific ways has burnout affected your decision making quality, emotional availability, or capacity for innovative thinking?
4. How have your personal relationships evolved as your leadership pressures have increased? What changes have others noticed in you that you may have overlooked?
5. What small but meaningful changes could you implement this week that would address the root causes of your stress rather than merely treating symptoms?

Team Reflection Questions

1. What patterns of burnout do we observe across our leadership team? Are there common triggers or pressures that affect multiple team members?
2. How does our organisational culture either contribute to or protect against leadership burnout? What unwritten rules exist about work hours, availability, or self care?
3. How do we currently support leaders who show signs of burnout? What organisational changes could create better early intervention?
4. In what ways might we be inadvertently rewarding behaviours that lead to burnout? How do our recognition and promotion practices influence wellbeing?
5. How can we create psychological safety for leaders to acknowledge when they're approaching burnout without fear of judgment or career consequences?

Key Takeaways

- **Leadership burnout is driven by chronic stress and emotional overload:** Burnout occurs when leaders face continuous pressure without adequate recovery, leading to mental and physical exhaustion. It often stems from excessive responsibilities, emotional strain, and prolonged periods of high stakes decision making.
- **Early warning signs include fatigue, emotional detachment, and cognitive decline:** Symptoms such as persistent tiredness, difficulty connecting with others, impaired decision making, and reduced emotional resilience signal the onset of burnout. Recognising these signs early allows for timely intervention.
- **Proactive identification is essential to prevent long term damage:** If left unchecked, burnout can have severe long term impacts on a leader's wellbeing and the organisation's performance. Addressing these symptoms early can prevent burnout from escalating, helping leaders maintain their health and effectiveness.
- **Burnout affects both personal and professional domains:** Leadership burnout doesn't only compromise the leader's capacity for decision making and innovation but also spills into their personal life, damaging relationships and mental health. Acknowledging the holistic impact is key to prevention.
- **Addressing leadership burnout requires organisational and personal interventions:** Effective prevention strategies include not only individual self care and emotional intelligence but also organisational changes that reduce stressors, such as workload management, psychological support, and fostering a healthy life work integration.

2

TYPES OF BURNOUT IN LEADERSHIP

Overview

Leadership burnout isn't a one-size-fits-all experience. For me, it manifested in several ways – emotional, physical, mental, and occupational burnout. Each layer compounded the others, leaving me drained and disconnected from my work and personal life. At the time, I didn't have the language to articulate what I was going through. I just knew I felt overwhelmed, exhausted, and completely detached from the leader I thought I was supposed to be.

In this chapter, I'll explore these types of burnout and others, drawing on both my personal experience and the research that helped me understand what was happening. By identifying the unique characteristics of these burnout types, I hope to provide insights and practical solutions to help other leaders navigate similar challenges.

DOI: 10.4324/9781003668626-4

Emotional Burnout in Leadership

Definition:
Emotional burnout occurs when leaders become emotionally drained from constantly managing team morale, resolving conflicts, and meeting support needs.

Relevance:
Leaders often find themselves carrying the emotional weight of their teams, expected to be the steady foundation that everyone relies on. I've felt it myself – the unspoken expectation to be calm, empathetic, and endlessly supportive, no matter how overwhelming the circumstances. In high pressure environments like healthcare, education, or corporate management, this constant emotional engagement can be draining. The effort to reassure, guide, and resolve conflicts without showing your own struggles takes a toll over time.

Research supports this reality. The *Harvard Business Review* notes that emotionally supportive leaders in high stress roles are especially vulnerable to burnout (Wiens, 2024). The exhaustion doesn't just stem from the workload; it's the emotional energy required to be "the rock" for everyone else while suppressing your own needs and vulnerabilities. Over time, this can lead to detachment, not because leaders stop caring, but because they simply have nothing left to give.

Real World Example:
A school principal, managing the emotional upheaval caused by the COVID-19 pandemic, faced significant emotional exhaustion from supporting her staff, students, and parents. Despite her dedication, the constant emotional strain left her feeling detached from her role (Reyes-Guerra et al., 2021).

Practical Solutions:

- **Emotional Intelligence (EQ) Coaching:** EQ training helps leaders manage their emotions and navigate conflicts, reducing emotional depletion (Goleman, 2018b).
- **Debrief Sessions:** Regular debriefs in leadership groups provide a safe space for leaders to offload emotional stress and receive peer support.

Physical Burnout in Leadership

Definition:
Physical burnout arises when leaders neglect their physical health due to long hours, constant availability, and the demands of leadership.

Relevance:
Leaders, myself included, often fall into the trap of pushing our physical limits in the name of getting things done. Late nights bleed into early mornings, and the idea of taking a break feels more like an indulgence than a necessity. I remember days when I'd skip meals or tell myself I'd exercise tomorrow, only to crash into bed utterly drained, knowing tomorrow would bring the same relentless pace.

It turns out, I'm not alone. A Mayo Clinic study found that 50% of senior leaders experience physical symptoms of burnout, including persistent tiredness, tension headaches, and muscle aches (Mayo Clinic, 2022). These are more than just inconvenient side effects, they're our bodies' way of signalling that we've pushed too far for too long. Chronic fatigue doesn't just appear out of nowhere; it's the cumulative result of neglecting sleep, exercise, and self care, all in the name of meeting professional demands.

Practical Solutions:

- **Time Blocking for Recovery:** Scheduling regular breaks and downtime for physical activity can alleviate strain and improve energy levels.
- **Sleep Hygiene:** Leaders should prioritise consistent sleep patterns and disengage from work in the evenings to promote recovery.

Cognitive Burnout in Leadership

Definition:
Cognitive burnout occurs when leaders become mentally exhausted from continuous decision making, problem solving, and strategy development.

Relevance:
Leadership often feels like an endless stream of decisions – big and small, urgent and strategic – all demanding your attention. I've experienced firsthand how this constant decision making can leave you mentally drained.

Even seemingly simple choices begin to feel overwhelming, and by the end of the day, creativity and clarity are replaced by a fog of exhaustion.

This isn't just a personal observation; research from McKinsey highlights how decision fatigue significantly reduces leaders' ability to think creatively and make effective choices (McKinsey & Company, 2023b). It's not surprising – when your mental resources are stretched thin, the sharpness and innovation that leadership demands start to erode. Decision fatigue is a silent drain, chipping away at your capacity until even the simplest tasks feel monumental.

Real World Example:
A CEO of a technology company experienced cognitive burnout after months of making high stakes decisions. This mental strain impaired their ability to think clearly and stifled creativity (Burke & Cooper, 2021).

Practical Solutions:

- **Cognitive Offloading:** Using task management tools such as Trello or Asana can help reduce mental strain.
- **Delegation:** Leaders can delegate less critical decisions to their teams, freeing mental capacity for more significant decisions.

Occupational Burnout in Leadership

Definition:
Occupational burnout arises when leaders face overwhelming workloads, organisational inefficiencies, or unrealistic expectations, leading to feelings of powerlessness.

Relevance:
Leadership often feels like walking a tightrope – high expectations pulling you forward while unclear goals leave you unsure of your next step. I've been there, juggling endless demands in an overwhelming work environment where success felt just out of reach. The pressure to meet lofty expectations, paired with the frustration of ambiguous direction, can create a perfect storm for burnout.

It's a challenge many leaders face. According to the American Psychological Association, 40% of executives report experiencing burnout, driven by the relentless pace and overwhelming demands of their roles

(APA, 2022). When the work environment feels unmanageable, the weight of responsibility can become crushing, leaving leaders feeling powerless and depleted.

Practical Solutions:

- **Workflow Restructuring:** Leaders should review workflows, delegate tasks, and streamline inefficiencies to reduce pressure.
- **Clearer Prioritisation:** Setting clear goals and expectations can help prevent burnout.

Relational Burnout in Leadership

Definition:
Relational burnout occurs when the demands of managing relationships with employees, peers, and other stakeholders become overwhelming.

Relevance:
As a leader, managing relationships often felt like an endless balancing act. Between staff, peers, stakeholders, and external partners, there was always someone needing guidance, reassurance, or a difficult conversation. I'd spend my days navigating these interactions, only to feel completely drained by the end of it. The emotional energy required to manage these relationships, especially in high stress environments, left little for myself or my family.

This experience isn't uncommon. *Forbes* highlights how leaders in high pressure roles are particularly vulnerable to relational burnout, as the demands of maintaining multiple connections can lead to emotional exhaustion (Robinson, 2024). When every relationship feels like a priority, the constant effort to meet others' needs can leave leaders feeling stretched too thin, struggling to maintain their own emotional wellbeing.

Practical Solutions:

- **Peer Support Networks:** Joining leadership circles or peer mentoring groups allows leaders to share challenges and gain insights from others in similar roles.
- **Emotional Intelligence Training:** Enhancing EQ helps leaders manage relational stress more effectively and improve communication.

Creative Burnout in Leadership

Definition:
Creative burnout arises when leaders are constantly expected to innovate and generate new ideas, leading to creative stagnation.

Relevance:
As a leader tasked with driving innovation, I often felt the unrelenting pressure to deliver fresh ideas and breakthrough solutions. At first, the challenge was exciting – an opportunity to push boundaries and inspire others. But over time, the constant demand for creativity, without time to recharge, became draining. Each brainstorming session felt like squeezing water from a stone, and frustration replaced the sense of possibility I once felt.

This experience is echoed in research. *Innovation Management* highlights that sustained creative pressure, especially without opportunities for recovery, is a major contributor to burnout (Innovation Management, 2020). Creativity thrives on inspiration and rest, but when leaders are constantly expected to innovate, the stress can stifle their ability to think expansively, leading to creative stagnation and exhaustion.

Practical Solutions:

- **Scheduled Downtime for Reflection:** Allowing time for ideas to develop without constant pressure can prevent creative burnout.
- **Cross Disciplinary Collaboration:** Engaging with teams from different sectors can stimulate creativity and innovation.

Compassion Burnout in Leadership

Definition:
Compassion burnout occurs when leaders are continually exposed to the emotional struggles of their teams, often in caregiving or non-profit sectors.

Relevance:
As a leader, I've experienced the weight of compassion burnout firsthand. Supporting a struggling team while managing my own challenges felt like an endless emotional marathon. Leaders in roles such as

healthcare and education often find themselves absorbing the emotional burdens of others, which takes a toll on their wellbeing. Harvard Medical School research confirms that prolonged exposure to emotional distress in teams is a significant factor contributing to burnout (Harvard Medical School, 2022).

Practical Solutions:

- **Self Compassion Practices:** I learned the value of practising self compassion, acknowledging my limits and giving myself permission to step back when needed. Leaders can benefit from mindfulness techniques to maintain emotional balance.
- **Team Resilience Programs:** Shared resilience initiatives help distribute the emotional load among team members, fostering collective strength rather than placing it all on the leader.

Decision Burnout in Leadership

Definition:
Decision burnout occurs when leaders are overwhelmed by the volume of decisions they must make, leading to mental exhaustion and impaired decision making.

Relevance:

> Decision fatigue, especially in high stakes environments, can erode a leader's clarity and confidence. Research from McKinsey shows that 85% of senior executives experience decision burnout, significantly reducing their capacity to think creatively and make sound choices (McKinsey & Company, 2023a, 2023b).

Practical Solutions:

- **Decision Making Tools:** Structured tools like decision matrices helped me streamline my choices and reserve mental energy for critical decisions.
- **Delegation:** Learning to trust my team with smaller decisions gave me the clarity to focus on what truly mattered.

Spiritual Burnout in Leadership

Personal Reflection:

> There was a time when my work no longer felt meaningful. The values I held close – faith, connection, impact, integrity – seemed out of sync. I began questioning my purpose as a leader, which left me feeling unmoored and disheartened.

Definition:
Spiritual burnout arises when leaders feel disconnected from their core values or the mission of their organisation, leading to a loss of purpose.

Relevance:
Leaders who feel misaligned with their organisation's mission often struggle to stay engaged. Research by Byrne (2024) shows that when leaders feel disconnected from their organisation's values, the resulting detachment can lead to spiritual burnout.

Practical Solutions:

- **Mission Realignment:** Reflecting on how my work aligned with my values helped me rediscover a sense of purpose. Leaders can engage in similar assessments to ensure their roles contribute to personal fulfilment.
- **Purpose Finding Exercises:** Coaching sessions were invaluable in helping me reconnect with my core values and redefine my leadership direction. Some people like to journal, but it was never quite me.

Moral Injury in Leadership

Definition:
Moral injury occurs when leaders are repeatedly forced to act against their core values or witness systemic harm they cannot prevent. Unlike other forms of burnout that deplete energy, moral injury damages a leader's sense of purpose and ethical integrity.

Relevance:
This concept is particularly significant in education and healthcare, where leaders often face impossible choices between organisational mandates and what they believe is right for those in their care. Recent research identifies moral injury as a distinct contributor to burnout among healthcare leaders (Dean et al., 2020). Sometimes what we call burnout is not just exhaustion; it is the emotional injury of watching things break and being powerless to fix them. That is not fatigue. That is moral injury. And it requires healing, not just rest.

Practical Solutions:

- Create ethical decision frameworks that align organisational policies with core values.
- Establish peer support groups specifically for processing moral distress.
- Develop advocacy skills to influence systemic change from within.
- Practise self compassion when facing impossible choices.

Organisational Burnout in Leadership

Definition:
Organisational burnout occurs when burnout permeates the entire organisation, placing additional pressure on leaders to maintain productivity and morale.

Relevance:
Gallup research highlights that organisational burnout is on the rise, affecting leaders who must manage both their own stress and their team's morale (Gallup, 2023a, 2023b). Leaders in these environments face the dual challenge of addressing their personal burnout while also trying to create a healthier culture for their teams.

Practical Solutions:

- **Organisational Wellness Programs:** Implementing wellness initiatives that support both employees and leadership can help address organisational burnout.
- **Team Check-Ins:** Regular team check-ins allow leaders to monitor stress levels and take proactive measures to alleviate burnout.

Cultural Burnout in Leadership

Definition:
Cultural burnout occurs when leaders face stress due to a misalignment between their personal values and the culture of their organisation.

Relevance:
Leaders working in environments that conflict with their values often struggle to stay engaged. Research from MIT Sloan highlights how this dissonance can contribute to cultural burnout (MIT Sloan, 2022).

Practical Solutions:

- **Cultural Awareness Training:** Leaders should engage in cultural awareness training to manage value conflicts within their organisations.
- **Inclusive Leadership Practices:** Promoting inclusive leadership can mitigate cultural burnout by ensuring alignment between organisational values and personal values.

Neurodivergent Burnout in Leadership

Definition:
Neurodivergent burnout occurs when leaders with neurological differences experience extreme depletion from the additional cognitive and emotional effort required to navigate workplace environments designed for neurotypical functioning.

Relevance:
Leaders who are neurodivergent, including those with ADHD, autism, or sensory sensitivities, face unique burnout risks that are often overlooked. Many engage in "masking" behaviours to conform to neurotypical norms, which can be mentally and emotionally exhausting. This invisible labour contributes to what researchers call "autistic burnout," a state of extreme exhaustion and sensory overload (Raymaker et al., 2020).

Practical Solutions:

- **Environmental Adaptations:** Creating sensory friendly work environments with options for quiet spaces and flexible lighting.

- **Communication Protocols:** Establishing clear, direct communication practices that reduce ambiguity.
- **Inclusive Practices:** Implementing flexible working arrangements that accommodate different cognitive styles.
- **Psychological Safety:** Developing a culture where disclosing neurodivergence and requesting accommodations is normalised and supported.

When Burnout Spreads: The Ripple Effect in Teams

While I managed to keep most of my burnout invisible, I have seen how stress in one leader can reshape an entire team. In several schools I've worked with, I have witnessed the ripple effects of leadership exhaustion, teams becoming more reactive, disconnected, or chronically on edge. This was not because of any intentional behaviour, but because emotions are contagious.

What I now think of as "burnout ripple" is not a formal diagnosis, but a real pattern: when a leader is running on empty, that strain often shows up in how their team thinks, feels, and works. Over time, the stress that begins in one person can become a shared team climate.

This insight is supported by research on emotional contagion, the phenomenon where people unconsciously mimic and absorb the emotional states of those around them, especially in close teams. A landmark study by Sigal Barsade (2002) showed how a leader's emotional tone can measurably shape group dynamics, engagement, and even cooperative behaviours.

We often think of burnout as a personal issue, but this research challenges that. Burnout has a social footprint. The emotional state of a leader, especially over time, helps shape the emotional state of their team. Recent research into psychological safety reveals that leaders' emotional states strongly influence whether team members feel safe to express concerns about workload or wellbeing. When leaders exhibit burnout symptoms, team psychological safety often deteriorates, creating a cycle where team members become less likely to voice their own stress signals until they too reach breaking point (Positive Group, 2023).

Practical Solutions:

- Build regular team check-ins focused on emotional tone, not just tasks.
- Model calm and recovery as much as urgency and drive.

- Introduce short reset rituals during stressful periods.
- Normalise conversations about workload and pressure.
- Establish "pressure release valves," structured opportunities for team members to safely discuss stress levels without judgment.
- Create team agreements about mutual support during high pressure periods.

Even when burnout feels personal, its effects are rarely contained. The ripple effect of leadership begins from within; our internal state inevitably shapes our external impact. As leadership psychologists emphasise, sustainable team cultures start with leaders who prioritise their own wellbeing not as a luxury, but as a fundamental leadership responsibility.

Practical Application: Addressing Your Burnout Type

To develop targeted strategies based on your specific burnout type:

1. **Identify your primary burnout type:** Review the types described in this chapter and identify which resonates most strongly with your experience. Most leaders experience a combination, but one type typically dominates.
2. **Implement type specific intervention:** Based on your primary burnout type, select one tailored strategy:

    - **Emotional burnout:** Schedule three 10 minute emotional regulation breaks daily, using deep breathing or brief journaling.
    - **Cognitive burnout:** Implement 25 minute focused work periods with 5 minute breaks, and batch similar decisions together.
    - **Physical burnout:** Prioritise sleep by establishing a consistent bedtime routine and scheduling three 30 minute exercise sessions weekly.
    - **Relational burnout:** Build in a 5 minute preparation period before interactions and schedule intentional connection time with positive relationships.
    - **Spiritual burnout:** Set aside 15 minutes weekly to reconnect with your core values and purpose.

3. **Share with a trusted colleague:** Briefly explain your burnout type and selected strategy to someone who can provide accountability and perspective on your progress.
4. **Review after two weeks:** Assess whether your targeted intervention is addressing the correct burnout type. If not, try an intervention for your secondary burnout type.

Use the **Burnout Type Assessment** in the Tools and Templates section to determine your primary burnout type and create a tailored recovery plan based on your specific needs.

Personal Reflection: When Burnout Had No Name

For the longest time, I could not articulate what was happening to me. I just knew something was profoundly wrong. I felt like I was drowning in plain sight, surrounded by colleagues and team members who saw me as capable and in control, while inside I was fragmenting in ways I could not explain.

The emotional weight hit first. As a leader, I felt compelled to shoulder everyone's burdens while keeping my own feelings carefully hidden. I spent so much energy managing others' emotions that I had nothing left for myself. The isolation was suffocating, not because I was physically alone, but because I felt disconnected from my work and the people around me, all while maintaining the facade that everything was fine.

My body began rebelling in ways I dismissed as simply part of leadership. The persistent fatigue, tension headaches, and sleepless nights seemed like badges of dedication rather than warning signals. I pushed through, skipping meals, working late, treating rest as a luxury I could not afford. I told myself that tomorrow I would slow down, but tomorrow always brought the same relentless pace.

Mentally, I was operating in a fog. Decision making, once energising, became paralysing. Even simple choices – what to prioritise, how to respond to an email, felt overwhelming. I would sit staring at my to-do list, unable to act, drained by the constant mental juggling. The creativity and strategic thinking leadership demanded were replaced by a grinding, mechanical effort to get through each day.

The sheer volume of work left me feeling trapped. Emails, meetings, and the ongoing pressure to perform created a sensation of drowning in responsibilities. I began to resent the work I once loved, feeling powerless to change the pace or reduce the demands. Managing relationships became exhausting, every interaction with staff, peers, and stakeholders felt like another drain on already depleted reserves.

Perhaps most devastating was the loss of meaning. My work no longer felt purposeful. The values I held close – faith, connection, impact, integrity – seemed completely out of sync with my daily reality. I began questioning my purpose as a leader, which left me feeling unmoored. I was putting on a mask every time I left the house, presenting a carefully constructed version of myself that I thought leadership required, but it was not really me. I got lost in that performance, forgetting where the mask ended and I began.

What made this experience particularly isolating was that I lacked the language to describe it. I knew I was struggling, but I could not name what was happening beyond feeling "stressed" or "overwhelmed," words that felt entirely inadequate for the depth of my depletion.

Everything shifted when I finally started researching burnout, not to write a book or develop a framework, but simply to try and make sense of what was happening to me. As I read about the different types, emotional, physical, cognitive, relational, spiritual, I experienced a profound sense of recognition. It was as if someone had taken my scattered, unnamed experiences and organised them into a coherent picture. I was not failing at leadership; I was experiencing multiple, overlapping forms of burnout, each requiring different approaches and understanding.

Learning about emotional burnout helped me understand why the isolation felt so profound: it was not that I had stopped caring, but that I simply had nothing left to give. Understanding physical burnout validated my body's rebellion and helped me recognise that rest was not weakness, but necessity. Recognising cognitive burnout explained the decision paralysis and mental fog that had become my daily reality.

The research on relational burnout illuminated why every interaction felt like a performance, and understanding spiritual burnout helped me see that my loss of meaning was not a character flaw but a natural response to misalignment. Even learning about concepts like moral injury, the damage that occurs when we are forced to act against our core values, helped me understand some of the deeper wounds I had sustained.

Most importantly, having names for these experiences meant I could address them systematically rather than hoping they would simply resolve with time. Each type of burnout had research-backed solutions, and suddenly what felt like an impossible, overwhelming problem became a series of manageable challenges. Understanding the ripple effect of burnout also helped me recognise how my state was unconsciously impacting my team, adding urgency to my recovery, not just for my sake, but for theirs.

That personal journey eventually became the foundation for what would later grow into the Leadership Reset Framework – but at the time, I was simply trying to survive.

The relief of finally having language for my experience cannot be overstated. It transformed my relationship with burnout from shame and self blame to understanding and action. It is why I remain passionate about helping other leaders recognise these patterns in themselves, because you cannot change what you cannot name.

Final Thoughts

Burnout in leadership is rarely one dimensional; it comes in many forms, each with unique challenges. Compassion, decision, spiritual, organisational, and cultural burnout represent just some of the pressures leaders face. Each type of burnout reveals different facets of the leader's experience, but they all share a common thread: the need for balance, self awareness, and support. Recognising these specific types of burnout and implementing targeted strategies is essential not just for leaders' wellbeing but also for the success and resilience of their teams and organisations.

Sharing my personal experiences, alongside research and practical solutions, I hope this chapter provides insights to help leaders not only identify the warning signs but also feel empowered to take action. Burnout is not a personal failure – it's a signal that something needs to change. Addressing it requires courage, a willingness to seek help, and a commitment to realigning priorities with values.

Leadership isn't about being invincible; it's about adapting, evolving, and leading by example. By taking deliberate steps to prioritise their own wellbeing, leaders can emerge stronger, more fulfilled, and more effective in their roles. More importantly, they can help create a culture where wellbeing is not an afterthought but a fundamental part of leadership and organisational success. As you reflect on these insights, I encourage you to think about your own journey: what burnout might look like in your context, how it's impacting you or those around you, and what small steps you can take today to foster a healthier, more sustainable approach to leadership.

In the Next Chapter

Understanding burnout is only the beginning. In Chapter 3, we explore how sustainable leadership starts with a shift in mindset, from outdated and traditional work life balance to a more integrated life first approach. You will be invited to consider what it looks like to lead in a way that honours your values, protects your wellbeing, and brings your whole life into alignment.

Reflection Questions

Personal Reflection Questions

1. Which type of burnout resonates most deeply with your experience? How has this specific form of burnout manifested in your leadership practice?
2. What recurring patterns have you noticed in how burnout affects you across different roles or seasons? Are there consistent triggers that precede your feelings of depletion?
3. Which of your current burnout management approaches address root causes vs. merely alleviating symptoms? How might you shift this balance?
4. How have your support networks evolved as your leadership responsibilities have grown? Where are the most significant gaps in your support system?
5. If you were to redesign your leadership role to prevent your primary type of burnout, what three elements would you transform first?

Team Reflection Questions

1. Which types of burnout are most prevalent in our leadership team, and what might this reveal about our organisational structure or culture?
2. How do different types of burnout impact team dynamics and decision making processes? What blind spots might emerge when multiple leaders experience similar burnout patterns?

3. What collective strategies could we implement to address the most common forms of burnout affecting our leadership team?
4. How might we better recognise and respond to different burnout types in each other before they reach critical levels?
5. What changes to our team structure, meeting formats, or communication patterns would help prevent the dominant burnout types we experience?

Key Takeaways

- **Leadership burnout manifests in multiple forms:** Emotional, physical, cognitive, relational, and organisational burnout are the most prevalent types, each affecting leaders in unique ways and requiring targeted prevention strategies.
- **Impact varies by type:** Each form of burnout impacts leaders differently. Emotional burnout drains empathy and compassion, while cognitive burnout impairs decision making and creativity, requiring customised approaches.
- **Overlapping burnout forms compound stress:** Different types of burnout often overlap and intensify stress effects. For example, cognitive burnout can exacerbate emotional fatigue, requiring holistic intervention approaches.
- **Targeted interventions are essential:** Solutions like emotional intelligence coaching, time blocking, delegation, and wellness programs effectively manage different burnout types when integrated into daily leadership routines.
- **Sustainable leadership practices prevent burnout:** Establishing clear priorities, setting boundaries between personal and professional life, and promoting team wellbeing are critical strategies that enhance resilience and organisational success.

3

LIFE BEFORE WORK

THE FOUNDATION OF SUSTAINABLE LEADERSHIP

Overview

In a world where professional success often overshadows personal wellbeing, the idea of work life balance has become a popular yet flawed goal for modern leaders. The term implies a constant tug-of-war between professional responsibilities and personal life, creating a misconception that they are opposing forces.

This chapter redefines the conversation, advocating for a life first approach to leadership. By embracing life work integration, where personal wellbeing, relationships, and purpose take precedence, leaders can cultivate resilience, emotional intelligence, and a fulfilling professional journey. This paradigm shift promotes sustainable leadership, enabling leaders to thrive without sacrificing their personal lives.

Rethinking the Balance: Life Comes First

The conventional notion of work life balance views work and life as competing priorities. This outdated perspective sets leaders up for an unending struggle to manage two separate spheres. Leadership expert Simon Sinek (2017) emphasises that effective leadership begins with self care; leaders cannot care for others if they neglect their own wellbeing. However, many leaders fall into a cycle of overwork, where professional demands become the primary source of stress, fatigue, and eventual burnout.

As I personally experienced, this imbalance leads to emotional exhaustion, strained relationships, and diminished decision making capabilities. The lesson was clear: prioritising personal wellbeing and fostering meaningful connections are essential foundations for professional success. Sue Langley's (2021) work in positive psychology echoes this, highlighting the transformative power of focusing on mental health, strong relationships, and self care for sustainable leadership. When life takes priority, leaders bring renewed energy, creativity, and resilience to their roles.

How We Got It Wrong: The Origins of Work Life Balance

The concept of work life balance emerged during the late 20th century, when work and personal life were more distinct. People often worked fixed hours in offices or factories, creating a physical and temporal boundary between professional and personal time. Balancing these two domains seemed logical and achievable in that context.

However, the rise of digital technology and remote work blurred these boundaries. Smartphones, email, and 24/7 connectivity have created an "always on" culture where leaders are expected to be accessible at all times. This shift has rendered the traditional idea of work life balance obsolete.

Instead, leaders need to embrace **life work integration**, a mindset that situates work within the broader context of life rather than the other way around (see Table 3.1). This approach acknowledges that periods of intense professional focus are sometimes necessary but should never come at the expense of long term wellbeing. Leaders who adopt life work integration design their professional lives to support their personal priorities, ensuring that they remain effective, present, and fulfilled.

Unlike the traditional model, life work integration doesn't assume balance means 50/50. Instead, it recognises that some seasons require more of one than the other – and that's okay, as long as life remains the anchor, not the afterthought.

Table 3.1 Comparing the Models: Life Work Integration vs. Work Life Balance

Dimension	Traditional Work Life Balance	Life Work Integration
Core Assumption	Life and work compete for time and attention	Work exists within the broader context of life
Goal	Equal time for both domains	Alignment of work with personal values and wellbeing
Structure	Set hours and fixed separation between work and home	Flexible boundaries that adapt to priorities
Stress Response	Tries to manage stress by compartmentalising	Reduces stress through intentional blending and autonomy
Definition of Success	Achieving preset targets regardless of personal cost	Creating sustainable impact while maintaining wellbeing
Leadership Focus	Performance driven, with personal needs managed on the side	Purpose driven, with personal needs at the centre
Decision Making	Based primarily on business outcomes	Integrates personal values with business needs
Technology View	Tools that can intrude on personal time	Tools that enable flexibility and presence
Recovery Approach	Scheduled vacations as the primary recovery method	Ongoing renewal practices integrated into daily routine
Team Culture Impact	Creates pressure for team members to also compartmentalise	Models sustainable practices that benefit the entire team
Adaptability	Struggles during crises when boundaries collapse	Provides resilience through flexible prioritisation
Long Term Outlook	Often leads to cyclical burnout and recovery	Sustains energy and effectiveness over career lifespan

Evidence-based Insights

Research supports the shift towards life first leadership. A 2022 study by Deloitte highlights that organisations prioritising leader wellbeing report higher productivity and lower burnout rates. Similarly, findings from Gallup (2021a) show that leaders who prioritise personal health and relationships foster more engaged and resilient teams. Neuroscience also reveals that chronic stress impairs decision making and creativity, underscoring the importance of practices like mindfulness, time blocking, and boundary setting for maintaining brain health.

Life Work Integration: A New Leadership Mindset

Rather than viewing life and work as conflicting priorities, life work integration redefines leadership by positioning life at the centre. Leaders who embrace this mindset intentionally design their professional roles to enhance, rather than detract from, their personal wellbeing.

Drawing on my own experiences with burnout, I've found practical strategies like time blocking invaluable. By treating personal priorities – such as exercise, family time, and hobbies – as immovable commitments akin to work meetings, leaders can carve out time for what truly matters. Evidence-based research supports this approach, showing that aligning daily schedules with core personal values not only improves wellbeing but also enhances professional effectiveness. Delegating tasks that misalign with values further empowers leaders to focus on meaningful work that enriches both their careers and personal lives.

Life work integration is not about rigid boundaries; it's about cultivating a harmonious relationship between personal and professional spheres. Leaders who adopt this flexible mindset can balance periods of intense professional focus with times when personal life takes priority, achieving greater resilience and fulfilment.

The Changing Nature of Work

The industrial revolution introduced a clear divide between work and personal life. Factories and offices imposed strict schedules, separating work hours from personal time. While this structure seemed logical in the 20th century, the advent of digital technology in the 21st century has blurred these boundaries.

The shift to remote work has created new challenges for maintaining boundaries. According to Spill (2024), 46% of people report that working from home contributes to burnout. Without the physical separation between work and home environments, leaders often struggle to disconnect. Furthermore, over a third of employees report that their employers expect them to work beyond reasonable hours, with younger employees particularly affected – 27% of 16–24 year olds and 19% of 25–34 year olds work at least five hours per week over their contracted hours.

The "always on" culture enabled by smartphones, emails, and remote work has made constant availability the norm, leaving many leaders struggling to disconnect. Research shows this relentless connectivity often leads to stress, burnout, and a diminished ability to lead effectively.

To counter these challenges, leaders must adopt life work integration, prioritising life over work. This evidence-based approach repositions work as a subset of life, ensuring that personal wellbeing becomes the foundation for sustainable leadership.

Scientific Backing on Mental Health

Scientific research underscores the dangers of chronic stress from overwork. Studies by the American Psychological Association (e.g., APA, 2020) reveal that prolonged workplace stress contributes to burnout, depression, and anxiety. Neuroscience further shows that chronic stress impairs the prefrontal cortex, the brain region responsible for decision making, emotional regulation, and creativity (McEwen & Akil, 2020).

Personal experience and evidence converge here: leaders who neglect their wellbeing are more likely to suffer cognitive declines, diminishing their leadership capacity. However, neuroscience also offers hope through neuroplasticity, the brain's ability to adapt and recover. Evidence-based practices such as mindfulness, sufficient rest, and life work integration can reset neural pathways, fostering resilience and creativity.

Sue Langley (2021), a leading expert in positive psychology, reinforces the importance of wellbeing. Her research links positive emotions and flourishing to enhanced leadership performance, underscoring the profound connection between life first leadership and emotional intelligence.

By integrating personal stories, practical tools, and robust research, this chapter offers leaders actionable strategies to redefine their approach to work and life, achieving both personal and professional success.

Integrating the Concept of "Flourishing"

The concept of flourishing, introduced by Martin Seligman (2011), defines living within an optimal range of functioning where individuals experience purpose, engagement, and fulfilment. Leaders who prioritise life over work align themselves with this principle, not only avoiding burnout but achieving growth and thriving both personally and professionally.

Building on Seligman's foundational work, recent scholarship in positive psychology has expanded the concept of flourishing beyond individual wellbeing to include broader societal dimensions. VanderWeele (2017) introduces a comprehensive model that encompasses happiness and life satisfaction, mental and physical health, meaning and purpose, character and virtue, close social relationships, and financial and material stability. For leaders, this multidimensional approach underscores the importance of fostering environments that support not only personal wellbeing but also the collective flourishing of their teams and organisations.

Drawing on my personal journey and experiences with burnout, it's clear that prioritising mental health and relationships unlocks new levels of creativity and problem solving. Research supports this: leaders who foster personal fulfilment and emotional wellbeing positively influence their teams, creating an environment where organisational success is underpinned by team flourishing.

Balanced Leadership Models from Diverse Cultures

Scandinavian leadership models, particularly those in Finland and Denmark, highlight the power of prioritising wellbeing over relentless performance metrics. Through initiatives like shorter workweeks, mandatory vacation policies, and wellbeing focused leadership, these nations consistently top global happiness and workplace satisfaction indexes (World Economic Forum, 2022).

These wellbeing first practices resonate with my experience as a leader seeking balance and sustainability. They demonstrate how prioritising personal health and emotional resilience leads to higher engagement, mental health, and productivity – not just for individuals but across entire organisations.

The global shift to remote work further amplifies the relevance of these models, offering lessons on integrating life first principles into leadership at scale.

Australian Perspectives on Life First Leadership

While Scandinavian models offer valuable insights, Australian leaders are developing their own approaches to life first leadership. Several Australian organisations are pioneering practices that prioritise wellbeing while maintaining high performance.

In the technology sector, Australian companies like Atlassian have implemented practices such as "ShipIt Days" and "FedEx Days" that encourage creativity while respecting work boundaries. Their "Team Playbook" includes specific strategies for maintaining team wellbeing alongside performance, demonstrating how innovation and balance can coexist (Atlassian, 2022).

Public sector organisations in Australia are also embracing life first approaches. For instance, many government departments now offer flexible work arrangements, wellbeing programs, and leadership development that specifically addresses life work balance. These initiatives acknowledge the unique pressures faced by public sector leaders and provide practical support for maintaining wellbeing (Australian Public Service Commission, 2023).

The University of Melbourne's Leading for Wellbeing initiative combines coaching, peer networking, and realistic workload models to support academic leaders, addressing the unique pressures of the higher education sector. Since implementation, they've reported improved retention and job satisfaction among faculty leadership (University of Melbourne, 2024b).

Bendigo and Adelaide Bank's Sustainable Leadership initiative includes regular wellbeing check-ins, structured mentoring for life work integration, and KPI frameworks that explicitly include leadership health alongside traditional performance metrics (Bendigo and Adelaide Bank, 2024).

What distinguishes these Australian examples is their pragmatic approach to balancing wellbeing with performance expectations. Rather than viewing these as competing priorities, these organisations demonstrate how performance and wellbeing can be mutually reinforcing, creating sustainable leadership models that benefit both individuals and organisations.

Global Perspectives: Cultural Variations in Leadership Sustainability

Leadership burnout and its prevention strategies are significantly influenced by cultural contexts that shape expectations, support systems, and recovery approaches. While we've examined Australian and Scandinavian models, a broader cultural perspective reveals diverse approaches to leadership sustainability worth considering.

The World Economic Forum (2022) identifies several cultural patterns that impact leadership sustainability. Japan's concept of "karoshi" (death from overwork) has led to significant reforms, including mandatory employee checks when working hours exceed established thresholds. This approach acknowledges the organisational responsibility for preventing burnout rather than leaving it to individual leaders.

In contrast, many African leadership traditions emphasise community support as central to leadership sustainability. Research from the *International Journal of Leadership Studies* (2022) highlights how ubuntu philosophy, which holds that a person is a person through other people, shapes leadership approaches that distribute emotional burden across networks rather than concentrating it on individuals.

German organisations often implement "unavailability protocols" that prevent contact with leaders during designated recovery periods, creating structural protection of personal time. This approach reflects the cultural value placed on clear boundaries between work and personal life, with companies like Volkswagen restricting email servers from contacting employees outside working hours.

These diverse approaches demonstrate that leadership sustainability is not universal but culturally embedded. Organisations with global operations should recognise these variations and adapt their leadership support systems accordingly. Rather than imposing a single model, multinational companies can learn from various cultural perspectives to create more nuanced and effective approaches to preventing leadership burnout across different contexts.

Leadership Styles and Emotional Intelligence

Emotional intelligence (EQ) is widely considered important to effective leadership, and a life first mindset supports the development of these emotional skills. Leaders who invest in their personal wellbeing are better equipped to regulate their emotions, lead with empathy, and make thoughtful, creative decisions under pressure.

Daniel Goleman's research on emotional intelligence suggests that leaders who model life first behaviours tend to foster open communication, empathy, and trust within their teams. These leaders often create environments where emotional wellbeing is prioritised, which may help reduce stress and improve team cohesion. Goleman's work indicates that when leaders emphasise emotional intelligence – particularly aspects like self awareness and empathy – they may positively influence both personal and team dynamics. Emotional wellbeing appears to play an important role in building trust, facilitating communication, and supporting team engagement and resilience when facing challenges (Goleman, 2013a).

Practical Steps for Prioritising Life Before Work

Life-first leadership requires more than good intentions, it demands concrete action. The following practical steps provide a framework for shifting from a work-dominated approach to one where personal wellbeing guides professional decisions and practices.

1. Time Blocking for Personal Priorities

Schedule activities such as family dinners, exercise, or hobbies into your calendar as non-negotiable commitments, treating them with the same importance as work meetings. This ensures that personal priorities are consistently addressed rather than being pushed aside when work demands increase.

2. Delegation and Task Management

Regularly assess your workload, focusing on tasks that align with your strengths and values. Delegate responsibilities that detract from your core competencies, freeing time for more meaningful and energising work. Effective delegation isn't about offloading work – it's about strategic allocation of leadership energy.

3. Boundary Setting

Establish firm boundaries around after-hours communication, creating technology-free zones during personal time. Clearly communicate these boundaries to your team to foster mutual respect and shared expectations. Consistent boundaries protect your capacity to lead effectively over the long term.

4. Values Based Decision Making

Reflect on your core values and align professional responsibilities with them. This approach ensures that work enhances rather than undermines personal wellbeing, creating a sense of purpose and fulfilment. When faced with competing priorities, let your values guide your choices.

5. Wellbeing as a Leadership KPI

Advocate for organisational metrics that measure success through wellbeing indicators, such as team engagement and personal health. By prioritising wellbeing as a key performance indicator, leaders can create a culture that values balance and sustainability for everyone.

By integrating these practices into daily routines, leaders can model a life first mindset that fosters resilience, emotional intelligence, and sustained effectiveness in both personal and professional realms.

Challenges and Balanced Arguments: Embracing Life First Leadership

Adopting a life first leadership model offers a transformative alternative to burnout-driven practices, but it is not without challenges. Critics, especially in high pressure industries like finance, technology, and corporate law, argue that prioritising personal wellbeing might signal a lack of commitment to career progression. Long hours are often equated with dedication, and leaders who set clear boundaries around personal time may fear missing career-enhancing opportunities or slower advancement in competitive environments.

In cultures where overwork is deeply ingrained, such as the United States and Japan, prioritising personal time may be misinterpreted as a lack of ambition or teamwork. According to *Harvard Business Review* (2021a), professionals often fear that openly maintaining work life balance could be seen as underperforming or less committed to organisational goals. These perceptions create significant barriers to adopting a life first mindset.

Evidence Supporting Life First Leadership

Despite these concerns, substantial research demonstrates that overworking without prioritising personal fulfilment results in burnout, diminished decision making, and reduced productivity. For instance, the American Psychological Association (2021) found that leaders facing chronic stress were 30% more likely to suffer cognitive decline, impacting leadership capacity and overall organisational outcomes.

Conversely, leaders who prioritise wellbeing report higher creativity, engagement, and resilience. Research from Deloitte's *Global Human Capital Trends* (2021a) shows that wellbeing first leadership enhances job satisfaction and team engagement, reducing turnover. In real world examples, Scandinavian countries like Finland and Denmark illustrate the success of prioritising personal time through shorter workweeks, generous leave policies, and a focus on mental health. These approaches yield higher productivity and sustained innovation while maintaining personal and team wellbeing.

A Balanced Approach to Leadership

The benefits of life first leadership outweigh the perceived risks. By reducing burnout and fostering resilience, organisations can cultivate leaders who sustain high productivity without sacrificing personal wellbeing. For competitive industries, adopting a balanced approach may require cultural shifts, but the long term benefits – greater innovation, stronger teams, and improved organisational health – justify the effort.

Practical Application: Setting Life First Boundaries

Boundary setting is often the most challenging aspect of life-first leadership, particularly in high pressure environments where "always on" expectations are the norm. The following framework provides a structured approach to establishing and maintaining boundaries that protect wellbeing without compromising leadership effectiveness.

Identify Your Non-Negotiables

To begin setting effective boundaries:

1. **Conduct a personal energy audit:** Track your energy levels throughout the week to identify when you need recovery time most critically.

2. **Define your core wellbeing requirements:** Determine the minimum sleep, exercise, family time, and personal activities you need to function at your best.
3. **Assess current boundary violations:** Note which areas of your life are most frequently compromised by work demands.

Boundary Implementation Strategy

Once you've identified your non-negotiables, implement them with this approach:

1. **Start with one clear boundary:** Select one specific boundary that would make the most significant difference to your wellbeing. Focus on a clear, measurable boundary such as "No work emails after 7pm" or "Uninterrupted family dinner three nights weekly."
2. **Block protected time:** Place non-negotiable blocks in your calendar for your most important personal priorities. Treat these appointments with the same commitment as your most important work meetings.
3. **Craft your communication:** Prepare a brief, confident explanation of your boundary: "To ensure I can deliver on our key priorities, I will be [specific boundary]. This helps me bring my best to [shared goal]."
4. **Create environmental supports:** Set up practical reminders and supports such as email auto-responders, notification settings, or visual cues in your workspace that reinforce your boundary.
5. **Start small and build:** Begin with one well-defined boundary that feels achievable, then expand gradually as you experience success.

Boundary Setting in High Pressure Environments

High pressure leadership roles require especially thoughtful boundary strategies:

Digital Boundaries

- Set specific times when you will not check or respond to emails (e.g., after 7pm or before 7am).
- Configure devices to only allow notifications from essential sources during personal time.

- Include your working hours and expected response times in your email signature.

Communication Scripts

When setting boundaries, clear communication is essential:

- With superiors: "To ensure I can deliver on our key priorities, I've identified that I need to protect time for [strategic work/family/recovery]. I'd like to [specific boundary]. How can we make this work while ensuring our core objectives are met?"
- With team members: "I'm implementing some changes to help our team work more sustainably. Going forward, I'll be [specific boundary]. This will help me be more present and effective during our working hours. I encourage you to establish similar boundaries that work for you."

Crisis-Period Boundaries

Even during high pressure periods:

- Schedule non-negotiable recovery periods during extended crisis periods.
- Implement leadership rotation during prolonged crises so team members take turns being "on call."
- Define what truly constitutes an emergency requiring immediate attention.
- Plan post-crisis recovery time that is protected as rigorously as any critical meeting.

Leaders who successfully implement these boundary strategies report not only improved wellbeing but enhanced leadership effectiveness, as they bring renewed focus and energy to their work during their engaged hours.

The **Boundary Setting Protocol** in the Tools and Templates section provides a structured framework for establishing, communicating, and maintaining different types of boundaries in your leadership role.

Final Thought

Leadership is a marathon, not a sprint as they say. Sustaining effectiveness and fulfilment requires more than sheer determination – it demands a conscious commitment to living a life that fuels your work, rather than one where work drains your life. I learned this lesson the hard way. For too long, I saw my personal needs as secondary, something to squeeze in around the edges of my professional responsibilities. It wasn't until I reached a breaking point that I realised the cost of this approach – not just to me but to those I led and cared about.

This chapter has been deeply personal because it speaks to a journey, I've walked myself. I've felt the exhaustion of blurred boundaries, the frustration of constant availability, and the loss of clarity that comes from trying to balance too much. But I've also experienced the freedom and renewal that comes from reclaiming control, setting boundaries, honouring personal priorities, and leading with purpose rather than pressure.

Life first leadership isn't a luxury; it's a necessity. It's about recognising that when you prioritise your life – your health, relationships, and sense of purpose – you bring your best self to work. This doesn't just benefit you; it creates a ripple effect, inspiring your team to do the same. The strategies shared in this chapter, like time blocking personal priorities and aligning decisions with your values, aren't abstract concepts – they're practical tools that have reshaped my own approach to leadership.

The outdated notion of balancing life and work as competing forces must give way to a more integrated perspective, where life takes precedence and work becomes a source of enrichment, not exhaustion. This is leadership reimagined, rooted in wellbeing, empathy, and emotional intelligence. When we embrace this approach, we set the stage not just for professional success, but for a life that feels meaningful and whole.

As you reflect on this chapter, I encourage you to consider your own journey. Are you living a life that fuels your work, or is work taking more than it gives? The answers to these questions can be transformative, and I hope the tools and insights shared here inspire you to lead with renewed energy, balance, and purpose. Leadership doesn't have to come at the cost of your wellbeing – in fact, the best leadership is born from it.

In the Next Chapter

With a life first foundation in place, we turn next to the science behind burnout. In Chapter 4, we explore how prolonged stress affects the brain, impacts decision making, and disrupts emotional regulation. Understanding the neuroscience of burnout gives leaders the insight they need to build habits that restore focus, clarity, and resilience from the inside out.

Reflection Questions

Personal Reflection Questions

1. In what specific ways do you currently prioritise work over personal wellbeing? Which of these patterns are conscious choices vs. unconscious habits?
2. What barriers prevent you from achieving genuine life work integration? How might these barriers reflect organisational expectations vs. personal beliefs?
3. Recall a time when prioritising your wellbeing transformed your leadership effectiveness. What principles about sustainable leadership did this experience reveal?
4. If you were to define your non-negotiable boundaries for a balanced life and leadership, what core principles would guide these boundaries?
5. What symbolic action could you take tomorrow that would signal to yourself and others your commitment to putting life before work?

Team Reflection Questions

1. How does our team culture either support or undermine life work integration? What messages do we send about the importance of personal wellbeing?
2. What formal or informal expectations exist about availability, response times, and work hours that might contribute to burnout?
3. How might we redesign our collective work practices to better honour life priorities while maintaining organisational effectiveness?
4. What team agreements could we establish that would support each member in maintaining healthy boundaries between work and personal life?
5. How can we hold each other accountable for maintaining life work integration without creating additional pressure or guilt?

Key Takeaways

- **Sustainable leadership begins with prioritising personal wellbeing:** Long term leadership success depends on aligning professional responsibilities with core life values, fostering resilience, and preventing burnout.
- **Life work integration surpasses traditional work life balance:** Rather than treating work and life as competing forces, leaders should create harmony between them, fostering a flexible approach where work enhances personal fulfilment.
- **Clear, non-negotiable boundaries protect personal wellbeing:** Establishing firm limits for work, family time, exercise, and rest helps leaders sustain energy and prevent burnout through consistent protection of personal time.
- **Emotional intelligence fosters cultures of empathy and trust:** Leaders who prioritise life before work set an example for their teams, creating healthier, more resilient, and more productive work environments.
- **Wellbeing centred leadership models demonstrate proven success:** Models from countries like Finland and Denmark show how prioritising employee wellbeing leads to greater job satisfaction, innovation, and sustainable organisational performance.

4

THE NEUROSCIENCE OF LEADERSHIP BURNOUT

HOW THE BRAIN REACTS TO STRESS

Overview

Burnout is more than a psychological challenge – it has measurable neurological impacts that can disrupt leadership effectiveness. I remember a time when the demands of leadership left me in a mental fog, struggling to make decisions and manage emotions effectively. The weight of stress was not just emotional – it felt as though my brain was working against me. Through personal experiences like these and evidence-based neuroscience, this chapter explores how chronic stress reshapes brain structure and function, reducing leaders' capacity to perform under pressure.

We delve into the science behind these changes and introduce actionable strategies that harness the brain's remarkable ability to adapt, known as neuroplasticity. Practices like mindfulness, meditation, optimised sleep, and physical exercise emerge as powerful tools for rebuilding resilience, enhancing emotional regulation, and improving cognitive performance. By weaving together personal anecdotes, cutting-edge research, and practical applications, this chapter offers leaders a roadmap to not only recover from burnout but thrive in high pressure environments.

Neuroplasticity: The Brain's Adaptation to Stress

Key Idea:
Neuroplasticity refers to the brain's ability to reorganise and form new neural connections in response to learning and experiences. This adaptability is crucial for overcoming the negative impacts of stress and burnout. Leaders who experience chronic stress can leverage neuroplasticity to reset their stress responses, enabling them to handle challenges with resilience.

How Neuroplasticity Works:
The brain's response to stress is adaptive, meaning it can reorganise its neural pathways to cope with challenging environments. However, prolonged exposure to stress can lead to maladaptive changes, particularly in the following areas:

- **Prefrontal Cortex:** This area, responsible for decision making, logical thinking, and self control, becomes impaired under chronic stress. Leaders with prolonged stress often experience decision fatigue, impulsivity, and difficulty in strategic thinking. These changes can impair a leader's ability to focus and prioritise tasks effectively (Harvard University, 2021).
- **Amygdala:** The amygdala regulates emotional responses and is involved in the brain's "fight-or-flight" mechanism. Chronic stress heightens the activity of the amygdala, leading to increased fear, anxiety, and emotional volatility. This makes leaders more reactive and prone to burnout (McEwen & Akil, 2020).

Reversing Stress Effects Through Neuroplasticity:
Fortunately, neuroplasticity offers a pathway for recovery. Engaging in activities like mindfulness, cognitive behavioural therapy (CBT), and regular physical exercise helps stimulate healthier neural pathways and reverse the effects of stress. Research from Harvard University shows that just eight weeks of mindfulness training can increase grey matter density in the prefrontal cortex, improving cognitive control, emotional regulation, and overall resilience (Harvard University, 2021).

Effects of Chronic Stress on the Brain

Key Idea:
Burnout causes structural changes in the brain. Understanding how stress impacts specific brain regions can help leaders identify burnout early and take proactive steps to protect their mental health.

The Prefrontal Cortex and Decision Making:
The prefrontal cortex is responsible for high level decision making, planning, and prioritisation. Chronic stress weakens its functioning, making it difficult for leaders to manage complex tasks, focus, and avoid procrastination. Leaders experiencing burnout often feel overwhelmed by cognitive overload, leading to diminished decision making abilities (McEwen & Akil, 2020).

The Amygdala and Emotional Regulation:
The amygdala becomes hyperactive when exposed to chronic stress, leading to heightened emotional reactivity. Leaders who suffer from burnout are more prone to irritability, anxiety, and emotional instability. This emotional volatility can disrupt leadership effectiveness, as reactions become less measured and more impulsive (American Psychological Association, 2020).

The Hippocampus and Memory:
The hippocampus, responsible for memory and learning, is another area significantly impacted by chronic stress. Prolonged stress leads to shrinkage in the hippocampus, resulting in difficulties with memory retention, cognitive fatigue, and forgetfulness. This can make it challenging for leaders to retain new information and perform effectively in dynamic environments (McEwen & Akil, 2020).

Frazzle: The Cognitive Cost of Chronic Stress

Neuroscientist Amy Arnsten describes a critical neural tipping point known as frazzle – a state where the brain's prefrontal cortex becomes overwhelmed by stress and temporarily shuts down (Arnsten, 2009). In this state, control shifts to more reactive, emotion-driven regions such as the amygdala. Leaders experiencing frazzle may find themselves unusually forgetful, emotionally volatile, or unable to access previously routine thinking. Decision quality drops. Reactions become automatic. Tasks that were once simple begin to feel impossible.

Recent research has validated Arnsten's model, showing that even mild but persistent stress can significantly impair prefrontal connectivity, disrupting attention, planning, and working memory (Liston et al., 2009). In school leadership, this often presents as irritability, mental fog, impulsive decisions, and a loss of perspective under pressure.

Frazzle also plays a role in burnout's early stages. It is a sign that the brain is no longer effectively regulating stress responses and is beginning to operate in survival mode. When leaders remain in this state without sufficient recovery, neural circuits begin to reorganise around dysfunction – what researchers call allostatic load (Juster et al., 2010). Allostatic load represents the cumulative impact of stress on the brain and body and often marks the shift from short-term strain to long term burnout.

Understanding frazzle as a neural state, not a personal failure, empowers leaders to intervene earlier and more effectively. Catching the signs of cognitive overload before they solidify into burnout is one of the most important steps towards long term leadership sustainability.

Reframing Stress – a Mindset Reset for Sustainable Leadership

One of the most powerful breakthroughs in leadership wellbeing research is the discovery that how we think about stress directly shapes its impact on our minds and bodies. Burnout is not caused by stress alone. It is caused by how we relate to it, and whether we recover from it.

While most leaders are taught to manage stress by reducing it, emerging research suggests that a more impactful intervention may be to reframe it. Psychologist Kelly McGonigal (2015) found that people who experienced high levels of stress but did not believe it was harmful were significantly healthier than those who feared stress – even healthier than people with low stress levels. It was not just the stress itself, but the mindset about stress that predicted their health outcomes.

This is echoed in studies by Crum et al. (2017), who coined the term "stress is enhancing mindset". When individuals view stress as a challenge rather than a threat, their performance, emotional regulation, and physiological resilience all improve. Leaders with this mindset demonstrate greater cognitive flexibility, more adaptive behaviour under pressure, and even healthier cortisol responses.

This shift is not abstract. A practical tool known as Implementation Intentions can make this mindset actionable. For example:

"If I feel tension before a team meeting, then I will take two deep breaths and remind myself that this stress means I care about the outcome."

These micro-strategies interrupt the automatic stress-threat response and reinforce a more constructive, intentional relationship with pressure.

For leaders, the implication is profound: Stress is not the enemy. Stagnation is. When leaders can shift from fear of stress to engagement with it, they are more likely to avoid frazzle and prevent the cascade into burnout. This mindset is not a denial of stress, but a redirection of its energy – a reset at the level of perception.

Mindfulness and Neuroplasticity: Building Neurological Resilience

Key Idea:
Mindfulness practices are proven to build neurological resilience by strengthening brain areas responsible for emotional regulation, self awareness, and decision making. By regularly engaging in mindfulness exercises, leaders can reverse the negative effects of stress and improve their mental clarity, resilience, and cognitive control.

Mindfulness and Brain Function:
Research from Stanford University shows that mindfulness enhances neuroplasticity in brain areas such as the prefrontal cortex, reducing activity in the amygdala, which lowers stress levels. Leaders who practise mindfulness report improved emotional regulation, better decision making abilities, and greater resilience to stress (Stanford University, 2022).

Practical Applications of Mindfulness:
Leaders can integrate mindfulness into their daily routines using the following practices:

- **Focused Breathing Exercises:** Focusing on diaphragmatic breathing quickly calms the nervous system by activating the parasympathetic response, reducing cortisol levels and restoring focus.
- **Body Scan Meditation:** This meditation encourages awareness of physical tension throughout the body, promoting relaxation and a sense of calm.

- **Meditation Apps:** Apps such as **Headspace** and **Calm** offer guided meditations designed to reduce stress and enhance focus, making it easier for leaders to practice mindfulness on the go (Headspace, Calm).

The Importance of Sleep for Brain Function and Stress Resilience

Key Idea:
Sleep is critical for maintaining cognitive function, emotional regulation, and stress resilience. Chronic sleep deprivation exacerbates the negative effects of burnout by impairing decision making, increasing emotional reactivity, and reducing resilience. Leaders need to prioritise sleep as an essential part of their stress management strategy.

How Sleep Affects the Brain:
During sleep, the brain performs several crucial functions, such as:

- **Memory Consolidation:** Sleep enables the hippocampus to store and retrieve memories, helping leaders retain and use new information effectively.
- **Toxin Removal:** The brain clears toxins and waste products during sleep, including proteins linked to neurodegenerative diseases.
- **Emotional Regulation:** Adequate sleep reduces activity in the amygdala, leading to improved emotional stability and less reactivity to stressors.

Sleep deprivation negatively affects the brain by:

- **Reducing Cognitive Function:** Leaders who are sleep deprived struggle with focus, creativity, and decision making, as the prefrontal cortex is particularly sensitive to lack of rest (McEwen & Akil, 2020).
- **Emotional Dysregulation:** Without sufficient sleep, the amygdala becomes hyperactive, leading to emotional reactivity and poor stress management.

Practical Sleep Optimisation Strategies:

- **Establish a Consistent Sleep Schedule:** Leaders should maintain regular sleep and wake times, even on weekends, to regulate their circadian rhythm.

- **Create a Sleep-Friendly Environment:** Ensuring a quiet, dark, and cool room promotes better sleep quality. Minimising screen time before bed helps avoid disrupting sleep patterns.
- **Prioritise Sleep Hygiene:** Leaders should avoid caffeine and large meals before bed and engage in relaxing activities like reading or light meditation before sleeping.

Social Connectivity and Brain Health: The Role of Relationships in Preventing Burnout

Key Idea:
Positive social interactions and supportive relationships play a crucial role in brain health and resilience. Leaders who cultivate strong social networks – both professionally and personally – are better equipped to manage stress and avoid burnout.

Social Connectivity and the Brain:
Research shows that social interactions trigger the release of oxytocin, a hormone that reduces stress and fosters feelings of trust and safety. Leaders who engage in meaningful social connections are more likely to experience reduced stress levels, improved emotional regulation, and enhanced cognitive resilience (Stanford University, 2022).

Benefits of Social Support for Leaders:

- **Emotional Regulation:** Social connections help reduce amygdala activity, allowing leaders to better manage their emotions in stressful situations.
- **Cognitive Resilience:** Supportive relationships act as a buffer against stress, helping leaders think more clearly and avoid cognitive fatigue.
- **Improved Team Dynamics:** Leaders who foster strong relationships within their teams create environments where psychological safety thrives, reducing burnout risks for both themselves and their teams.

Beyond Exhaustion: The Disillusionment Factor

An often overlooked dimension of modern leadership burnout is systemic disenchantment – the progressive loss of faith in the very systems leaders are tasked with upholding. This goes beyond individual exhaustion to a deeper question of meaning and purpose.

It was not just my body that was tired. It was my belief in the system. Burnout was not just about workload. It was about disillusionment. Watching promising initiatives fail due to structural barriers, seeing the same issues resurface despite best efforts, and struggling to create meaningful change within constraining parameters all contributed to this form of burnout.

The Gallup *State of the Global Workplace* report (2023b) confirms this trend, with 60% of leaders reporting disconnection from their organisation's mission, a figure that has risen steadily over the past decade.

The antidote to disenchantment is not blind optimism, but a clear eyed commitment to what matters most, coupled with realistic expectations about the pace and scale of change. Leaders who navigate this form of burnout often redefine success on their own terms, focusing on spheres where they can create meaningful impact while acknowledging systemic limitations.

Practical Neuroscience Based Tools for Leaders

Key Idea:
Leaders can adopt neuroscience based tools to manage stress and prevent burnout. These practices promote resilience and protect against the cognitive and emotional effects of chronic stress.

Breathing Exercises:
Practicing deep belly breathing (diaphragmatic breathing) activates the parasympathetic nervous system, lowering cortisol levels and helping leaders stay calm during stressful situations (Stanford University, 2022).

Cognitive Behavioural Techniques:
CBT helps leaders reframe negative thought patterns and develop healthier responses to stress. For example, a leader might challenge the belief that they must immediately resolve every issue, learning to prioritise tasks effectively and delegate when necessary (Tang et al., 2015).

Physical Exercise:
Exercise stimulates neurogenesis (the growth of new neurons), particularly in the hippocampus, and reduces cortisol levels, enhancing emotional wellbeing and cognitive function. Leaders who exercise regularly experience reduced stress levels and improved brain resilience (Sapolsky, 2004).

The Neuroscience of Recovery: From Damage to Rebuilding

While the tools and strategies outlined above are vital for managing stress, cutting-edge neuroscience research now offers profound insights for leaders who have already experienced burnout. The brain's remarkable neuroplasticity, its capacity to reorganise and form new neural pathways, provides a biological foundation for recovery even after significant stress related damage has occurred.

Recent studies from Stanford University (2022) demonstrate that targeted recovery protocols can accelerate the restoration of prefrontal cortex function following burnout. This research builds upon what we've discussed regarding how stress affects brain structure, but focuses specifically on rehabilitation and rebuilding neural capacity. These structured approaches include:

1. **Cognitive Reset Periods:** Research shows that complete disengagement from work-related thinking for at least 7–10 consecutive days begins to reverse the neurological patterns associated with chronic stress. Unlike typical holidays, which often involve planning and decision making, these reset periods must minimise cognitive load through simple activities in nature or meditative practices. The key factor is the complete absence of work-related problem solving, which allows overtaxed neural circuits to recover.
2. **Micro-Recovery Practices:** Beyond longer reset periods, implementing brief but frequent recovery moments throughout the workday strengthens neural pathways associated with resilience. Even 5–10 minutes of mindfulness practice four times daily can reduce cortisol levels and improve executive function, according to findings from Tang et al. (2015). These micro-breaks interrupt the cycle of stress accumulation and promote a return to baseline cortisol levels before they reach damaging thresholds.
3. **Cognitive Restructuring:** Targeted cognitive behavioural techniques help leaders identify and reconstruct stress inducing thought patterns. This process physically rewires neural circuits, improving emotional regulation capacity during challenging leadership situations. Brain imaging studies show actual structural changes in the amygdala and prefrontal cortex following consistent cognitive restructuring practice,

demonstrating that these techniques are not merely psychological but neurological interventions.

For leaders rebuilding after burnout, understanding these neurological processes offers both hope and direction. Recovery is not merely about feeling better, it's about actual structural restoration of the brain's capacity for focus, decision making, and emotional regulation. When leaders understand that burnout causes physical changes to their brain architecture, they can approach recovery with the same intentionality they would bring to physical rehabilitation after an injury.

Organisations that incorporate these findings into leadership development programs support both prevention and recovery by recognising that neurological wellbeing is fundamental to sustainable leadership. By viewing leadership burnout through a neuroscience lens, organisations shift from purely psychological interventions to comprehensive approaches that address the physical substrate of leadership capability, the brain itself.

Practical Application: Brain Based Recovery Strategies

To leverage neuroscience for leadership recovery and resilience:

1. **Implement daily mindfulness practice:** Begin with just five minutes of focused breathing daily to strengthen your prefrontal cortex and reduce amygdala reactivity. Even this brief practice has been shown to improve executive function when done consistently.
2. **Structure brain friendly workdays:** Plan your schedule to align with cognitive patterns:

    - Schedule complex thinking work during your peak alertness period.
    - Take a ten minute movement break after 90 minutes of focused work.
    - Avoid scheduling important decisions when emotionally triggered.

3. **Prioritise sleep quality:** Enhance your neural recovery by improving sleep:

    - Maintain consistent sleep and wake times, even at weekends.

- Create a 30 minute technology free buffer before bedtime.
- Keep your bedroom cool, dark, and quiet to optimise sleep architecture.

4. **Track cognitive recovery:** Note improvements in decision quality, emotional regulation, and mental clarity as you implement these practices. Recognising positive change reinforces neural recovery pathways.

Use the **Recovery Micro Practices** in the Tools and Templates section to implement brain based interventions throughout your workday, matching the duration to your available time and specific recovery needs.

Final Thought

Leadership burnout is not just emotional or mental – it is neurological. Chronic stress reshapes the brain, impairing decision making, emotional regulation, and the very capacity to lead with clarity and connection. I recall a period when the weight of leadership blurred my thinking, narrowed my focus, and left me emotionally depleted. At the time, I thought I just needed more rest. What I needed was a reset – grounded in both reflection and science.

This chapter has integrated personal insight with neuroscience to show how the brain responds to prolonged stress, and, importantly, how it can recover. Through practical strategies like mindfulness, sleep optimisation, social connection, cognitive behavioural tools, and movement, leaders can actively rewire their brains to restore function, improve focus, and regain resilience.

The journey from burnout to breakthrough is not just about endurance. It is about learning how to work with your brain, not against it. With insight and intention, leaders can rebuild the cognitive and emotional foundations needed to thrive, even in demanding environments.

In the Next Chapter

Now that we understand the neurological cost of burnout, we turn to its wider consequences. In Chapter 5, we explore the broader impact of burnout on leaders, teams, and organisations. From productivity losses to cultural erosion, this next chapter outlines why addressing burnout is not just a personal priority, but a strategic imperative.

Reflection Questions

Personal Reflection Questions

1. How have prolonged periods of stress affected your cognitive functions, particularly your ability to think strategically or regulate emotions during challenging interactions?
2. Which specific habits in your daily routine most significantly contribute to your chronic stress? What neurological patterns might these habits be reinforcing?
3. What evidence have you noticed of stress impacting your brain function, such as memory lapses, decision fatigue, or emotional reactivity?
4. Which neuroscience based resilience strategies have you meaningfully incorporated into your routine, and which remain intellectual concepts rather than embodied practices?
5. How might you leverage your understanding of neuroplasticity to design leadership practices that promote brain health alongside organisational effectiveness?

Team Reflection Questions

1. How does our collective work environment either support neural recovery or exacerbate stress responses? What specific environmental factors could we modify?
2. What team practices might we implement to support healthy brain function, such as meeting structures that respect attention spans or communication protocols that reduce cognitive load?
3. How can we create a culture that values recovery time as essential for cognitive performance rather than viewing it as unproductive?
4. What neuroscience informed approach might we take towards leadership development that accounts for how the brain functions under pressure?
5. How might our understanding of stress effects on the brain influence how we structure workloads, deadlines, and performance expectations?

Key Takeaways

- **Chronic stress alters brain function:** Prolonged stress reshapes key brain regions like the prefrontal cortex, amygdala, and hippocampus, impairing decision making, emotional regulation, and memory, with effects reversible through targeted interventions.
- **Neuroplasticity enables recovery:** The brain's ability to rebuild neural pathways weakened by chronic stress allows leaders to recover through practices such as mindfulness, physical exercise, and cognitive behavioural therapy.
- **Mindfulness enhances cognitive control:** Regular mindfulness practice improves brain function, enhancing decision making abilities, emotional regulation, and stress resilience by promoting healthy restructuring of neural pathways.
- **Quality sleep is crucial for recovery:** Sufficient sleep maintains cognitive function, consolidates memory, and balances emotions. Leaders who prioritise sleep experience better mental clarity and greater stress resilience.
- **Social connections reduce stress impact:** Positive interactions and strong support networks lower amygdala activity and improve emotional regulation, enabling leaders to manage stress more effectively through enhanced cognitive resilience.

5

THE COST OF LEADERSHIP BURNOUT

IMPACT ON ORGANISATIONAL SUCCESS AND FINANCIAL STABILITY

Overview

Leadership burnout has far-reaching consequences that extend beyond individual wellbeing, threatening the foundation of organisational success. Reflecting on my own experience, I vividly recall the personal toll of burnout – feeling overwhelmed, emotionally depleted, and constantly on edge. While I managed to shield my organisation from immediate fallout by hiding my struggles, the strain was unsustainable. Had I not stepped away when I did, I feared my burnout would have begun to erode the very culture and stability of the school I led.

This chapter delves into these pervasive impacts, particularly in the Australian context, to illustrate how leadership burnout, if unchecked, can ripple through an organisation, undermining productivity, innovation, and team morale. By connecting personal insight with broader trends, we uncover how prioritising leader wellbeing is not just beneficial but essential for organisational success.

DOI: 10.4324/9781003668626-7

Drawing on real world examples from domestic and global organisations, we unpack how burnout diminishes productivity, erodes innovation, and undermines employee morale. The financial costs are stark: increased turnover, recruitment expenses, absenteeism, and healthcare outlays. These figures underscore the urgency for organisational preventative measures.

Incorporating evidence-based research and practical applications, this chapter bridges the gap between theoretical understanding and actionable strategies. From case studies featuring organisations like Google and Unilever to insights tailored for Australian workplaces, it provides readers with tools to mitigate burnout's impact. Leaders will discover how prioritising wellbeing fosters resilience, boosts team engagement, and enhances long term organisational stability. By integrating personal narrative, cutting edge research, and practical solutions, this chapter offers a comprehensive roadmap to address leadership burnout's profound organisational implications.

Loss of Productivity and Innovation

Key Idea:
Burnout among leaders directly impairs their capacity to maintain high levels of productivity and creativity. Cognitive exhaustion and emotional fatigue impede decision making and problem solving abilities, which are essential for driving organisational success.

Productivity Decline:
Research demonstrates that burnt out leaders are prone to decision fatigue, which results in compromised judgment and inefficient task prioritisation. A study from the *Harvard Business Review* (2021a) shows that leadership burnout can lead to a 25–30% reduction in productivity, as stressed leaders struggle to meet deadlines and fulfil strategic goals. In Australia, sectors like healthcare and education – where decision making is critical and time sensitive – have reported significant performance declines due to leadership fatigue. The Principal Health and Wellbeing Survey (2023) revealed that 45% of Australian school leaders experience high levels of emotional exhaustion, leading to disruptions in both teacher performance and student outcomes.

Innovation Stifled:
The loss of innovation is another critical consequence of leadership burnout. Innovation requires mental clarity, cognitive flexibility, and the ability to approach problems with fresh perspectives – capacities that are diminished in overworked and burnt out leaders. Neuroscientific studies conducted by

McKinsey & Company (2021) indicate that chronic stress reduces activity in the prefrontal cortex, impairing creativity and the executive function necessary for strategic innovation. In industries such as technology and creative services, where innovation is the key to competitive advantage, leadership burnout can result in stagnation. The World Economic Forum (2022) found that burnt out leaders contribute to a 45% reduction in innovation output, leaving teams without the strategic direction needed to excel.

Impact on Team Morale

Key Idea:
Leadership burnout undermines not only the leader's effectiveness but also the overall wellbeing and performance of their team. The emotional disengagement that accompanies burnout erodes trust and collaboration, lowering team morale and productivity.

Disengagement and Absenteeism:
When leaders disengage, their teams follow suit. Burnt out leaders often become emotionally detached, which can create a cascade of disengagement within the team. The Gallup (2021a) report highlights that teams led by burnt out leaders experience a 21% decrease in productivity and double the risk of absenteeism. In Australia, the education sector again provides a stark example: according to the Principal Health and Wellbeing Survey (2023), school leaders suffering from burnout see increased rates of teacher absenteeism, and as a result, a deterioration in student learning outcomes.

> **CASE STUDY**
>
> **AUSTRALIAN EDUCATION SECTOR**
>
> In high stress environments like education, leadership burnout can be particularly damaging. The high emotional toll on principals, as evidenced in the Australian Principal Occupational Health, Safety and Wellbeing Survey (Australian Catholic University, 2024), has led to increased teacher turnover, absenteeism, and poor student performance. Burnt out school leaders become less engaged with their teaching staff, resulting in a trickle down effect that compromises the overall effectiveness of the school. This case illustrates how burnout at the leadership level can lead to widespread organisational dysfunction and poor outcomes across various metrics.

Erosion of Company Culture

Key Idea:
Burnt out leaders often unintentionally erode the fabric of organisational culture. Trust, collaboration, and psychological safety are all at risk when leaders are unable to model healthy engagement.

Breakdown of Trust and Collaboration:
A leader's emotional withdrawal due to burnout can undermine the very culture they've worked to build. According to research by *Forbes* (2021), nearly 80% of employees working under burnt out leaders report higher levels of stress, lower job satisfaction, and reduced teamwork. As teams become less cohesive, collaboration suffers, and silos form. In Australia, this phenomenon is evident in high pressure industries like healthcare and finance, where the competitive and time sensitive nature of the work environment exacerbates the negative effects of leadership disengagement.

Long Term Cultural Damage:
Cultural damage caused by burnt out leadership can take years to repair. A study by the Chartered Institute of Personnel and Development and Simplyhealth (CIPD & Simplyhealth, 2022) found that organisations with burnt out leaders experience a 20% decline in employee engagement over time, leading to increased turnover and decreased loyalty. In the Australian context, where industries such as construction and resource management face high levels of leadership burnout, the loss of cohesive culture leads to a slower recovery from economic downturns and weaker competitive positioning.

Financial Costs of Burnout

Key Idea:
Burnout not only affects the human elements of an organisation but also imposes substantial financial costs. These include increased turnover, recruitment and onboarding expenses, lost productivity, and growing healthcare costs.

Turnover Costs:
Leadership turnover is expensive, particularly when it results from burnout. This concern has become increasingly urgent, with the 2024 Australian Principal Occupational Health, Safety and Wellbeing Survey revealing that

more than half of school principals intend to quit or retire early, with experienced leaders (15+ years) leading this trend (Australian Catholic University, 2024). The costs go beyond recruiting and onboarding; they encompass the lost productivity during the transition period, as well as the disruption of team dynamics. With burnout now attributed to 40% of employee resignations across sectors (Foremind, 2024), organisations face significant financial repercussions.

Research from the Center for American Progress found that very highly paid jobs and those at the senior or executive levels tend to have disproportionately high turnover costs – up to 213% of annual salary. In industries like healthcare and finance, where leadership expertise is specialised, the cost of replacing a leader is even higher due to the extended onboarding process and strategic disruption this causes.

Lost Productivity:
Burnout-related declines in productivity can cripple an organisation. The World Economic Forum (2022) reported that productivity loss from burnt out leaders could reach up to 30%. This is particularly damaging in industries where agile decision making and fast paced innovation are key to survival, such as Australia's tech and creative sectors. The ripple effect of leadership burnout often spreads through departments, causing delays in projects, missed deadlines, and lost revenue.

Healthcare Costs:
The financial burden of leadership burnout has grown increasingly significant for Australian organisations. Recent data reveals that more than half of Australian school principals intend to quit or retire early, with experienced leaders (15+ years) leading this trend (Australian Catholic University, 2024). This leadership exodus creates substantial financial implications beyond recruitment costs, including knowledge loss, transition disruption, and reduced organisational performance during leadership gaps.

With burnout now increasingly driving employee resignations across sectors, organisations face multiple financial consequences. Gallup research confirms that burnt out employees are 2.6 times more likely to be actively seeking a different job (Gallup, 2022). The direct costs of replacing a senior leader can range from 150–200% of their annual salary when accounting for recruitment, onboarding, and productivity losses during transitions (Harvard Business Review, 2023).

Beyond replacement costs, leadership burnout impacts organisational performance through decreased innovation, reduced team engagement, and lower productivity. Burned-out employees are 63% more likely to take a sick day and significantly more likely to disengage at work (Gallup, 2022), creating substantial financial implications for organisations' competitive positioning and market adaptability.

Real World Case Studies

Google:
In high performance sectors like technology, leadership burnout has been linked to delays in product development and reduced market competitiveness. Industry research highlights that burnout among senior leaders can impair strategic execution and innovation. In response, many organisations have introduced wellness initiatives, such as executive coaching and streamlined meeting schedules, to support leadership wellbeing. These interventions have been associated with improved engagement and faster delivery timelines (*Harvard Business Review*, 2021a).

Microsoft: Microsoft faced leadership burnout as senior executives struggled to manage global operations across time zones. To combat this, the company introduced digital wellbeing programs focused on mindfulness, flexible working hours, and encouraging digital detoxes. These initiatives led to a 50% reduction in burnout symptoms among senior leaders (Pontefract, 2024).

The Wellbeing Perception Gap: Recent research highlights a concerning disconnect in how leaders perceive wellbeing compared to their teams. The State of Workplace Burnout 2024 report found that 68% of managers believe their people's wellbeing is the same or better compared to 12 months ago, while 45% of employees report their wellbeing has worsened in the same period (Infinite Potential, 2024). This perception gap can lead to inadequate support measures and contribute to higher burnout rates. Organisations must implement regular, anonymous wellbeing assessment tools to ensure accurate understanding of employee experiences.

Unilever: After a period of rapid expansion, Unilever experienced a drop in leadership productivity linked to burnout. By introducing mental health programs and flexible working policies, Unilever saw a 25% reduction in absenteeism and improved employee satisfaction (Unilever, n.d.).

Demographic Dimensions of Leadership Burnout

Leadership burnout manifests differently across demographic groups, reflecting how various sociocultural factors influence stress and recovery patterns. Understanding these nuances is essential for developing inclusive support strategies.

Gender Dimensions: Beyond the general statistics on women's increasing burnout rates (42% compared to men's 30%), research reveals more nuanced patterns. Women in leadership positions frequently report experiencing "compound pressure," the expectation to demonstrate exceptional competence while maintaining emotional support for teams. This often translates to women spending 25–30% more time on people management issues than male counterparts in equivalent roles (McKinsey & Company, 2023c).

Cultural and Ethnic Considerations: Leaders from culturally diverse backgrounds often face "representation fatigue" the added burden of being expected to represent entire communities while navigating majority culture environments. In Australian contexts, Indigenous leaders report 37% higher burnout rates, often citing the emotional labour of bridging cultural divides alongside standard leadership responsibilities (Diversity Council Australia, 2023).

Age and Generation: Cross generational research reveals significant differences in burnout manifestation:

- Gen Z leaders (under 30) experience higher levels of anxiety but greater willingness to discuss mental health openly.
- Mid-career leaders (30–45) report the highest work family conflict.
- Late career leaders (55+) demonstrate greater emotional resilience but more physical manifestations of stress.

Neurodiversity Considerations: Neurodivergent leaders (including those with ADHD, autism, or dyslexia) report unique burnout patterns. While often possessing exceptional problem solving abilities, the constant "masking" required in traditional work environments creates significant cognitive load. Studies show neurodivergent leaders benefit particularly from clear boundaries, reduced sensory overload, and explicit communication protocols (Harvard Business Review, 2023).

Organisations developing burnout prevention strategies must accommodate these diverse experiences rather than implementing one size fits all approaches. Successful programs recognise that leadership wellbeing initiatives need to be as diverse as leaders themselves.

Industry Specific Burnout Impact: Australian Case Studies

Healthcare Sector:
Burnout among healthcare professionals in Australia remains a pressing concern. Mental Health Australia's 2022 survey revealed that 84% of healthcare workers reported increased stress and pressure in the workplace due to the pandemic (Mental Health Australia, 2023). This heightened stress has contributed to significant workforce challenges, particularly in remote areas. For instance, turnover rates in remote Aboriginal Community Controlled Health Services have exceeded 150%, underscoring the urgency of addressing burnout to improve staff retention and patient care. (Healthcare Professionals Association of Australia [HPAA], 2025).

In response, some healthcare organisations have implemented comprehensive leadership wellbeing programs, incorporating structured peer support, realistic workload assessments, and mandatory recovery periods after intensive care cycles. These initiatives aim to address burnout and improve overall clinical outcomes.

Resources Sector:
Leadership fatigue in the Australian resources sector has been directly linked to increased safety risks. In Western Australia, fatigue was identified as a contributing factor in 2.5% of all notifiable mining incidents, often during periods of extended managerial shifts without breaks (Mining Magazine Australia, 2023).

In response, leading mining companies have adopted leadership rotation systems for remote sites, introduced comprehensive fatigue management policies, and established routine wellbeing assessments. Although industry-wide statistics on outcomes remain limited, these measures align with national safety recommendations and reflect best practice in reducing operational risk (Mining Magazine Australia, 2023).

Financial Services:
Leadership burnout in the financial services sector has had measurable effects on engagement, performance, and client outcomes. A 2023 study by the Corporate Mental Health Alliance Australia found that 44% of

professionals in the sector experienced burnout symptoms, with consequences for both retention and innovation (Corporate Mental Health Alliance Australia [CMHAA], 2023).

In response, some institutions have taken an organisational approach. They have separated client-facing responsibilities from internal leadership functions, introduced quarterly wellbeing retreats for executive teams, and embedded wellbeing indicators into leadership KPIs. These initiatives reflect a growing understanding that sustainable leadership cannot be achieved without structural support (CMHAA, 2023).

These diverse examples demonstrate how leadership burnout impacts different sectors in unique ways, while highlighting the common thread that organisational performance is directly linked to leadership wellbeing across all industries.

Practical Application: Building Your Business Case

To translate the costs of burnout into a compelling case for organisational change:

1. **Quantify personal impact:** Estimate the productivity impact of your own experience with burnout or stress. Consider:

    - Hours of reduced productivity weekly
    - Percentage decline in decision quality
    - Time spent recovering from stress related challenges

2. **Calculate team effect:** Assess how leadership stress cascades to your team by noting:

    - Changes in team engagement metrics
    - Increases in team conflict or misunderstandings
    - Impact on innovation and creative thinking

3. **Frame in organisational terms:** Translate these effects into language that resonates with key stakeholders:

    - For executives: Emphasise financial and strategic implications
    - For HR: Focus on retention and engagement metrics
    - For operations: Highlight reliability and quality impacts

4. **Propose targeted solutions:** Suggest 1–2 specific, achievable interventions rather than wholesale change, focusing on those with highest potential return.

The **Organisational Burnout Assessment** in the Tools and Templates section helps you identify organisational factors contributing to burnout and prioritise interventions with the highest potential impact.

Final Thought

The cost of leadership burnout is far reaching, affecting not just individual leaders but entire teams, organisational culture, and long term performance. From reduced productivity and increased staff turnover to cultural decline and financial strain, burnout is a challenge no organisation can afford to overlook. Reflecting on my own experience, I recognise how the pressure to perform without prioritising wellbeing placed both my health and the stability of the school I led at risk.

To address burnout effectively, organisations must take a proactive approach. This includes embedding mental health support, tailoring leadership development, and integrating structured wellbeing initiatives into daily practice. Evidence-based strategies, such as building emotional resilience and fostering psychological safety, are essential, not optional.

In the Australian context, with its unique cultural dynamics and sector specific pressures, local solutions matter. Case studies from both global organisations and our own education systems highlight the clear benefits of investing in leader wellbeing. These investments lead to stronger outcomes, greater innovation, and more resilient workplace cultures.

This chapter is a call to action. It is not only about protecting those who lead, but about ensuring the long term health and success of the organisations they serve.

In the Next Chapter

Burnout recovery begins with clarity and direction. In Chapter 6, we introduce the Leadership Reset Framework, a four-phase model designed to help leaders shift from overwhelm to alignment. You will explore the foundation of this framework and how it provides a practical, sustainable path forward for those ready to lead differently.

Reflection Questions

Personal Reflection Questions

1. How has your experience with burnout affected your team's performance, innovation capacity, or engagement levels in ways that might not be immediately apparent?
2. What hidden costs of your leadership burnout have you observed beyond your personal wellbeing, such as impacts on team trust or organisational culture?
3. How might you quantify the cost of your burnout in terms that would resonate with key stakeholders in your organisation?
4. What organisational factors in your organisational structure contribute most significantly to your experience of burnout? Which of these factors could you influence?
5. How does your approach to wellbeing set the tone for your team's culture? What messages might your behaviour be sending about sustainable leadership?

Team Reflection Questions

1. What are the quantifiable costs of leadership burnout in our organisation in terms of turnover, absenteeism, lost innovation, or reduced engagement?
2. How has leadership burnout affected our organisational culture in ways that might not appear in financial metrics but impact our long term sustainability?
3. What business case could we develop for investing in leadership wellbeing that would appeal to various stakeholders in our organisation?
4. Which structural or cultural factors in our organisation most significantly contribute to leadership burnout? What collective action could address these factors?
5. How might we better measure and communicate the relationship between leadership wellbeing and organisational performance?

Key Takeaways

- **Leadership burnout has wide-reaching organisational impact:** Burnout undermines productivity, stifles innovation, and erodes team morale, creating ripple effects throughout the organisation that threaten long term success.

- **Significant financial costs burden organisations:** Leadership burnout incurs substantial expenses through increased turnover (up to 200% of annual salary), absenteeism, productivity losses (up to 30%), and rising healthcare costs.
- **Real world solutions demonstrate positive outcomes:** Companies like Google, Microsoft, and Unilever show how structured wellness programs, executive coaching, and flexible work policies yield measurable improvements in leadership sustainability.
- **Australian organisations face sector specific challenges:** Education, healthcare, and technology sectors in Australia must implement targeted interventions to address concerning trends, including the high proportion of leaders planning early retirement.
- **Preventative measures yield better returns than reactive approaches:** Organisations that invest proactively in leadership wellbeing experience higher engagement, increased innovation, and sustained competitive advantage compared to those addressing burnout after it occurs.

PART 2

THE LEADERSHIP RESET FRAMEWORK

6

INTRODUCTION TO THE LEADERSHIP RESET FRAMEWORK

Overview

The Leadership Reset Framework (Figure 6.1) is not just a model; it's a lifeline for leaders navigating the relentless demands of modern leadership. I know this firsthand. At the height of my own burnout, I felt like I was running on fumes, unable to see a way forward. That experience became the foundation for creating a framework that doesn't just help leaders recover but equips them to emerge stronger, more self aware, and purpose driven.

This four-phase journey – **Recognition, Reflection, Realignment, and Reinvention** – provides a structured yet personal path to transform what feels like a breaking point into a breakthrough. These phases are designed to guide you through the RESET process I introduced earlier – **R**ecognising burnout's reality, **E**xploring your authentic leadership through reflection, **S**hifting priorities through realignment, and **E**mbedding sustainable practices through reinvention – ultimately helping you **T**hrive as a leader who balances wellbeing with impact.

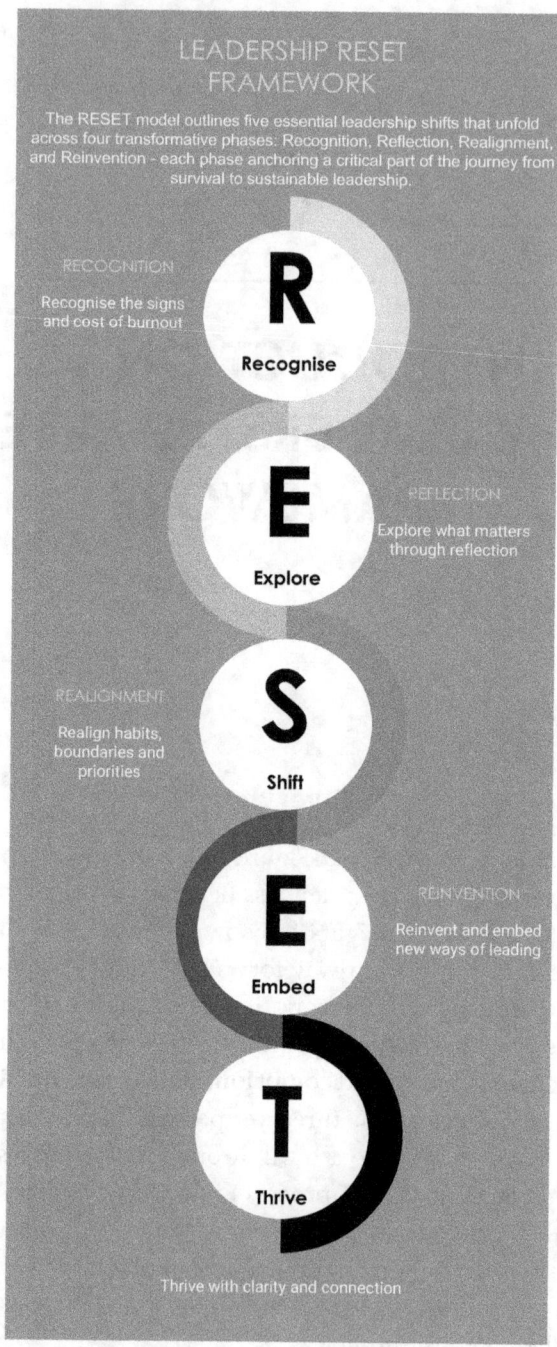

Figure 6.1 The Leadership Reset Framework

Each phase builds upon the other, guiding leaders to confront their challenges, redefine their priorities, and reimagine their leadership with resilience and sustainability at its core. This chapter introduces the framework, sharing practical insights from my experience and from leaders who've faced similar struggles.

Today's leadership landscape is more demanding than ever. The pressure to innovate, manage complex teams, and meet expectations leaves little space to pause and recalibrate. Burnout, long dismissed as a personal failing, is now recognised as an organisational issue. Gallup (2020) highlights that nearly 76% of employees experience burnout, with leaders bearing a disproportionate share of the burden. Similarly, the World Health Organization (2019) officially identifies burnout as an "occupational phenomenon," underscoring its profound impact on wellbeing and performance.

The Leadership Reset Framework is a response to these challenges. It empowers leaders to turn burnout into a springboard for growth, offering actionable steps to regain control, realign their purpose, and reinvent their approach to leadership. This chapter invites you to explore how this transformative process can lead to long term success, both personally and professionally.

Personal Reflection: Why This Framework Mattered to Me

My journey through burnout and recovery has followed what I now recognise as the RESET path – a framework that captures the full arc of moving from crisis to renewal:

Recognise the reality of burnout. This was perhaps the hardest step. For too long, I mistook my exhaustion, irritability, and disconnection as temporary challenges rather than warning signs of a deeper problem. The breaking point on Military Road, when panic overwhelmed me while driving, became impossible to ignore. True recognition came when my GP used the term *major depressive disorder*, forcing me to confront what I had been minimising for months. Recognition requires honesty, the courage to acknowledge when we are not okay. I want to be clear, this book is not a clinical exploration of depression. For me, the diagnosis was a jarring confirmation of how far burnout had gone unchecked. The heart of this book remains leadership burnout – what causes it, how to recognise it, and how to recover in a way that leads to sustainable reinvention.

Explore through reflection and self awareness. Once I admitted I was burnt out, I began the process of exploration. Through journaling, therapy, and conversations with trusted colleagues, I examined the patterns and beliefs that had led me to this point. I explored the disconnect between my stated values and my actual behaviours. This exploration was not comfortable; it required facing uncomfortable truths about my drive for validation, my difficulty setting boundaries, and my tendency to derive worth from achievement. Yet this exploration provided essential insights without which change would have been impossible.

Shift priorities and establish new boundaries. With greater awareness came the need for decisive action. I shifted my relationship with time by restructuring my calendar to include recovery periods. I learned to delegate responsibilities I had previously clung to, trusting others with tasks I had considered exclusively mine. Perhaps most challenging was shifting my mindset around availability, learning that being constantly accessible was not a requirement of effective leadership. These shifts were not minor adjustments but fundamental realignments that challenged long-established habits.

Embed new practices into daily leadership. Shifts become sustainable only when embedded into routine. I created systems that reinforced my new boundaries, from calendar blocks that others could not override to communication protocols that clarified my availability. I established a regular reflection practice, setting aside time each week to assess my alignment and make adjustments as needed. These were not one-time decisions but ongoing commitments requiring constant renewal. The embedding process transformed occasional good intentions into consistent leadership practices.

Thrive with clarity, purpose, and balance. The ultimate goal of RESET is not merely to avoid burnout but to create a leadership approach that enables true flourishing. Today, I experience leadership differently. I remain ambitious and driven, but my ambition is tempered by wisdom about sustainability. I measure success not just by achievements but by whether I can maintain alignment between my values and actions. I find greater satisfaction in my work because it no longer comes at the expense of my wellbeing. This thriving state is not perfect, challenges remain, and vigilance is required, but it represents a fundamental transformation in how I approach leadership.

The Leadership Reset framework is not a linear progression but a cycle of growth. Even now, I revisit these elements regularly, recognising new areas that need attention, exploring deeper patterns, shifting priorities as circumstances change, embedding new practices, and continuing to redefine what it means to thrive as a leader.

What began as a personal crisis has become a template for renewal, not just for me but for other leaders facing similar challenges. The journey from burnout to breakthrough is not about returning to where we were before; it is about emerging with a wiser, more sustainable approach to leadership, one that honours our humanity while maximising our impact.

Why Burnout Is a Critical Leadership Issue

Burnout, especially in leadership roles, goes beyond personal exhaustion – it has organisational implications. Leaders are responsible for decision making, setting the tone for team culture, and driving productivity. When they are burnt out, their cognitive abilities, emotional regulation, and interpersonal relationships all suffer. This, in turn, impacts the teams they lead. *Harvard Business Review* (2022b) found that burnout in leaders often results in higher turnover rates, reduced team engagement, and overall lower morale.

Leaders often feel the need to push through their exhaustion, mistakenly believing that showing vulnerability or slowing down is a sign of weakness. However, by not addressing burnout early, leaders risk long term damage to both their wellbeing and the health of the organisation. McKinsey & Company (2021) highlights that burnout is one of the most significant factors leading to leadership attrition, making it essential for both leaders and organisations to prioritise mental health and sustainable leadership practices.

The Leadership Reset Framework is needed because it helps leaders take a step back, assess their physical, emotional, and mental states, and make deliberate adjustments to their leadership approach. The framework doesn't simply offer a temporary fix – it equips leaders with the tools to avoid future burnout and foster a more resilient, balanced leadership style.

The Four Phases of the Leadership Reset Framework

1. Recognition: Recognising the Breaking Point

This is the foundational phase where leaders **Recognise** the early signs of burnout – whether it's emotional exhaustion, physical fatigue, or cognitive overload. Many leaders dismiss these symptoms as temporary or part of the job, but ignoring them can lead to deeper issues. This phase is crucial because it allows leaders to identify the breaking point before it causes irreparable damage to their health and their leadership effectiveness.

In this phase, leaders are encouraged to ask themselves tough questions:

- Am I constantly feeling drained or overwhelmed?
- Have I become disengaged from my work and team?
- Is my decision making impaired due to stress?
- Am I sacrificing my personal time or relationships for work regularly?
- Do I feel a sense of fulfilment or accomplishment in my role, or is it diminishing?
- Am I neglecting self care (exercise, sleep, hobbies) because of work demands?
- Have I noticed changes in my mood or behaviour, such as irritability, frustration, or withdrawal?
- Is my work affecting my physical health, such as headaches, sleep disturbances, or chronic stress?
- Am I finding it difficult to concentrate or maintain focus on tasks?
- Do I feel like I'm constantly in crisis mode or firefighting instead of leading proactively?
- Am I avoiding important tasks or decisions because they feel too overwhelming?
- Have my colleagues, peers, or family expressed concern about my wellbeing or work habits?
- Do I feel disconnected from the passion or purpose that initially drove me to this leadership role?

Recognising these signs early allows leaders to take immediate steps towards resetting and regaining balance. According to the World Economic Forum (2021), the ability to recognise and address burnout early is critical for preventing long term mental health issues and ensuring the sustainability of leadership.

2. Reflection: Gaining Clarity Through Self Awareness

Once burnout is recognised, the next phase involves deep self **Reflection**. Leaders must explore what led them to burnout in the first place. Was it overcommitment? A lack of boundaries? Misaligned values? Self awareness is at the heart of emotional intelligence (EQ), which Goleman (2013b) identifies as a key leadership trait. Reflection helps leaders uncover the internal and external factors contributing to their burnout, giving them the insights needed to move forward.

In this phase, leaders ask themselves reflective questions:

- What patterns or habits contributed to my burnout?
- Are there stress triggers in my work environment that I haven't addressed?
- Am I neglecting personal wellbeing in pursuit of professional success?
- What are the values that are most important to me, and am I honouring them in my leadership?
- How have my boundaries between work and personal life been compromised?
- What assumptions about success or leadership have contributed to my overcommitment?
- What support systems (personal or professional) am I not fully utilising?
- Are there tasks or responsibilities that I can delegate or let go of?
- How have my leadership responsibilities aligned (or misaligned) with my personal strengths?
- What emotions or feelings have I been suppressing in order to maintain my leadership role?
- How has my leadership style been affected by stress, and how has that impacted my team?
- What recurring feedback have I received from peers or colleagues that I've overlooked?
- Am I more focused on managing crises than on long term vision and strategy?

Reflection fosters EQ, allowing leaders to better understand their own emotional responses and how these impact their leadership. Research shows that reflective practices strengthen leaders' resilience and self awareness, key factors in preventing burnout (Ruderman et al., 2014). Leaders who engage in regular reflection develop greater capacity to navigate challenges and maintain perspective during high pressure situations.

3. Realignment: Setting Clear Boundaries and Priorities

The third phase focuses on **Realignment** – redefining priorities and setting clear boundaries to protect personal wellbeing while maintaining professional responsibilities. Many leaders fall into burnout because they take on too much or fail to delegate. Realignment encourages leaders to focus on what matters most, eliminate or delegate non-essential tasks, and protect their personal time.

Realignment isn't just about time management; it's about values based leadership. McKinsey & Company (2020b) notes that leaders who realign their work with their values and strengths are significantly more effective and experience greater job satisfaction.

In this phase, leaders ask themselves:

- What tasks are essential to my role, and what can be delegated?
- Are my current priorities aligned with my long term goals?
- What boundaries do I need to set to prevent burnout in the future?
- Which tasks or responsibilities no longer align with my values or strengths?
- How can I restructure my day to focus on high impact activities?
- What steps can I take to ensure my personal time is non-negotiable?
- Am I allowing space for reflection and strategic thinking in my daily routine?
- What areas of my leadership need to be realigned with my personal values?
- What support do I need to maintain healthy boundaries in the future?
- Are there areas where I'm sacrificing personal wellbeing for short term gains?

- How can I ensure that delegation empowers my team without creating dependency?
- Which activities energise me, and how can I prioritise those in my leadership role?

Practical strategies like time blocking, boundary audits, and the Eisenhower Matrix are introduced to help leaders restructure their workdays and realign their efforts with their core values and capacities.

4. Reinvention: Adopting a New Leadership Approach

The final phase, **Reinvention**, is where leaders take everything they've learned from the previous phases and apply it to a new, more resilient leadership model. Reinvention is about creating a leadership style that prioritises not just results, but also wellbeing, emotional intelligence, and sustainable success. Leaders who have gone through burnout often come out the other side with deeper insights into their strengths, values, and leadership style.

Reinvention ensures that leaders not only avoid future burnout but thrive in their roles by adopting practices that promote long term wellbeing. This phase challenges leaders to shift from a reactive leadership style – constantly responding to pressures and demands – to a proactive one, where emotional regulation, empathy, and resilience are at the core of their approach.

Leaders in this phase ask themselves:

- How can I lead with empathy and emotional intelligence?
- What leadership practices will ensure my long term health and success?
- How can I model resilience and life work balance for my team?
- What habits can I adopt to sustain emotional and physical wellbeing in leadership?
- How can I shift from reactive leadership to a proactive, values based approach?
- What systems or routines can I implement to maintain focus on both results and wellbeing?

- How can I create a leadership legacy based on empathy, resilience, and sustainability?
- What new skills or mindsets have I developed from my burnout experience?
- How can I use my personal growth to inspire and support my team's development?
- How can I ensure I remain adaptable and open to change in my leadership style?
- What practices can I implement to cultivate continuous learning and growth?
- How can I use my leadership journey to create a positive ripple effect throughout my organisation?

Research by the World Economic Forum (2021) shows that emotionally intelligent leaders who prioritise reinvention post-burnout are more effective in crisis management and fostering innovation. This phase is about adopting a leadership approach that not only prevents future burnout but creates a ripple effect of positivity and resilience throughout the organisation.

The Leadership Reset Framework: Visual Overview

The circular diagram in Figure 6.2 visually represents the four phases of the Leadership Reset Framework, showing their interconnected nature and progressive development:

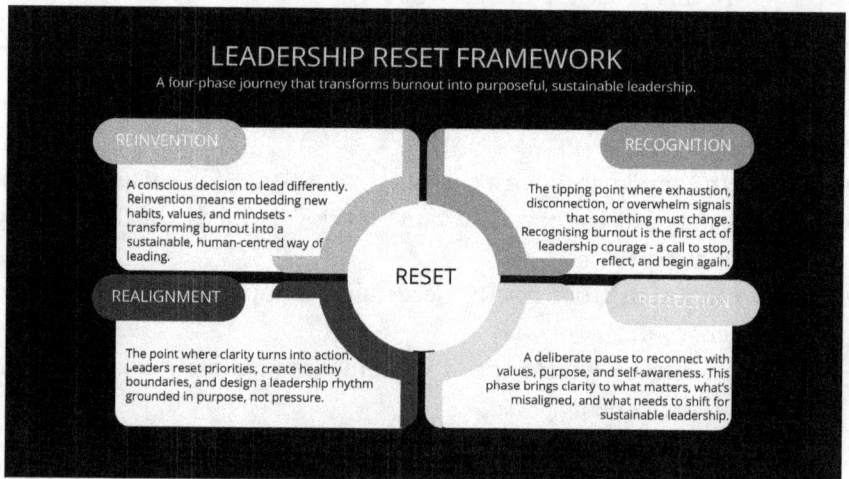

Figure 6.2 Four Phases of the Leadership Reset Framework

Phase 1: Recognition

- Identifying warning signs
- Understanding personal breaking points
- Acknowledging emotional and physical symptoms
- Monitoring energy levels

Phase 2: Reflection

- Exploring underlying causes
- Clarifying personal values
- Examining leadership patterns
- Developing emotional intelligence

Phase 3: Realignment

- Setting clear boundaries
- Prioritising high impact work
- Delegating effectively
- Aligning tasks with values

Phase 4: Reinvention

- Creating sustainable practices
- Building emotional resilience
- Embedding wellbeing routines
- Leading with purpose and balance

The diagram uses connecting lines to show the cyclical, ongoing nature of the framework, emphasising that leadership reset isn't a one time event but a continuous practice of awareness and adjustment.

Why the Leadership Reset Framework Works

The Leadership Reset Framework works because it is designed as a cyclical, holistic approach to leadership that addresses the root causes of burnout and provides practical solutions. Its effectiveness lies in its focus on emotional intelligence, self awareness, and strategic realignment, all critical components in sustainable leadership.

1. **Addressing Burnout Proactively:** By recognising burnout early, the framework enables leaders to intervene before the damage becomes irreversible. Leaders who implement these practices report lower stress levels, improved decision making, and greater team engagement (Gallup, 2020).
2. **Building Emotional Intelligence:** Emotional intelligence is a core focus throughout the framework. Goleman's (2013b) research confirms that leaders with high EQ are better equipped to manage stress, foster collaboration, and lead with empathy – all key factors in preventing burnout.
3. **Sustainable Change:** Reinvention ensures that the changes leaders make are not temporary fixes but long term strategies for leading with resilience. This phase transforms burnout from a crisis into an opportunity for lasting leadership growth.

Practical Application: Framework Readiness Assessment

To determine your starting point within the Leadership Reset Framework:

1. **Assess your current phase:** Review the four phases (Recognition, Reflection, Realignment, Reinvention) and identify which best describes your current state. While the phases are sequential, your journey may start at any point depending on your circumstances.
2. **Evaluate phase specific readiness:** Consider these questions for your identified starting phase:

   - **Recognition Phase:** Am I ready to honestly acknowledge signs of burnout?
   - **Reflection Phase:** Can I create regular space for meaningful reflection?
   - **Realignment Phase:** Am I prepared to establish new boundaries?
   - **Reinvention Phase:** Am I open to adopting a new leadership identity?

3. **Identify potential obstacles:** For your starting phase, note 1–2 challenges that might hinder your progress, such as organisational culture, personal habits, or external pressures.

4. **Create enabling conditions:** Establish 1–2 supports that will help you engage fully with your starting phase, such as an accountability partner, scheduled time for framework activities, or specific resources.

The **Leadership Reset Weekly Check-In** in the Tools and Templates section provides a structured way to track your progress through each phase of the framework and make necessary adjustments to your approach.

RESET at a Glance

Throughout this chapter, we've explored the four phases of the Leadership Reset Framework. These phases – Recognition, Reflection, Realignment, and Reinvention – together, they form the RESET path:

- **Recognise** the signs and cost of burnout in your leadership.
- **Explore** what matters most through deep reflection and self awareness.
- **Shift** your leadership habits, boundaries, and priorities towards sustainability.
- **Embed** new ways of leading through consistent, values based practice.
- **Thrive** as both a leader and a human being, with clarity, courage, and connection.

This model is a practical compass for leaders navigating burnout – each phase designed to support your recovery and long term reinvention.

Final Thought

The Leadership Reset Framework offers more than a roadmap to navigate burnout. It provides a meaningful opportunity to redefine what it means to lead with purpose, clarity, and sustainability. While burnout is undoubtedly confronting, it can also serve as a turning point – a moment for leaders to pause, reflect, and choose a new path.

Through its four interconnected phases – **Burnout, Reflection, Realignment,** and **Reinvention** – the framework equips leaders with the tools to recover and grow. I have felt how burnout can erode resilience and clarity, but I have also experienced the power of a structured, intentional reset. This is not about returning to business as usual. It is about creating a new normal where wellbeing and performance are no longer in conflict.

The framework empowers leaders to prioritise health alongside their responsibilities. It invites a leadership style shaped by self awareness, empathy, and long term resilience. In today's demanding and fast paced environments, this approach is not a luxury. It is a necessity. This is leadership reimagined for a more sustainable and human future.

In the Next Chapter

With the framework now introduced, we begin by examining the first phase: Recognition. In Chapter 7, we explore what burnout looks and feels like, how to recognise it in yourself and others and why facing it honestly is the essential first step on the path to recovery and reinvention.

Reflection Questions

Personal Reflection Questions

1. Where in the Leadership Reset Framework do you currently find yourself, and what evidence suggests you're ready to progress to the next phase?
2. Which personal factors are either facilitating or impeding your progress through the framework? How might your beliefs about leadership be contributing to this?
3. What subtle resistance or unacknowledged fears might be preventing you from fully embracing the framework? How could addressing these deepen your reset journey?
4. How do your current levels of emotional resilience and self awareness influence your leadership effectiveness? Which dimensions need development?
5. What one immediate action would create meaningful momentum in your leadership reset journey? What's stopping you from taking this step today?

Team Reflection Questions

1. How can we support each other through different phases of the Leadership Reset Framework while maintaining team performance?

2. What organisational barriers might prevent team members from successfully moving through the framework stages? How can we address these collectively?
3. How might we create mutual accountability for progress through the reset journey without creating additional pressure?
4. What team agreements could we establish that would support sustainable leadership practices across our group?
5. How can we recognise and celebrate progress through the framework stages in ways that reinforce the value of wellbeing alongside performance?

Key Takeaways

- **Burnout represents an organisational leadership crisis:** Burnout impacts not only individual leaders but also team morale, productivity, and organisational success, requiring proactive, structured intervention approaches.
- **The four-phase process enables comprehensive recovery:** The Leadership Reset Framework – Recognition, Reflection, Realignment, Reinvention – provides a structured path for leaders to recover from burnout and build sustainable resilience.
- **Self awareness and reflection form the foundation:** The framework emphasises identifying root causes of burnout through reflective practices that align leadership style with personal values and authentic strengths.
- **Realignment establishes sustainable boundaries:** Setting clear priorities, defining boundaries, and strategic delegation create balance between personal wellbeing and professional responsibilities to prevent future burnout.
- **Reinvention creates lasting leadership transformation:** Developing leadership practices centred on emotional intelligence, empathy, and resilience ensures sustainable effectiveness and prevents burnout recurrence.

7

PHASE 1 – RECOGNITION

RECOGNISING THE BREAKING POINT

Overview

In this first phase of the Leadership Reset Framework, recognition transforms general burnout awareness into personal insight. While Chapter 1 provided broad understanding of burnout symptoms, this phase focuses on identifying your personal breaking point and early warning signs.

Burnout in leadership is not merely a fleeting response to an intense week or a challenging project; it is a deeply rooted condition that develops over time under relentless demands and expectations. Leadership roles often come with expansive responsibilities, high stakes, and the unrelenting pressure to deliver results, manage complex team dynamics, and navigate crises – all while juggling personal commitments. This unyielding strain frequently leads to severe physical, emotional, and mental exhaustion, gradually eroding a leader's capacity to perform effectively.

Drawing on personal anecdotes and evidence-based research, this chapter explores the insidious nature of burnout, particularly in leadership contexts where professional and personal boundaries often blur. Recognising burnout at its earliest stages is critical to prevent long term harm to both individuals and their organisations. When left unchecked, burnout doesn't just hinder decision making and emotional regulation – it compromises the very foundation of organisational culture, productivity, and performance. The ripple effects extend beyond the individual leader, affecting team morale, creativity, and overall success.

Burnout is now recognised as an occupational phenomenon by the World Health Organization, and leaders, who bear the weight of organisational expectations, are especially vulnerable. The statistics outlined in Chapter 1 reveal the scope of this challenge, but the Leadership Reset Framework addresses what those numbers represent: real leaders struggling to sustain effectiveness while maintaining wellbeing. In leadership roles, burnout manifests in all facets of wellbeing: physical, emotional, cognitive, psychological, behavioural, and relational. Early warning signs like fatigue, irritability, and decision fatigue are often dismissed as temporary, but when ignored, these symptoms can escalate into more severe consequences for both the individual and their teams.

Through an integration of global data, practical tools, and deeply personal insights, this chapter equips leaders with strategies to recognise personal breaking points, implement preventative measures, and foster resilience. Understanding how burnout manifests and addressing it early empowers leaders to safeguard their own wellbeing, maintain team engagement, and uphold organisational success. Far from being a sign of weakness, identifying burnout is a critical step towards sustainable leadership. By reframing burnout as an opportunity for intervention and growth, leaders can protect not only their health but also the effectiveness and culture of their organisations.

Recognising Your Personal Breaking Point: Self Analysis

Before we revisit the symptoms of burnout, take a moment to reflect on your own experience with the following questions. These reflections will help you connect a general understanding of burnout to your unique situation:

1. When do you feel most depleted in your leadership role? Consider specific situations, times of day, or interactions that consistently drain your energy.

2. What aspects of leadership have changed for you recently? Think about tasks or responsibilities that once energised you but now feel burdensome.
3. How do others respond to you when you're under stress? Sometimes those around us notice changes in our behaviour before we do. Have colleagues, team members, or family commented on changes in your demeanour?
4. What physical sensations do you experience during high pressure periods? Pay attention to tension, fatigue, or other physical symptoms that might be signalling burnout.
5. In what ways has your emotional response to leadership challenges shifted? Consider whether you're experiencing more impatience, detachment, or frustration than before.
6. How effectively can you "switch off" from work? Reflect on whether work thoughts intrude during personal time, or if you find yourself unable to mentally disconnect.
7. What matters most to you in your leadership role, and are you able to prioritise it? Consider the gap between what you value and how you actually spend your time and energy.
8. When was the last time you felt truly engaged and energised by your work? The distance from these moments can be a powerful indicator of burnout.

These questions aren't just academic – they're designed to help you recognise patterns in your own experience that may indicate you're approaching or experiencing burnout. Your answers will help you identify which specific aspects of burnout are most relevant to your situation and guide your journey through the remaining phases of the Leadership Reset Framework.

Generational Perspectives on Leadership Burnout

Leadership burnout manifests differently across generational cohorts, reflecting varying expectations, values, and approaches to work. Understanding these differences enables more targeted interventions and support systems for leaders across all career stages.

Research from Gallup (2023a) reveals distinct patterns in how different generations experience and respond to leadership pressure:

Generation Z and Younger Millennials (born 1997–2012 and 1981–1996) report higher levels of burnout than older colleagues, with nearly

60% experiencing symptoms. However, they are also more likely to openly discuss mental health concerns and prioritise wellbeing in their leadership approach. These leaders tend to question traditional "always on" expectations and seek integrated approaches to life and work. For this cohort, burnout often manifests as disillusionment when organisational cultures don't align with their values around flexibility and purpose.

Generation X (born 1965–1980) leaders frequently experience what Gallup terms "sandwich pressure" simultaneously managing significant organisational responsibilities while caring for both children and ageing parents. This generation reports the highest levels of work-family conflict, with burnout often manifesting as physical exhaustion rather than emotional detachment. However, their extensive workplace experience often provides valuable perspective on navigating organisational challenges.

Baby Boomers (born 1946–1964) in leadership positions typically report lower burnout levels but may be less likely to recognise or acknowledge symptoms. This generation often associates leadership with self sacrifice and may view burnout prevention practices as indulgences rather than necessities. When burnout does occur, it frequently appears after prolonged periods of overwork with fewer early warning signs.

These generational differences highlight the importance of tailored approaches to leadership sustainability. Organisations with multigenerational leadership teams should develop burnout prevention strategies that account for these varying perspectives, creating cultures where wellbeing is valued across all age groups. This diversity of experience can become a strength, with each generation contributing different insights into sustainable leadership practices.

Common Symptoms of Leadership Burnout

While we covered key signs and symptoms in Chapter 1, here is a quick overview.

1. **Physical Symptoms:**

These are often the first to emerge, though they may be overlooked as part of a "high pressure" job:

- **Chronic fatigue:** Persistent tiredness that sleep doesn't alleviate.
- **Headaches or migraines:** Linked to prolonged stress.

- **Muscle tension:** Particularly in the neck and back, often due to stress.
- **Disrupted sleep:** Difficulty falling or staying asleep, or waking up feeling unrested.

2. **Emotional Symptoms:**

Burnout significantly affects a leader's emotional state, impairing their ability to connect with their work and teams:

- **Irritability:** Increased frustration, often triggered by minor setbacks.
- **Apathy or disillusionment:** Loss of passion for the work and detachment from organisational goals.
- **Emotional numbness:** A coping mechanism that can result in leaders becoming detached from their emotions, team, and work.
- **Hopelessness:** Feeling that no matter how hard they try, things won't improve.

3. **Cognitive Symptoms:**

Cognitive impairment is one of the hallmarks of burnout, often surfacing after prolonged stress:

- **Decision fatigue:** Difficulty making decisions, even small ones, as if each choice feels overwhelming.
- **Memory lapses:** Forgetting key details or struggling to recall critical information.
- **Difficulty concentrating:** Feeling scatterbrained or struggling to focus on tasks for extended periods.
- **Overwhelm:** Feeling paralysed by seemingly minor tasks that previously seemed manageable.

4. **Behavioural Symptoms:**

Burnout also manifests in the way leaders behave, often becoming less effective or taking on unhealthy habits as a means of coping:

- **Increased absenteeism:** Avoiding the workplace or meetings.

- **Procrastination:** Delaying important decisions or tasks because they seem too overwhelming.
- **Workaholism:** Ironically, some leaders try to compensate for their exhaustion by working longer hours, which exacerbates the issue.
- **Risk-taking:** Taking shortcuts or making impulsive decisions as a way to speed up processes or outcomes.

5. **Psychological Symptoms:**

Leadership burnout can result in psychological distress, often leading to more severe mental health conditions if not managed:

- **Anxiety:** Constant worry or dread about work or decisions, often disproportionate to the actual situation.
- **Depression:** A deepening sense of sadness or lack of interest in once-enjoyed activities.
- **Self doubt:** A growing lack of confidence in one's abilities, often leading to imposter syndrome.
- **Paranoia:** Feeling that others are conspiring against them or that their leadership is being unfairly scrutinised.

6. **Relational Symptoms:**

Burnout doesn't only affect the individual leader; it reverberates through their relationships, both personal and professional:

- **Detachment from colleagues:** Leaders may withdraw from team interactions, failing to engage in meaningful conversations or decision making processes.
- **Conflict escalation:** Small issues that would have previously been handled with grace may now lead to outbursts or disputes.
- **Neglect of personal relationships:** Leaders may stop engaging with their family or friends, focusing solely on work even outside of work hours.
- **Inability to empathise:** Burnt out leaders may struggle to connect emotionally with their teams, resulting in a lack of empathy or understanding for the challenges their team members face.

Quick Tips – How to Reset: Practical Tools for Managing Burnout

Burnout Monitoring Worksheet

A **Burnout Monitoring Worksheet** allows leaders to track their symptoms daily, weekly, and monthly to identify fluctuations in their emotional and physical wellbeing. Regular reflection helps leaders spot trends before burnout becomes critical.

Steps to Implement:

1. Track symptoms daily and identify your personal energy patterns to predict and prevent burnout episodes.
2. Rate each symptom from 1 to 5 (1 being minimal, 5 being severe).
3. At the end of each week, review trends to identify stressors or symptoms that intensified as the week progressed.
4. Adjust schedules or take proactive steps, such as breaks or shifting responsibilities.

Energy Audit

An Energy Audit is an excellent way for leaders to track their energy levels at different times of the day. Burnout often manifests through depleted energy, and recognising when these dips occur can help leaders realign their daily tasks with their natural energy levels.

Steps to Implement:

1. Divide the day into morning, afternoon, and evening blocks.
2. Rank your energy levels from 1 to 10 at the end of each block.
3. After one week, look for patterns in energy dips and adjust workloads to match periods of high energy.

By matching task intensity to natural energy rhythms, leaders can sustain performance while preventing cognitive overload.

Daily Recharge Breaks

Integrating Recharge Breaks into the daily routine can prevent burnout from building up unnoticed. These breaks should involve full disengagement from work, allowing mental and physical recovery.

Steps to Implement:

1. Use reminders (e.g., apps like Stretchly) to prompt breaks every hour for stretching, hydrating, or breathing exercises.
2. Schedule at least one significant break (e.g., 20–30 minutes) during the day to fully detach from work-related thoughts and tasks.

Nightly Shutdown Ritual

The Nightly Shutdown Ritual helps leaders mentally disconnect from work, reducing anxiety and promoting better sleep. By setting clear boundaries, leaders can create a definitive end to their workday.

Steps to Implement:

1. Write down the tasks you completed today and the tasks you will focus on tomorrow.
2. Reflect on one positive accomplishment from the day.
3. Turn off all work devices and set a specific "shutdown" time each evening.

Research from *Harvard Business Review* indicates that leaders who maintain clear boundaries between work and personal life are 30% less likely to experience chronic burnout.

The Stress Trigger Journal

Stress triggers can exacerbate burnout. The Stress Trigger Journal enables leaders to reflect on what specific events or situations are contributing to their stress and develop coping strategies for future triggers.

Steps to Implement:

1. Log stress inducing events, noting what happened and how you felt emotionally and physically.
2. Review the journal weekly to identify recurring triggers.
3. Create a strategy to mitigate these triggers, whether through delegation, adjusting workloads, or mindfulness practices.

Resilience Building Activities

Resilience is a key component in preventing burnout and ensuring long term leadership effectiveness. Practices such as Progressive Muscle

Relaxation or Yoga Nidra help reset the nervous system and provide much needed mental recovery. These exercises can be accessed through apps like Insight Timer, which offers guided sessions tailored to building resilience (Insight Timer, n.d.).

Recognition as the Foundation of Your Reset Journey

Recognising and understanding your personal burnout patterns is the critical first step in the Leadership Reset Framework for several key reasons:

It Creates a Baseline for Measurement: By clearly identifying your current state, you establish a reference point against which you can measure progress as you move through reflection, realignment, and reinvention.

It Personalises Your Approach: Burnout manifests differently for each leader. Your recognition of specific symptoms helps tailor the subsequent phases to address your unique challenges rather than applying generic solutions.

It Builds Emotional Self Awareness: The act of recognising burnout develops the emotional intelligence that will be crucial throughout your recovery journey, particularly as you move into the reflection phase.

It Validates Your Experience: Acknowledging burnout removes the shame or denial that often accompanies it, creating psychological safety for your recovery process.

It Motivates Change: When you clearly recognise the impact burnout is having on your leadership, relationships, and wellbeing, you create the motivation necessary to commit to the deeper work of the subsequent phases.

As you complete this recognition phase and move into reflection, you'll build on this foundation of self awareness. The patterns, triggers, and symptoms you've identified here will become the focus of your deeper reflection work in Phase 2, where you'll explore not just what is happening, but why – uncovering the root causes that will inform your realignment and reinvention.

Personal Reflection

I remember being the brunt of a practical joke at work. Normally, this would have been fine, something I actively encouraged to build team morale and create a positive atmosphere. I prided myself on maintaining good humour and resilience in these situations.

However, this particular instance sent me into an unexpected spiral. Before I could process what was happening, I found myself sitting in the corner of my office, sobbing uncontrollably. I couldn't articulate why something I would typically laugh off suddenly felt like a knife through my heart.

To make matters worse, I then realised it was my first panic attack at work. A new wave of fear washed over me: What if people noticed? What if they realised their supposedly strong leader was crumbling? The anxiety about having another panic attack at work became almost as debilitating as the attack itself.

While it wasn't a full-scale breakdown in a clinical sense, that moment was a breaking point. The facade I had carefully constructed was finally cracking. I had become so disconnected from my role that I was merely going through the motions. On paper, I appeared successful and in control. The reality could not have been further from the truth.

Recognising that disconnect was the hardest part. It felt like failure, an admission that I wasn't the leader I portrayed myself to be.

While I needed to reach a breaking point to recognise something was wrong and to begin my journey of healing, it is possible to recognise signs of burnout at an earlier stage. Let's explore how to recognise and proactively treat burnout.

Practical Application: Creating Your Early Warning System

To develop a personal system for catching burnout before it escalates:

1. **Identify your unique warning signs:** Review the burnout symptoms discussed in this chapter and circle the 3–5 that appear earliest for you. These are your personal "canaries in the coal mine" that signal when stress is becoming unhealthy.
2. **Create simple tracking:** Rather than complex monitoring, establish a quick daily check-in. Rate each of your warning signs on a 1–5 scale at the same time each day. A notes app or the Burnout Symptom Tracker works well.
3. **Set specific thresholds:** Decide what numbers will trigger action. For example: "Any score of 4+ requires immediate intervention" or "Three consecutive days of 3+ scores means I need support."

4. **Pair warnings with specific actions:** For each warning sign, identify one concrete action that helps address it. For example, if decision fatigue is your early warning, your response might be "No major decisions after 3pm" or "Use the delegation checklist for the next 48 hours."

The **Leadership Burnout Prevention and Recovery Cheat Sheet** in the Tools and Templates section provides a quick reference guide to warning signs and appropriate recovery strategies that you can keep accessible for daily reference.

Final Thought

Phase 1 of the Leadership Reset Framework highlights the importance of recognising burnout before it leads to deeper personal or organisational consequences. While earlier chapters provided the foundation to understand burnout conceptually, this phase has helped translate that understanding into personal insight and practical awareness.

Drawing from both lived experience and evidence-based strategies, this phase equips you to identify early warning signs and take meaningful action. Tools such as the Burnout Monitoring Worksheet and the Nightly Shutdown Ritual offer practical ways to regain control and move towards a more sustainable, values aligned leadership rhythm.

Recognition is more than noticing symptoms. It is the moment of truth where you acknowledge that something must change. This is not a sign of weakness, but a mark of courage and self awareness – qualities that define exceptional leadership. Recognising burnout is not admitting failure. It is taking the first step towards transformation.

True leadership begins with the ability to lead yourself. Preventing burnout calls for a deliberate balance of emotional intelligence, reflective practice, and strategic action. By placing your wellbeing alongside your responsibilities, you create the conditions for both personal and organisational resilience. Sustainable leadership begins with self care, and Phase 1 lays the groundwork for everything that follows.

In the Next Chapter

With recognition in place, we now turn to Phase 2: Reflection. In Chapter 8, you will explore the deeper patterns, values, and beliefs that have shaped your leadership. Through guided tools and reflective practices, this next phase invites you to gain clarity, reconnect with purpose, and create space for realignment and change.

Reflection Questions

Personal Reflection Questions

1. What experiences have led you to moments of extreme burnout, and how did your self perception shift during these periods? What did you discover about yourself?
2. How can you distinguish between organisational factors and personal tendencies in your experience of burnout? How might these factors interact and reinforce each other?
3. What internal narratives or deeply held beliefs reinforce your tendency to push through stress rather than address burnout? Where did these narratives originate?
4. What subtle signs of approaching burnout have you learned to recognise in yourself that others might not notice? What early intervention strategies work best for you?
5. How might reframing burnout as an opportunity for transformation rather than a personal failure change your approach to recovery and growth?

Team Reflection Questions

1. What early warning signs of burnout can we identify in our team members, and how might we create supportive conversations around these observations?
2. How can we collectively identify organisational factors in our organisation that contribute to leadership burnout without creating blame or defensiveness?
3. What team protocols could we establish for supporting a leader who has reached or is approaching their breaking point?
4. How might we adjust our collective expectations and work allocation when a team member shows signs of burnout?
5. What regular check in practices could we implement that would normalise discussions about stress levels and capacity?

Key Takeaways

- **Burnout develops gradually through chronic stress:** Leadership burnout is not a temporary reaction but a condition that builds over time through constant demands, leading to profound physical, emotional, and cognitive exhaustion.
- **Early recognition prevents escalation:** Identifying burnout signs like chronic fatigue, irritability, and cognitive impairment helps prevent long term damage to both leaders and their organisations.
- **Leadership burnout creates organisational ripple effects:** Burnout affects not only the leader but cascades through team morale, productivity, and overall organisational performance, requiring timely intervention.
- **Multiple symptoms indicate developing burnout:** Physical symptoms (disrupted sleep), emotional changes (detachment), and cognitive impairment (decision fatigue) collectively undermine leadership effectiveness and relationships.
- **Practical monitoring tools enable prevention:** Implementing structured approaches like burnout tracking, energy audits, and scheduled recovery breaks helps leaders manage wellbeing before burnout becomes unmanageable.

8

PHASE 2 – REFLECTION

GAINING CLARITY THROUGH SELF AWARENESS

Overview

Having recognised burnout's presence in the previous phase, reflection creates the foundation for meaningful change through increased self awareness. This second phase of the Leadership Reset Framework moves from acknowledgment to understanding. Reflection is one of the most powerful yet often overlooked tools in leadership. I learned this the hard way during a particularly challenging phase of my career. Caught up in a relentless cycle of meetings, deadlines, and decisions, I rarely paused to consider how I was truly feeling or how my emotions were influencing my actions. It wasn't until I hit a breaking point – feeling irritable, overwhelmed, and disconnected – that I realised the importance of stepping back and taking stock of my mental and emotional state.

Reflection goes beyond merely reviewing past actions; it's about cultivating self awareness to understand how thoughts, emotions, and behaviours shape leadership style and contribute to burnout. When I began incorporating reflection into my routine, I noticed a shift. Journaling about my day, taking quiet moments to breathe, or simply asking myself, "How am I really feeling?" became transformative practices. They helped me detect early signs of stress and misalignment, enabling me to course-correct before reaching exhaustion.

In today's fast paced environment, where quick decisions often overshadow thoughtful pauses, reflection provides the clarity needed to sustain effective leadership. It creates the space to analyse actions, recognise unhealthy patterns, and reconnect with purpose. Without it, leaders risk long term emotional detachment and decision fatigue – key contributors to burnout. For me, reflection became not just a tool but a lifeline, reminding me that leadership starts with leading myself.

What Does Reflection Mean for Leadership?

Reflection, in the context of leadership, goes beyond reviewing past decisions or performance metrics. I've learned this firsthand. For years, I fell into the trap of constant activity – solving problems, managing crises, and driving results without pausing to assess how I felt or why I reacted to certain situations. I told myself I was being productive, but in truth, I was operating on autopilot, losing touch with my core values and leadership goals.

Reflection creates the mental space to reconnect with these essential elements. It allows leaders to understand the deeper "why" behind their actions, fostering clarity in decision making and emotional self regulation. Reflection isn't just a tool; it's a lifeline that helps leaders navigate the complexity of their roles while staying true to their purpose.

Self Awareness: The Key to Emotional Intelligence

I remember a moment when frustration got the better of me in a team meeting. My irritation over a minor issue spilled into my tone, leaving the team visibly uncomfortable. That evening, as I reflected, I recognised the underlying stress that had triggered my response. This moment of self awareness was humbling but transformative – it allowed me to address my stress and repair the team dynamic.

Self awareness is the cornerstone of emotional intelligence (EQ). Leaders who reflect regularly can manage their stress, regulate their emotions, and empathise with others more effectively. Reflection doesn't eliminate challenges, but it equips leaders with the insight needed to respond with emotional clarity. By catching early signs of burnout – like emotional exhaustion or irritability – leaders can intervene before they spiral into deeper crises.

How Does Reflection Prevent Burnout?

Burnout often stems from running on autopilot. Leaders, myself included, can fall into routines that prioritise others' expectations over their wellbeing. I vividly recall pushing through a period of overwhelming work, convincing myself it was temporary. It wasn't. Reflection broke that cycle for me. It forced me to question why I was working that way and whether it aligned with my values.

For example, during one particularly intense year, I realised through reflection that I was taking on excessive responsibilities. This realisation was uncomfortable but necessary. It allowed me to reset my boundaries, prioritise downtime, and reengage with my family – steps that not only improved my wellbeing but also enhanced my leadership effectiveness.

Reflection allows us to recognise these harmful patterns and adjust our behaviours, creating a pathway to better self care, clearer boundaries, and more meaningful leadership.

The Role of Reflection in Fostering Growth and Resilience

Growth doesn't happen without pause. Without reflection, I might still be repeating patterns that drained my energy and limited my potential. Reflection has allowed me to learn from mistakes, adapt to challenges, and evolve as a leader.

One of the most powerful aspects of reflection is its ability to build resilience. By examining past experiences, I've gained insights into what triggers my stress and how I can cope more effectively. For instance, I now use journaling to identify patterns in my reactions and adjust my strategies accordingly. These small but intentional steps have made me more adaptable and less vulnerable to burnout over time.

Reflection fosters a growth mindset, transforming setbacks into learning opportunities. It equips leaders to face future challenges with clarity and emotional strength, ensuring sustained leadership success.

Why Reflection and Self Awareness Are Crucial in Leadership Development

Leadership without reflection is like driving blindfolded – you might move fast, but you're likely heading in the wrong direction. I've experienced the difference firsthand. Before I prioritised reflection, I made decisions that aligned with short term pressures rather than long term values. Now, regular reflection acts as my compass, ensuring I stay aligned with my goals and wellbeing.

As Harvard Business School Professor Bill George emphasises in his book *True North*, self awareness is fundamental to authentic leadership. Leaders who understand themselves inspire trust, empathy, and loyalty in their teams (George & Sims, 2007). Reflective leaders exhibit higher emotional resilience and make decisions more aligned with their values (Fernandez et al., 2020).

By fostering self awareness through reflection, leaders not only prevent burnout but also unlock their full potential. Reflection empowers leaders to lead with integrity, empathy, and purpose, creating stronger, more sustainable organisations.

The Link Between Self Awareness and Burnout Prevention

Self awareness has been my greatest ally in understanding burnout. It's not always easy to admit when something is off, but recognising the root causes of stress – whether it's work overload, emotional strain, or a lack of support – has been transformative.

I've learned that reflection isn't just about identifying stressors; it's about building the emotional resilience needed to navigate them. Research by *Harvard Business Review* (2022a) supports this, showing that reflective leaders are significantly less likely to experience emotional exhaustion.

Burnout isn't inevitable. With regular reflection, leaders can stay attuned to their needs, adjust their habits, and create a leadership style that supports both their wellbeing and their team's success. It's a powerful reminder that leadership begins with knowing – and caring for – yourself.

Quick Tips – How to Reset: Practical Tools for Self Reflection

Structured Reflection Journaling

Journaling is a powerful tool for exploring emotions and gaining insight into leadership behaviours. By answering guided prompts, leaders can pinpoint the factors contributing to stress or burnout, helping them learn from experience and adjust their behaviour going forward.

Steps for Structured Reflection Journaling:

- **Identify recurring challenges:** What personal values are you compromising for work? Are there areas where your leadership is misaligned with your purpose?
- **Examine emotional triggers:** What situations consistently lead to frustration or anxiety?
- **Balance reflection:** How are you balancing your personal wellbeing with professional responsibilities?

Example prompt: "What decisions did I make this week that left me feeling energised? What choices drained my energy?"

- **Practical Tip:** Platforms like Penzu and Reflectly provide guided prompts tailored to leadership journaling. They help focus on specific stressors and trigger points, making it easier to map out emotional highs and lows during the week.

Reflection Tracker

A **Reflection Tracker** allows leaders to track emotional states and insights over time, providing an overview of how stress and emotions fluctuate. By capturing daily reflections, leaders gain insight into their emotional wellbeing trends, helping them take action before stress becomes overwhelming.

Steps for Reflection Tracking:

- **Create a daily log:** Record your stress level (1–5), emotional state, and reflection on the day's events.

- **Identify patterns:** After a week, review the tracker to spot trends, such as days when your stress levels peaked or emotional responses that triggered specific behaviours.
- **Action planning:** Based on insights, create an action plan for managing stress and improving emotional resilience.

Example: A leader might notice that stress consistently peaks before important team meetings. By reflecting on this pattern, they can identify the source of the stress and take steps to mitigate it, such as preparing earlier or seeking feedback from team members.

- **Practical Tip:** Use **Google Sheets** or **Trello** to set up reflection tracking templates.

The Pause and Reflect Method

The Pause and Reflect Method helps leaders integrate reflection into their daily leadership routine by taking small, intentional pauses to evaluate their emotional state and decision making. By pausing after key meetings or decisions, leaders can better understand the emotions driving their actions.

Steps for Pause and Reflect:

- **Set intentional pauses:** After a stressful meeting or before making a significant decision, take 2–5 minutes to assess your emotions.
- **Ask key questions:** How am I feeling right now? What am I focusing on? What triggered this emotional state?
- **Adjust accordingly:** If you notice feelings of frustration, pause to regain composure before responding or making a decision.

- **Practical Tip:** Apps like Mindful Break can send reminders to pause and reflect throughout the day.

Daily Debrief with a Peer

Leaders benefit from talking through their daily emotional experiences with a trusted colleague or peer. The Daily Debrief helps leaders articulate their emotional highs and lows, providing an outlet for reflection and mutual support.

Steps for Daily Debrief:

- Partner with a trusted colleague to spend 10–15 minutes at the end of the day discussing emotional experiences.
- Focus on both challenges and successes, reflecting on what led to certain emotional states.
- Use the debrief to gain outside perspectives and emotional clarity.

  - **Practical Tip:** Incorporating the debrief into a peer mentoring program helps formalise this practice, ensuring that emotional insights are regularly discussed.

The Emotional Awareness Map

An Emotional Awareness Map helps leaders visualise how specific emotions affect their leadership and decision making. By connecting emotional responses to leadership situations, leaders develop greater self awareness and strategies for emotional regulation.

Steps for Building an Emotional Awareness Map:

- **List your core emotions:** Start with common emotions you experience in leadership (e.g., stress, frustration, satisfaction).
- **Map emotions to situations:** Identify the situations that trigger these emotions, such as high pressure meetings or tight deadlines.
- **Analyse impacts:** Reflect on how these emotions influence your decisions, relationships, and leadership style.

Example: A leader might map frustration to moments when team members miss deadlines, which impacts their decision making by causing reactive rather than strategic decisions. They can then develop strategies to address their frustration before making critical decisions.

Additional Strategy: Audio Journaling

For leaders who prefer to process their thoughts verbally, Audio Journaling offers an alternative to written journaling. Apps like Otter.ai allow leaders to voice record their reflections after meetings or stressful events. This enables real time insight capturing without the need to sit and write.

Research Insight: Studies from *Psychology Today* (2021a, 2021b) found that leaders who engage in audio or written journaling improve their emotional intelligence by 40%, enhancing their ability to self regulate and develop resilience.

Personal Reflection: My Personal Reflection Process

One of the most powerful things I did during recovery was writing. Not just a to-do list – but honest reflections. I began to write down moments that triggered strong emotional reactions – anger, anxiety, helplessness – and asked, "What's really going on here?"

I noticed patterns. Every time I felt out of control, it was usually because I had overcommitted or failed to set a boundary. Every time I got irritable, it was because I ignored my own need for rest. Slowly, I began to reconnect the dots. Reflection gave me language for what I couldn't explain before.

Personal Reflection: Rebuilding from What Wasn't Broken

I still remember my first appointment. I sat down, looked at him, and basically said, "I'm broken." Over the coming sessions, the psychologist made me realise that I wasn't completely broken. He helped me understand that parts of me were broken, but many parts weren't. For a while, we focused on what wasn't broken, and that was affirming.

The hard conversations came when he wanted to dig deeper into what I thought was broken. These were probably some of the hardest conversations I've ever had. I tried to avoid them. At one point he said, "Stop avoiding the real conversations and the topics that need to be discussed." He almost told me off. In subsequent sessions after that, he really helped me unpack what was going on in my mind.

Sessions weren't about lying on a couch talking about childhood. They were strategic, focused conversations about leadership patterns, stress responses, and decision making under pressure. It felt more like executive coaching than traditional therapy. We worked on practical leadership skills: how to have difficult conversations without absorbing others' emotions, how to delegate without guilt, how to separate my identity from my role. These weren't just mental health strategies. They were leadership competencies.

He introduced me to cognitive behavioural approaches, recognising thought patterns that amplified stress. For instance, I learned I was catastrophising minor setbacks, turning small problems into organisational crises in my mind. He taught me to challenge these thoughts: *Is this actually a crisis, or just a problem that needs solving?* This simple reframe changed how I approached daily challenges.

I initially saw therapy as an admission of failure. He reframed it: "You're investing in your most important leadership tool, your mind. Athletes have coaches, musicians have teachers. Why would leaders try to figure everything out alone?" That perspective shift was liberating. I wasn't broken. I was getting professional development.

The key isn't waiting until you're broken. It's recognising when patterns aren't serving you. If you're consistently reactive, exhausted, or disconnected from your purpose, that's data worth exploring with a professional. Not all therapists understand leadership pressures. Look for someone with experience in executive coaching or high pressure roles. The investment in finding the right fit is worthwhile.

Seeking help isn't weakness. It's strategy. And sometimes, it's the smartest leadership decision you'll ever make.

Practical Application: Establishing a Reflection Practice

To develop meaningful self awareness through reflection:

1. **Choose your reflection method:** Select an approach that feels natural and sustainable for you – journaling, audio recording, mindful walking, or structured thinking time. The best method is one you will actually use consistently.
2. **Start with three key questions:** Begin your reflection practice with these foundational questions:

    - "What situations this week caused me to feel most depleted?"
    - "When did I feel most energised and engaged?"
    - "What patterns am I noticing in my responses to pressure?"

3. **Schedule specific reflection time:** Identify one consistent 15-minute slot weekly where you can reflect without interruption. Many leaders find early mornings or the end of the workweek most effective.
4. **Link reflection to action:** Conclude each reflection session by identifying one specific insight and the corresponding action you will take in the coming week.

The **Reflective Leadership Journal** in the Tools and Templates section provides a structured format with prompts for energy assessment, emotional awareness, leadership challenges, and value alignment to guide your weekly reflection practice.

Final Thought

Reflection is not a passive exercise. It is an active and often deeply confronting process of self discovery. I remember clearly how difficult it was the first time I truly stopped to reflect during a particularly challenging period of leadership. Admitting that I was not fine felt like a betrayal of the composed, capable persona I thought I needed to maintain. Facing the discomfort of vulnerability, missteps, and long held habits was unsettling. Yet it proved to be one of the most transformative steps I have ever taken.

For many leaders, slowing down to reflect feels counterintuitive. Leadership often demands constant action, decision making, and visible results. But without space to process experiences, emotions, and patterns, we risk running on autopilot, disconnected from the purpose that brought us here in the first place. Reflection gives us the courage to acknowledge when things are off track, recognise stress triggers, and make meaningful changes.

Through structured reflection, leaders uncover patterns and misalignments that would otherwise go unnoticed. It is not just about preventing burnout. It is about building the emotional resilience needed to lead well and live well. While it may be uncomfortable to admit that everything is not all right, those moments of honesty are often where growth truly begins.

Reflection is the bridge between recognising burnout and reclaiming sustainable leadership. It is through this brave act of self awareness that leaders plant the seeds for transformation, foster clarity and reconnect with their purpose. These are the moments that shape not just what we do, but who we become.

In the Next Chapter

With deeper self awareness established, Chapter 9 focuses on realignment. You will explore how to set clearer boundaries, reset your priorities and begin rebuilding a leadership rhythm that supports both wellbeing and effectiveness. This phase is about turning insight into action and designing a more intentional way of leading and living.

Reflection Questions

Personal Reflection Questions

1. How has your level of self awareness shaped pivotal leadership decisions and affected your wellbeing? What patterns emerge when you examine these moments?
2. Which reflection practices have you attempted but abandoned, and why? What would make reflection sustainable within your particular leadership context?
3. Where do you notice the greatest gaps between your espoused values and your lived leadership practice? What specific tensions create these misalignments?
4. Which recurring emotional triggers in your leadership role have the most profound impact on your mental health? How might understanding their origins transform your response?
5. What specific changes to your daily structure would create genuine space for intentional reflection rather than reactive thinking?

Team Reflection Questions

1. How might we incorporate reflective practices into our team routines without them becoming perfunctory exercises?
2. What collective blind spots might exist in our team that limit our self awareness? How could we respectfully bring these to light?
3. How can we create psychological safety for honest reflection about team dynamics, leadership practices, and emotional experiences?
4. What team reflection protocols could help us identify misalignments between our stated values and our actual practices?
5. How might we use collective reflection to anticipate and prevent burnout patterns rather than merely responding to them?

Key Takeaways

- **Reflection builds essential emotional intelligence:** Regular reflective practices develop self awareness, enabling leaders to recognise stress patterns and burnout signs before they escalate to crisis levels.
- **Reflective practices disrupt burnout cycles:** Reflection allows leaders to step back from autopilot routines, examine habitual responses, and adjust behaviours that contribute to exhaustion and reduced effectiveness.
- **Self awareness fosters adaptability and growth:** Leaders who engage in reflection cultivate a growth mindset that enhances learning from experiences, building resilience and leadership effectiveness.
- **Clear insights improve decision quality:** Reflection provides clarity about emotional triggers and leadership patterns, helping leaders maintain alignment with values and sustain emotional wellbeing.
- **Regular reflection prevents emotional detachment:** In high pressure environments, reflection helps leaders maintain connection to core values and emotions, preventing the detachment that contributes to burnout.

9

PHASE 3 – REALIGNMENT

SETTING CLEAR BOUNDARIES AND PRIORITIES

Overview

With deeper self awareness established through reflection, realignment focuses on reshaping priorities and boundaries to prevent burnout recurrence. This third phase of the Leadership Reset Framework translates insight into structural change. Leadership burnout often creeps in when leaders overcommit, blur boundaries, and lose sight of their personal values. I learned this the hard way, navigating a relentless cycle of demands that left me physically and emotionally drained. Realignment became my lifeline – a process of recalibrating goals, behaviours, and boundaries to protect my energy and focus on what truly mattered.

This phase is essential for leaders to prioritise high impact tasks, delegate non-essential responsibilities, and establish firm boundaries. Realignment isn't just about recovering from burnout; it's about preventing its recurrence by aligning actions with values and maintaining a sustainable leadership approach. It empowers leaders to regain clarity and build resilience for the long haul.

DOI: 10.4324/9781003668626-12

What Realignment Means for Leaders

Realignment is a critical juncture where leaders step back to ask: "Am I spending time on what truly matters?" and "Does my current leadership role align with my values and purpose?" When I took this step, I had to confront the fact that I was prioritising external expectations over personal fulfilment – a difficult but transformative realisation.

By realigning, leaders can break free from the pressure to keep up with demands that no longer serve their mission. Setting boundaries, streamlining priorities, and letting go of non-aligned tasks create the space needed for renewed focus and energy. This process enables leaders to recalibrate their actions, ensuring they're not just busy, but purposeful.

Why Is Realignment Key in Preventing Burnout?

Burnout doesn't just stem from working too hard; it arises when leaders spend time on work that feels disconnected from their values. For me, recognising this disconnect was the turning point. Without realignment, leaders risk continuing on autopilot – pouring energy into tasks that lead to disillusionment and exhaustion.

Realignment interrupts this cycle by focusing efforts on meaningful goals. It encourages leaders to ask tough questions about their priorities, enabling them to shift focus, embrace self care, and avoid overextension. In the long term, this process fosters resilience, enhances decision making, and builds a sustainable leadership style adaptable to evolving challenges.

By regularly realigning their goals and actions, leaders ensure that their work fuels their mission rather than drains their wellbeing. This clarity and adaptability not only prevent burnout but also make leadership more impactful and fulfilling. For me, realignment became a non-negotiable habit that restored my sense of purpose and transformed how I lead.

Quick Tips – How to Reset: Practical Tips for Realignment

Priority Matrix (Eisenhower Matrix)

The **Eisenhower Matrix** is a powerful tool to help leaders prioritise tasks based on urgency and importance. By using this tool, leaders can focus on high priority work and eliminate or delegate tasks that are less essential.

Steps to Create and Use a Priority Matrix:

1. **Divide your task list into four quadrants:**

   - *Urgent and important*: Immediate tasks that require attention and have significant consequences.
   - *Not urgent but important*: Strategic tasks that are essential for long term success but don't require immediate action.
   - *Urgent but not important*: Tasks that require immediate action but have low long term value – these are often distractions.
   - *Neither urgent nor important*: Tasks that can be eliminated or delegated.

2. **Reassess weekly:** At the start of each week, review your task list and place each task in the appropriate quadrant.
3. **Adjust priorities:** Focus on high impact tasks in the "not urgent but important" quadrant, delegate or eliminate tasks in the last two quadrants.

Example: If your week is filled with non-strategic meetings or responding to minor emails, realign your priorities to spend more time on strategic planning or personal development.

- **Practical Tip:** Create your Eisenhower Matrix using Google Sheets, Notion, or other task management platforms like Trello.

Energy-Task Alignment for Sustainable Performance

Leaders often struggle to disconnect from work, which leads to burnout. Energy-task alignment involves matching your most demanding work to your peak energy periods while protecting recovery time for restoration. This approach recognises that sustainable performance comes from working with your natural rhythms rather than against them.

Steps for Energy-Task Alignment:

1. **Map your energy patterns:** Track when you feel most alert and focused vs. when you feel depleted throughout the day.
2. **Categorise tasks by energy requirement:** Identify which tasks need high mental energy (strategic thinking, difficult conversations) vs. low energy (routine admin, email).

3. **Design your schedule around energy peaks:** Schedule high demand work during your peak energy windows and routine tasks during lower-energy periods.
4. **Build in recovery protocols:** Plan intentional restoration activities between intensive work sessions.

Example: If your peak energy is 9–11am, schedule strategic planning then, not routine emails. Save emails for your 2–3pm energy dip and protect 11am–12pm for recovery before afternoon meetings.

Practical Tip: Use energy tracking apps or simple journaling to identify your personal energy patterns over a two-week period.

Boundary Setting Through "No" Lists

Saying no is one of the hardest skills for leaders to develop, yet it is critical for avoiding overcommitment. By creating a No List, leaders can clearly define which tasks, meetings, or requests they will decline in order to protect their time and energy.

Steps for Creating a No List:

1. **Identify non-essential tasks:** Make a list of tasks or projects that don't align with your long term goals or core responsibilities (e.g., attending meetings without an agenda, responding to non-strategic queries).
2. **Practice saying no:** Use clear, polite language to decline additional responsibilities, focusing on your core priorities.
3. **Review weekly:** At the end of each week, review how well you adhered to your No List and adjust as needed.

Example: A leader might add "declining non-strategic meeting requests" to their No List. By saying no to meetings without a clear agenda or purpose, they protect their time for more important work.

- **Practical Tip:** Use task management apps like Todoist to manage your No List and remind yourself to decline non-essential requests.

The Boundary Audit

A **Boundary Audit** helps leaders assess whether their personal and professional boundaries are being respected. By regularly auditing your boundaries, you can ensure that work is not encroaching on your personal time and that you are not overcommitting.

Steps for Conducting a Boundary Audit:

1. **Identify current boundaries:** List the boundaries you've set (e.g., no work emails after 6pm, no weekend meetings).
2. **Assess violations:** Reflect on where these boundaries are being ignored, either by you or others.
3. **Communicate clearly:** If boundaries are being violated, create a plan to communicate them more effectively to your team or colleagues.
4. **Reassess weekly:** Conduct weekly audits to ensure that boundaries are being respected and adjust them if needed.

Example: If a leader finds themselves consistently working past 7pm despite setting an end time, they need to review what's causing these disruptions and communicate more effectively with their team.

- **Practical Tip:** Use tools like Notion or Evernote to track and reassess your boundaries.

Personal Reflection: A Leadership Calendar in Crisis

At one point, I decided to print out a week of my calendar and colour-code it: red for meetings, blue for leadership admin, green for breaks. There was no green. Not a single green block.

That visual hit hard. It was a simple but powerful exercise that forced me to rethink how I was using my time – and who I was giving it to. I began blocking space for "thinking time" and "reset hours." These weren't luxuries – they became lifelines.

Delegation Matrix

Delegation is a critical skill for realignment. The Delegation Matrix helps leaders identify tasks that can be handed off to their team, focusing their own energy on high priority tasks that require their expertise.

Steps for Creating a Delegation Matrix:

1. **List your weekly tasks:** Write down all of your regular tasks, from high priority strategic work to administrative duties.

2. **Categorise tasks:** Divide tasks into "High Impact" (tasks only you can do) and "Low Impact" (tasks you can delegate).
3. **Delegate systematically:** Assign low impact tasks to team members and monitor progress using a project management tool like Asana or Trello.

Example: A leader might delegate routine administrative tasks to an assistant, freeing up time for strategic decision making or personal development.

- **Practical Tip:** Explore delegation templates using Trello.

Practical Application: Priority Realignment Process

To realign your time and energy with your core values and leadership priorities:

1. **Conduct a time audit:** For one week, track how you actually spend your time compared to what matters most. Note patterns of misalignment between your values and your calendar.
2. **Create your priority matrix:** Sort your current responsibilities into four categories:

    - **Important and Urgent:** Handle promptly and develop systems to reduce future urgency.
    - **Important but Not Urgent:** Schedule protected time for these high value activities.
    - **Not Important but Urgent:** Delegate with clear guidelines and expectations.
    - **Neither Important nor Urgent:** Eliminate or severely minimise.

3. **Implement boundary protocols:** For each priority category, establish specific boundaries. For example:

    - Block 90 minutes daily for important but not urgent work.
    - Create a delegation plan for tasks that others could handle.
    - Develop standard responses for declining low-value requests.

4. **Communicate your realignment:** Share your approach with key stakeholders: "To ensure I can focus on [strategic priorities], I am adjusting my involvement in [lower value areas]. This will allow me to contribute more meaningfully to our most important goals."

The **Priority Matrix Worksheet** and **Delegation Decision Tree** in the Tools and Templates section provide practical frameworks for implementing this realignment process effectively.

Final Thought

Realignment is not a one time fix. It is an essential and ongoing practice for sustainable leadership. I have learned firsthand that realignment is not just about correcting course when things go off track. It is about maintaining a rhythm where personal values and professional responsibilities remain in harmony. This alignment is vital in preventing burnout from becoming a repeating cycle.

For leaders, realignment is both an act of self preservation and a catalyst for growth. By regularly reviewing boundaries and priorities, I have found the clarity to make changes that support my wellbeing and long term leadership goals. It is not always easy. Letting go of tasks or redefining expectations can feel uncomfortable. But in these moments of recalibration, resilience and purpose driven leadership take shape.

Flexibility is central to realignment. Life and work are constantly shifting, and leaders must learn to adapt while staying anchored in their values. Whether it is delegating more effectively, redefining roles, or responding to unexpected demands, realignment helps leaders navigate complexity with intention and confidence. By embedding realignment into your leadership rhythm, you not only reduce the risk of burnout but create a sustainable foundation for lasting impact and fulfilment.

In the Next Chapter

With new priorities and boundaries now established, Chapter 10 focuses on the final phase of the Leadership Reset Framework: Reinvention. This phase invites you to adopt a new way of leading that is built on everything you have learned. It is about turning recovery into transformation and leading with renewed clarity, energy, and purpose.

Reflection Questions

Personal Reflection Questions

1. Which aspects of your current leadership role feel fundamentally misaligned with your values or sense of purpose? What specific changes would create meaningful realignment?
2. How do you currently communicate and enforce boundaries with your team? Where might ambiguity or inconsistency be undermining these boundaries?
3. In what ways do time management and prioritisation challenges contribute to your stress? Which stem from external demands vs. internal habits?
4. Which strategy would address your most significant leadership challenge, and what specific form would this take in your context?
5. What cultural or organisational barriers might undermine your boundary setting efforts? How will you navigate these while maintaining your commitment to realignment?

Team Reflection Questions

1. How do our team priorities align with our stated values and purpose? Where do we notice misalignments that create tension or burnout?
2. What collective boundaries could we establish around meetings, communications, and availability that would support sustainable leadership?
3. How might we redesign our decision making processes to focus team energy on truly important matters while reducing cognitive load on routine decisions?
4. What permission do we need to give each other to establish and maintain healthier boundaries within our team and with external stakeholders?
5. How can we realign our team structure and roles to better match individual strengths and reduce areas of unnecessary friction or stress?

Key Takeaways

- **Realignment prevents burnout recurrence:** Strategic recalibration of priorities and boundaries stops leaders from returning to patterns that lead to burnout, ensuring sustainable leadership practices.
- **Value alignment guides effective leadership:** Leaders must regularly assess whether tasks and responsibilities align with personal values and long term goals, eliminating non-essential duties that don't serve their mission.
- **Boundary setting protects leadership energy:** Establishing clear demarcations between work and personal life is crucial for wellbeing, with time blocking and regular boundary audits serving as effective protection tools.
- **Strategic delegation enhances leadership focus:** Delegating low-impact tasks enables leaders to concentrate on high priority, strategic work, preventing overcommitment and optimising resource allocation.
- **Realignment requires ongoing attention:** Rather than a one-time solution, realignment demands regular reassessment as leaders adapt to evolving challenges while maintaining alignment with core values.

10

PHASE 4 – REINVENTION

ADOPTING A NEW LEADERSHIP APPROACH

Overview

Burnout was my wake up call, forcing me to confront the reality that I couldn't lead effectively while neglecting my wellbeing. I realised recovery wasn't about returning to the same patterns that led to exhaustion – it was an opportunity to rethink how I approached leadership entirely. Reinvention, the final phase of the Leadership Reset Framework, transforms recovery into sustainable transformation. Having recognised, reflected, and realigned, this phase embeds new practices into your leadership identity.

In today's fast paced and complex work environments, burnout is increasingly common, and for many leaders, it can feel inevitable. But recovering from burnout requires more than just resting or resuming old routines; it demands a fundamental shift in how leaders view and execute their roles. Reinvention is about reimagining leadership, where personal wellbeing, life work integration, and organisational effectiveness coexist harmoniously.

DOI: 10.4324/9781003668626-13

This phase equips leaders with the tools and mindset to create a new leadership style — one that prioritises sustainable practices, values driven decision making, and authentic connection with their teams. Reinvention is not just about surviving burnout; it's about emerging stronger, more self aware, and ready to lead with purpose and resilience. By reframing burnout as a pivotal moment of transformation, leaders can redefine their leadership journey in ways that align with both personal and professional fulfilment.

Reinvention as a Phase of Transformation

Reinvention is the moment where the experience of burnout transforms from a setback into an opportunity for profound growth. I vividly recall standing at a crossroads after my own burnout — returning to my old ways wasn't an option, yet stepping into an unfamiliar and untested leadership style felt daunting.

But reinvention isn't about going back; it's about evolving into a leader who thrives, even in high pressure environments, without sacrificing mental or emotional wellbeing. For me, that crossroads was not just metaphorical. It led to the decision to step away from my role as a school principal. As much as I loved the community, I had to acknowledge that continuing in that role, under the circumstances, would not allow me to recover or lead sustainably. It was not a retreat from leadership, but a shift towards it on my own terms. That decision created space for me to rediscover purpose, redefine impact, and ultimately build a more sustainable way to lead.

This phase marks a shift from surviving burnout to becoming a more empathetic, emotionally intelligent, and resilient leader. Leaders who embrace reinvention break free from habits and practices that led to burnout, replacing them with strategies that prioritise sustainability and wellbeing. Reinvention requires courage, but it also offers a chance to redefine leadership by embedding personal values, emotional regulation, and purposeful action into every decision.

Reinvention is about fostering a culture of wellbeing within teams and reshaping organisations from the top down. It represents a leadership evolution grounded in self awareness, enabling leaders to proactively manage stress while building environments that encourage resilience, creativity, and collaboration. By adopting a reinvention mindset, leaders move from reactive to intentional leadership, creating a legacy where wellbeing and success coexist.

Through reinvention, leaders don't just recover from burnout – they chart a new path forward, one where they inspire others by embodying the principles of sustainable and transformative leadership.

Why Reinvention Matters

Reinvention matters because it goes beyond temporary fixes and leads to profound, lasting transformation. I remember the turning point after my own burnout – a moment when I realised that resuming my previous approach to leadership would only lead me back to the same challenges. This realisation was both humbling and empowering. Burnout had forced me to confront the unsustainable habits that had become my norm and gave me the clarity to redefine my leadership style in a way that prioritised balance and wellbeing.

Burnout recovery isn't just about regaining lost energy; it's about leveraging hard-earned insights to create meaningful change. During this phase, leaders gain a deeper understanding of their emotional triggers, strengths, and blind spots. They learn to build a leadership style rooted in emotional intelligence, wellbeing, and sustainable strategies. Reinvented leaders not only avoid future burnout but thrive in high pressure environments by fostering balance and protecting their mental health.

This transformation doesn't just benefit the individual; it ripples throughout the organisation. Leaders who embrace reinvention inspire their teams by modelling a healthier, more sustainable approach to work. Their leadership encourages cultural shifts where wellbeing becomes a priority, resulting in teams that are more engaged, innovative, and resilient.

Reinvention moves leadership from being transactional – focused solely on outputs and tasks – to being deeply relational, prioritising people and long term sustainability. By redefining success through this lens, leaders not only sustain their effectiveness but also create workplaces that enable everyone to thrive. Reinvention, at its core, is not just recovery – it is leadership reborn.

From Survival to Thriving: The Path of Reinvention

Burnout forced me into survival mode – a state where every task felt like a mountain, and I was focused solely on making it through the day. I recall moments of sheer exhaustion, where the weight of my responsibilities overshadowed any sense of purpose or fulfilment. But survival isn't sustainable, and it certainly isn't thriving. Reinvention became my lifeline, shifting my perspective and redefining my approach to leadership.

Reinvention is a pivotal phase that moves leaders beyond the reactive patterns of survival mode. It's about redefining leadership as an opportunity for growth, connection, and fulfilment rather than a relentless checklist of tasks. This requires a fundamental mindset shift: leadership isn't just about managing crises or meeting deadlines; it's about fostering emotional intelligence, resilience, and wellbeing for both yourself and your team.

In this phase, leaders adopt a proactive approach. Instead of being consumed by daily challenges, they focus on creating sustainable practices that prioritise mental health, set clear boundaries, and promote team wellbeing. I learned to collaborate more deeply with peers and mentors, realising that leadership isn't a solitary journey. Reinvention often involves co-creating healthier environments with those around you, breaking the cycle of overwork and burnout by building a leadership style rooted in shared values and collective wellbeing.

According to research by Deloitte (2021c), leaders who embrace reinvention post-burnout are significantly more likely to sustain practices that enhance both personal and organisational wellbeing. This aligns with my experience: the more I focused on building resilience and emotional intelligence, the stronger my leadership became – not just for myself, but for the people I led.

Reinvention isn't just about bouncing back; it's about transforming the way leaders think, act, and connect. It's about thriving in a way that's sustainable, fulfilling, and deeply impactful.

Micro Recovery Science

I used to believe recovery meant long holidays or weekends disconnected from work. But what actually shifted my wellbeing was something much smaller – micro recovery.

Micro recovery involves short, intentional moments of mental, physical, or emotional reset built into the day. These quick interventions have been shown to improve focus, mood, and decision making under pressure (Fritz et al., 2011). The benefit is not in the length of the break, but in the frequency and quality of the recovery.

In high pressure environments, leaders who use micro strategies report lower cognitive fatigue and higher clarity throughout the day (Reid, 2023). These tiny changes can lead to significant shifts in performance and well-being over time.

Practical Micro Recovery Strategies:

- 90 second breathing resets between meetings
- 5 minute nature breaks (even through a window)
- 2 minute non-work chats with a colleague
- Stretching or movement between tasks
- Intentional transitions between work blocks

Reinvention and recovery is not something you wait for. It is something you build in.

Quick Tips – How to Reset: Practical Tools for Reinvention

Leadership Reinvention Blueprint

Create a **Leadership Reinvention Blueprint** in Evernote or Notion, where you map out the changes you want to implement in your leadership style based on the lessons from burnout. Include sections for:

- Emotional Intelligence Development.
- Delegation and Empowerment.
- Self Care and Wellbeing Practices.
- Team Culture and Psychological Safety.

Steps:

- Identify areas where burnout was a result of leadership gaps (e.g., lack of delegation or emotional regulation).
- Write a personal action plan for each area, focusing on how you will reinvent your approach moving forward.
- Set measurable goals for how you will implement changes and track progress.

Emotional Intelligence and Empathy Training

Sign up for Emotional Intelligence (EQ) Training through BetterUp or Daniel Goleman's EQ course to develop skills in self regulation, empathy, and social awareness. Emotional intelligence is key to reinventing your leadership style and building stronger, more resilient teams.

Steps:

- Take an EQ assessment to benchmark your current skills.
- Enrol in an EQ training course.
- Apply new EQ skills in your daily leadership interactions and reflect on their impact.

Leadership Reboot Meetings

Host a Leadership Reboot Meeting with your team to share your new leadership vision and changes you plan to implement. Encourage open dialogue about how you can support your team's wellbeing moving forward and what cultural changes can be made to foster a more balanced work environment.

Steps:

- Prepare an outline of the lessons you've learned from burnout and how you plan to lead differently.
- Invite your team to share feedback and suggestions for improving team culture.
- Set clear actions for implementing changes and revisit them monthly.

The Leadership Legacy Reflection

Create a Leadership Legacy Reflection where you articulate the type of leader you want to be post-burnout. Reflect on:

- What qualities do you want to be remembered for as a leader?
- How will your leadership impact the wellbeing of your team?
- What lasting changes will you make to ensure sustainable success?

Continuous Learning for Leadership Growth

Reinvention requires ongoing learning. Commit to a continuous learning journey by attending leadership workshops, enrolling in courses on resilience and wellbeing, or reading books on emotionally intelligent leadership. Use platforms like LinkedIn Learning or Coursera to stay informed and inspired.

Steps:

- Choose one course per quarter to enhance your leadership skills.
- Attend leadership webinars or conferences to stay current on trends.
- Reflect on each learning experience and how it applies to your role.
- Explore LinkedIn Learning for leadership growth.

Research Insight:

According to the World Economic Forum (2021), emotionally intelligent leaders who focus on reinvention are 30% more effective at navigating crises and fostering resilient teams. Emotional intelligence is not just a personal skill — it is a leadership superpower.

Personal Reflection: Stepping Away to Find a New Purpose

My reinvention as a leader took a path I never expected. As I struggled with burnout, I came to a difficult realisation: I was no longer the principal I had once been or aspired to be again. Despite the external appearance of competence, I knew internally that something fundamental had shifted. I wasn't firing on all cylinders. My passion, energy, and effectiveness had diminished in ways perhaps not yet visible to others, but painfully apparent to me.

I could have continued, pushed through, maintained the mask I had become so skilled at wearing. Many would have expected this of me, and part of me felt obligated to soldier on. But I had to confront an uncomfortable question: at what cost? Not just to myself, but to my family who had already sacrificed so much, and to the school community that deserved leadership at full capacity.

If I couldn't give my role the 120% that had always been my standard, I knew I needed to make a change. This wasn't about lowering expectations or accepting mediocrity. It was about integrity, about acknowledging my limitations during this period of my life, and about making a difficult choice with both humility and courage.

The decision to step away from being a principal wasn't taken lightly. It meant letting go of a role that had defined my professional identity for years. It meant acknowledging vulnerability in a system that often prizes resilience above all else. But sometimes the most courageous leadership decision isn't to persevere regardless of the personal cost, but to recognise when a different path is needed.

What I didn't fully understand then, but see clearly now, was that stepping away wasn't the end of my leadership journey but the beginning of its reinvention. I transitioned into a role where I could support other principals, drawing on my experience to help them navigate their own leadership challenges. This shift allowed me to contribute meaningfully while rebuilding my own reserves.

As I worked alongside other principals, a new purpose began to emerge. I found myself increasingly passionate about advocating for their wellbeing, for creating systems and cultures that supported sustainable leadership. I began to see patterns in their struggles that mirrored my own, and I realised that my experience with burnout, painful as it had been, had given me insight and empathy that I could now channel into preventing others from reaching that breaking point.

This reinvention wasn't about abandoning leadership but transforming how I expressed it. Rather than leading a single school community, I was now contributing to leadership sustainability across many schools. My influence became less direct but potentially more far-reaching. I was no longer responsible for the day-to-day decisions of school management, but I was helping shape how school leadership itself was understood and practised.

Only later did I fully understand what this reinvention meant: my struggle had become a platform for change. By being open about my experience, by naming burnout and speaking about the toll it takes, I could help destigmatise these conversations in educational leadership. I could challenge the notion that exhaustion is simply the price of dedication. I could advocate for systems that value leader wellbeing not as a peripheral concern but as central to sustainable school improvement.

This reinvention wasn't always smooth or straightforward. There were moments of doubt, of wondering whether stepping away had been the right choice. But with time, I saw how this new path allowed me to serve education in ways that aligned with both my values and my capacity. I could contribute meaningfully without sacrificing my health and wellbeing in the process.

The greatest lesson in this reinvention has been that sometimes our most powerful leadership contribution comes not from pushing through regardless of the cost, but from making difficult choices that honour both our commitment to service and our need for sustainability. True reinvention isn't about doing the same things differently; sometimes it's about finding the courage to do different things entirely, guided by the wisdom that comes from both success and struggle.

Practical Application: Crafting Your Leadership Identity

To begin the reinvention process with clarity and purpose:

1. **Articulate your leadership purpose:** Complete this statement: "At my best, my leadership creates…" Focus on the impact you want to have rather than specific actions or traits.
2. **Identify core principles:** Select 3–4 principles that will guide your leadership decisions and behaviours. These might include values like transparency, empowerment, wellbeing, or growth.
3. **Establish non-negotiables:** Define what you will no longer compromise on, such as "No after-hours emails," "No micromanagement," or "No compromising on core values in decision making."
4. **Create a daily reminder practice:** Develop a brief daily ritual that reinforces your new leadership identity, such as reviewing your principles each morning or asking reflection questions at day's end.
5. **Implement key practices:** Identify specific practices that embody your new leadership approach and integrate them into your daily, weekly, and monthly routines.

The **Leadership Identity Canvas** and **Daily Leadership Practice Plan** in the Tools and Templates section provide comprehensive frameworks for developing your full leadership identity statement and embedding sustainable practices into your routine.

The Evolved Leader: Leading After Burnout

Burnout is not the end of your leadership story, it can be the beginning of a more grounded, sustainable and authentic version of it.

Leaders who recover from burnout often emerge with a deeper clarity about what matters. They no longer lead for approval, perfection, or pressure; they lead from alignment, empathy, and purpose.

These are the evolved leaders:

They model boundaries and recovery, not just resilience.
They cultivate psychological safety, because they've known the cost of silence.
They lead through presence, not performance.
They say no without guilt, delegate without shame, and ask for help without fear.
They see leadership not as a role to perform, but a relationship to nurture.

This transformation isn't instant, but it is possible. Burnout strips away illusion. What's left is real. And that's where the most powerful leadership begins.

Beyond Recovery: Leadership Transformation

Burnout recovery is not about returning to how things were. For many, including myself, the experience of burnout creates conditions for profound transformation.

Burnout did not just break me. It remade me. What emerged was not the same leader with better boundaries. It was someone clearer, softer, sharper. The pain of burnout stripped away what was not essential, leaving behind a more authentic and grounded leadership presence.

Recent findings highlight the value of integrating self compassion and reflective practice into leadership development. When leaders reframe adversity as growth, they develop stronger emotional intelligence and more sustainable leadership behaviours (Reid, 2023). This mirrors the concept of post-traumatic growth, where individuals emerge from disruption with renewed clarity, depth, and perspective.

This transformation is not instant. It requires time, reflection, and a willingness to rebuild leadership identity from the inside out. But if embraced, burnout becomes not the end of leadership, but a turning point.

Final Thought

In today's relentless and high pressure work environments, I have experienced the toll that leadership stress can take physically, emotionally, and mentally. The complexity and demands placed on leaders have never been greater, leaving many on the edge of burnout. Through my own experience of navigating these challenges, I came to realise that recovery is not just about rest. It is about transformation.

The Leadership Reset Framework provides a structured roadmap for leaders who want not only to recover, but to thrive. By recognising burnout as a signal rather than a failure, leaders can begin a process of self reflection, realignment, and reinvention. Each phase represents a step towards reshaping leadership into a practice that is sustainable, purposeful and aligned with personal values.

The tools, strategies, and reflective exercises offered throughout this book are more than a recovery plan. They empower leaders to prioritise wellbeing while still making a meaningful professional impact. Reinvention becomes the path to building resilience, strengthening team dynamics and fostering cultures that thrive under pressure. For me, reinvention meant rethinking everything from how I structured my calendar to how I engaged with my team. I stopped measuring success by how busy I was and started focusing on impact, presence, and sustainability. I began protecting non-negotiable wellbeing time, trusting my team more deeply and choosing clarity over control. These were not instant fixes, but deliberate choices I continue to practise every day.

Even now, I revisit the Leadership Reset framework regularly, not just when things go wrong, but as part of how I lead. I use a quarterly reset to check in on my boundaries, reflect on alignment, and recalibrate before pressure builds again. These habits have become part of my leadership rhythm, helping me stay grounded, intentional, and connected to what matters most.

Leadership is not about perfection. It is about adaptation. The Leadership Reset Framework is an invitation to lead in a more balanced and sustainable way, where success is measured not only by outcomes, but by the wellbeing and integrity of the journey itself.

In the Next Chapter

Having completed the four phases of the Leadership Reset Framework, we now shift focus to the bigger picture. In Chapter 11, we move from personal action to organisational responsibility, exploring how organisations can embed wellbeing into culture, leadership development, and strategic planning at every level.

Reflection Questions

Personal Reflection Questions

1. If you were to describe your ideal vision of sustainable leadership, what essential elements would it contain? How does this vision differ from conventional leadership models?
2. Which aspects of your current leadership approach no longer serve you or your team? What evidence suggests these approaches are undermining rather than enhancing your effectiveness?
3. How might you integrate continuous learning about leadership wellbeing into your routine without it becoming another obligation? What structures would support this?
4. What underlying fears or concerns might be preventing you from embracing a reinvented leadership approach? How do these fears relate to your core identity?
5. What small but symbolically important step could you take today that would signal your commitment to a reinvented leadership approach?

Team Reflection Questions

1. How might we collectively reinvent our leadership approach to better integrate wellbeing with high performance? What would success look like?
2. What aspects of our team leadership culture need transformation rather than mere adjustment? How would these changes affect our broader organisation?
3. How can we support each other in experimenting with new leadership approaches without fear of judgment when we face challenges?

4. What collective leadership identity might we develop that prioritises sustainability, emotional intelligence, and wellbeing alongside results?
5. How could we redesign our leadership practices to better align with emerging research on sustainable high performance?

Key Takeaways

- **Reinvention transforms leadership beyond recovery:** The reinvention phase moves leaders from surviving burnout to thriving through fundamental shifts in leadership approach, prioritising sustainable practices and emotional intelligence.
- **New leadership identity embedding sustainable practices:** Creating a leadership identity based on wellbeing, empathy, and resilience helps leaders integrate sustainable practices into their fundamental approach rather than temporary adjustments.
- **Emotional intelligence becomes the leadership foundation:** Developing emotional awareness and regulation enables stronger team connections, more effective responses to challenges, and psychologically safer environments.
- **Wellbeing integration requires systematic approach:** Successful reinvention includes structured incorporation of wellbeing practices through tools like leadership reboot meetings, shared accountability, and continuous learning.
- **Transformed leaders drive cultural change:** Reinvented leaders inspire broader organisational shifts by modelling sustainable practices and championing wellbeing focused approaches throughout their teams.

Part 3

ORGANISATION SOLUTIONS

11

ORGANISATIONAL SOLUTIONS

HOW ORGANISATIONS CAN PREVENT LEADERSHIP BURNOUT

Overview

Leadership burnout is not just an individual challenge – it's an organisational issue shaped by organisational structures, cultures, and expectations. However, the path to sustainable, resilient leadership requires a shared effort between organisations and individuals. While I am fortunate to work for an organisation that genuinely prioritises health and wellbeing – through both formal programs and informal support networks – I've learned that these resources alone are not enough. Leaders also need to take personal responsibility for their wellbeing by recognising their limits and making proactive choices to safeguard their health.

This chapter explores how organisations can support their leaders in preventing burnout, while emphasising the crucial role of individual accountability. From fostering a culture that values emotional intelligence (EQ) to embedding wellbeing as a key performance indicator (KPI), the chapter highlights organisational changes that enable leaders to thrive. Practical strategies such as flexible work policies, mental health initiatives,

DOI: 10.4324/9781003668626-15

and leadership coaching are paired with tools for tracking leadership wellbeing. Global examples, including Scandinavian life work integration models and innovative Australian practices, illustrate how organisational and individual efforts can work together to create healthier, more resilient organisations.

The role of Human Resources (HR) in championing these initiatives is also examined, showcasing how HR can create environments where leaders feel supported, engaged, and empowered to succeed.

From Individual to Organisation: A Shift in Focus

Much of this book has focused on the individual journey, recognising burnout, setting boundaries, fostering emotional intelligence, and redefining success. But as many leaders quickly realise, even the most well intentioned personal strategies will falter in systems that are broken, overloaded, or misaligned with wellbeing. Leadership burnout is not simply a personal failing; it's often a product of organisational issues, unsustainable expectations, outdated cultures, and invisible pressures embedded in organisational life.

This chapter marks a shift. From here, we focus on the broader context: how organisations, through their cultures, policies, and structures, can either contribute to burnout or actively prevent it. These organisational solutions are the foundation for long term, sustainable change, and they begin not just with policy, but with purpose.

Personal Reflection

Access to proactive health and wellbeing support has been invaluable in my leadership journey. One such initiative, the Ford Health Program, offered me comprehensive executive health assessments, personalised medical advice, and evidence-based strategies for maintaining resilience in high pressure roles (Ford Health, n.d.). Designed specifically for leaders, this program helped me better understand my health baselines, anticipate stress related risks, and adopt preventative habits that support long term performance.

While I haven't participated in every type of organisational wellbeing program, I've observed the positive impact of initiatives such as structured peer support, leadership retreats, and life work integration coaching in other sectors. Organisations like Unilever and the University of Melbourne have embedded wellbeing into their leadership development frameworks, recognising that sustainable leadership depends on more than individual effort; it requires supportive systems, clear priorities, and cultural alignment.

However, as I've learned firsthand, even the best programs can only go so far. Ultimately, my wellbeing was, and is, my responsibility. I had to set boundaries, say no when necessary, and actively engage with the support tools available. Recognising when I needed help, even when it was uncomfortable to admit, became an essential leadership practice.

Burnout taught me a powerful truth: wellbeing is a partnership. Organisations must provide the structures and resources that support healthy leadership, but leaders must also take ownership of their choices and capacity. When organisational systems and personal accountability align, we lay the foundation for a leadership culture where wellbeing and performance can thrive together.

Why Organisational Change Matters

Organisations play a pivotal role in shaping the conditions under which leaders work. Without organisational solutions, even the most resilient leaders will struggle to sustain their performance. But organisational change is not about removing all responsibility from the individual. Instead, it creates an environment where leaders can take meaningful action to maintain their wellbeing without feeling overwhelmed or unsupported.

By fostering a culture that values balance, wellbeing, and emotional intelligence, organisations can address the root causes of burnout. Combined with individual accountability, this creates a powerful partnership for preventing burnout and ensuring that leaders, and their teams, can thrive. Together, organisations and individuals can create a sustainable model of leadership that benefits everyone involved.

Australian Organisations Leading Wellbeing Change

Several Australian organisations have successfully implemented organisational approaches to leadership wellbeing, offering valuable models for preventing burnout while maintaining high performance.

The University of Melbourne's Leading for Wellbeing initiative provides coaching, peer networks, and realistic workload models to support academic leaders. As a result, retention and job satisfaction among faculty leadership have both improved (University of Melbourne, 2024b).

Bendigo and Adelaide Bank's Sustainable Leadership program includes regular wellbeing check-ins, structured mentoring for life work integration, and KPI frameworks that explicitly include leadership health. These measures aim to embed wellbeing as a strategic leadership priority rather than an optional benefit (Bendigo and Adelaide Bank, 2024).

VicHealth, Victoria's health promotion foundation, has embedded leadership wellbeing into its internal people strategy. Their Healthier Workplaces initiative offers psychological safety training, flexible work options, and wellbeing leadership coaching, leading to higher staff engagement and reduced turnover (VicHealth, 2023).

The Australian Public Service Commission (APSC) has introduced a comprehensive APS Mental Health Capability Framework to guide leadership behaviour and decision making. It includes system-wide resources for emotionally intelligent leadership, burnout prevention, and mentally healthy work design across all federal agencies (APSC, 2023).

These examples demonstrate a clear trend: sustainable leadership is no longer about individual stamina, but about how organisations design systems that allow leaders to thrive. When wellbeing is embedded into organisational frameworks, leadership becomes more resilient, ethical, and future fit.

Organisational Culture Shift: Prioritising Wellbeing Over Performance Metrics

Traditionally, organisational success has been measured through performance-driven metrics like profitability, productivity, and efficiency. However, in high stakes leadership roles, this relentless focus on outcomes often overlooks the mental and emotional wellbeing of leaders. Leadership burnout has become a byproduct of cultures that prioritise performance at all costs.

Organisations that invest in mental health resources see tangible results – employees who believe their employer cares about their wellbeing are three times more engaged and 71% less likely to report burnout (Spill, 2024). However, implementation remains a challenge, with 36%

of employees reporting their companies have nothing in place to prevent employee burnout, and only three out of ten managers making an effort to tackle employee burnout directly.

Cultural Shift Towards Wellbeing: To address burnout effectively, organisations need to reframe their priorities by embedding wellbeing into their organisational culture. This shift requires more than just policy changes; it calls for a reassessment of what success looks like. Wellbeing should not be seen as a peripheral concern but as a central driver of sustainable leadership.

Companies that have adopted a wellbeing centric approach – such as Patagonia and Buffer – are leading the way by integrating wellness initiatives into leadership roles. These organisations measure success not only by financial metrics but by the emotional and mental health of their leaders. Leaders are evaluated on their ability to foster a supportive environment, maintain balance, and drive productivity through empathy and engagement rather than sheer output.

> **CASE STUDY**
>
> **PATAGONIA**
>
> Patagonia offers flexible work schedules and a focus on work life balance as key leadership metrics. Leaders at Patagonia are expected to model this balance, setting an example for their teams. By prioritising mental health and sustainability, Patagonia has seen lower turnover rates, higher leadership satisfaction, and improved team morale (HumanSmart, n.d.).

Human Sustainability: A New Leadership Focus

Human sustainability has emerged as a critical focus for preventing leadership burnout. Research from Deloitte (2024) demonstrates the connection between wellbeing centred leadership and organisational success, with employees who trust their leaders being 2.5 times more likely to report that their company is advancing human sustainability. The impact extends beyond individual wellbeing – approximately 70% of workers report that increased organisational commitment to human sustainability would improve their productivity, engagement, and desire to remain with the company long term (Deloitte, 2024).

Organisations are recognising that sustainable leadership requires more than wellness programs. As Johns Hopkins Carey Business School's 2024 Wellbeing at Work report concludes, "successful organisations create a climate of wellbeing not by providing perks or benefits, but by creating a culture where people feel acknowledged, supported, and connected" (Johns Hopkins Carey Business School, 2024).

Human Sustainability: A Holistic Approach to Organisational Wellbeing

Human sustainability represents an evolution in how organisations conceptualise leadership wellbeing, moving beyond individual resilience towards a comprehensive framework that nurtures human capacity across entire systems. Deloitte's research reveals that approximately 70% of workers report increased organisational commitment to human sustainability would improve their productivity, engagement, and desire to remain with the company long term (Deloitte, 2021a).

This approach emphasises that sustainable leadership is not merely about preventing burnout but about creating conditions where people can flourish personally and professionally over extended periods. Human sustainability connects leadership wellbeing to broader organisational goals in several dimensions:

1. **Integration with ESG Frameworks:** Rather than treating wellbeing as separate from environmental, social, and governance objectives, organisations are increasingly incorporating human sustainability metrics into their broader ESG reporting. This integration acknowledges that social impact begins with how organisations treat their own people.
2. **Measurement Evolution:** Leading organisations are moving beyond simplistic wellbeing surveys to more sophisticated measurements that track recovery time, decision quality, and leadership longevity. These metrics create accountability for sustainable leadership practices at the highest organisational levels.
3. **Organisational Interventions:** Human sustainability requires examining how work is structured, including meeting practices, communication

expectations, and decision making processes. Organisations committed to this approach regularly audit these systems to identify and address structural causes of burnout.

By embracing human sustainability as a framework, organisations acknowledge that leadership wellbeing is not a personal responsibility but a strategic imperative requiring organisational support. This shift represents a significant evolution from traditional wellness initiatives, recognising that sustainable leadership requires fundamental changes to how work is designed, valued, and measured.

Emotional Intelligence: A Tool for Preventing Burnout

EQ is increasingly studied as a potential factor in preventing leadership burnout. Research suggests that leaders who develop their EQ may be better equipped to navigate stress, manage emotions, and support team resilience. EQ, as conceptualised by researchers like Goleman, typically encompasses five components: self awareness (recognising one's emotions), self regulation (managing emotional responses), empathy (understanding others' perspectives), motivation (internal drive), and social skills (building effective relationships).

EQ training typically includes developing self awareness, practicing emotional regulation, strengthening empathy through reflective conversations, and learning communication strategies that foster team trust and psychological safety.

The Role of EQ in Leadership: Leaders who develop their EQ may become more adept at recognising early signs of stress and burnout in both themselves and their teams. Recent research confirms the effectiveness of this approach, with leadership training participants experiencing a 25% increase in learning and 20% improvement in overall job performance, along with a 28% increase in leadership behaviours (Research.com, 2025). EQ development often focuses on emotional regulation techniques, which can help leaders navigate high pressure situations more effectively. The growing evidence for engaging leadership styles further demonstrates how emotionally intelligent approaches can improve work recovery and resilience during organisational changes (Ruiz-Palomino et al., 2025; Selander et al., 2025).

Empathy, another aspect of EQ, may enable leaders to build stronger connections with their teams, potentially creating environments where team members feel more valued and supported.

Building EQ: While some components of EQ may be innate, others can be strengthened through reflective practices, coaching, and structured feedback.

- **Reflective practices** such as journaling allow leaders to track their emotional responses to various situations and adjust their behaviours accordingly.
- **Coaching** provides a structured environment for leaders to explore emotional challenges, receive feedback, and develop better emotional regulation.
- **360-degree feedback** offers leaders insights into their social interactions, helping them understand how others perceive their emotional management.

CASE STUDY

GOOGLE

Google has implemented EQ training programs for its leadership teams, with the belief that fostering emotional intelligence supports resilience and equips leaders to better manage stress. These programs, combined with regular feedback and coaching, have resulted in lower burnout rates and higher engagement levels among leadership teams (Groth, 2015).

Wellbeing as a Key Performance Indicator

Traditional KPIs for leaders often revolve around financial outcomes, operational efficiency, and team productivity. However, these metrics fail to capture a crucial element of sustainable leadership: wellbeing. Organisations need to redefine KPIs to include metrics that assess a leader's mental and emotional health.

Incorporating Wellbeing into KPIs: Wellbeing focused KPIs should measure a leader's ability to maintain a healthy life work integration, support their team's wellbeing, and demonstrate emotional resilience. These metrics can be included in leadership evaluations to ensure that wellbeing is prioritised alongside performance. Research from Deloitte (2022) indicates that organisations adopting wellbeing as a KPI report a 40% reduction in leadership burnout cases.

> **CASE STUDY**
>
> **UNILEVER**
>
> Unilever (n.d.) has been a pioneer in integrating wellbeing into leadership evaluations. The company tracks leadership wellbeing metrics such as emotional engagement, team morale, and life work integration. Following this shift, Unilever experienced a 25% reduction in absenteeism and a significant increase in leadership satisfaction.

Universal Organisational Changes

To prevent burnout, universal changes must be implemented. These changes should not only focus on reducing stress but also on promoting flexibility, reducing administrative burdens, and embedding mental health support within the organisation.

1. **Flexible Work Policies:** Flexible work policies are one of the most effective tools in preventing burnout. Remote work options, compressed workweeks, and flexible hours provide leaders with the autonomy to manage their personal and professional commitments, helping them avoid the chronic stress that leads to burnout.
   Global Example: Finland is a global leader in life work integration, with many organisations offering flexible work arrangements as a standard practice. As a result, Finnish leaders report 30% lower burnout rates than their global counterparts (Helsinki Times, 2024).
2. **Reducing Administrative Burdens:** Leadership burnout is often exacerbated by excessive administrative tasks that detract from strategic decision making. Organisations can alleviate this burden by automating routine tasks and delegating non-essential responsibilities.
   Example: Northern Health, one of Melbourne's major public hospital networks, undertook a digital transformation initiative that reduced the administrative burden on clinical leaders by streamlining rostering, performance reporting, and incident tracking through automated dashboards. This allowed department heads to redirect their time

towards strategic leadership and clinical oversight. Following implementation, reported administrative time for senior leaders decreased by 25%, and job satisfaction scores among clinical leadership increased by 19% (Northern Health, 2023).
3. **Mental Health Support Systems:** Mental health support should be embedded within the organisation's framework. Access to counselling, wellness programs, and mental health days should be standard practice to ensure that leaders have the resources to manage stress before it escalates into burnout.
   Global Example: Canada has introduced comprehensive workplace wellness programs that provide access to mental health resources, counselling services, and regular wellbeing check-ins. These initiatives have reduced leadership turnover by 50% in participating organisations (Rosanes, 2024).

Practical Tools for Leadership Wellbeing

Organisations must offer practical tools to help leaders manage their wellbeing effectively. These tools include:

1. **Wellness Programs:** Structured wellness programs that offer mental health support, fitness initiatives, and stress management techniques can greatly enhance leadership wellbeing. Leaders should be encouraged to participate in these programs regularly.
2. **Leadership Coaching and Mentorship:** Coaching and mentorship are crucial in helping leaders navigate the emotional complexities of their roles. Leadership coaches provide personalised strategies for managing stress, building resilience, and improving emotional intelligence.
   Example: International Coaching Federation (ICF) A study by the ICF found that leaders who engage in regular coaching reported 60% lower burnout rates, demonstrating the effectiveness of coaching in leadership development (Garcia, 2024).
3. **Digital Tools for Tracking Wellbeing:** Digital tools such as wellbeing apps and time tracking software can help leaders monitor their life work integration, track their stress levels, and set boundaries. These tools provide real time data on wellbeing, enabling leaders to make proactive adjustments.

The Role of HR and Leadership Support

HR plays a pivotal role in fostering a culture that prioritises wellbeing. HR teams should be at the forefront of implementing wellness initiatives, conducting regular check-ins, and ensuring that leadership development includes mental health support.

HR Led Wellness Initiatives: HR teams should lead the charge in promoting a culture of wellbeing by offering programs that prioritise mental health and provide leaders with the tools they need to thrive. Regular leadership health check-ins, wellness workshops, and access to counselling should be embedded into the organisational framework.

Leadership Support and Development: Leaders who feel supported by their organisation are less likely to experience burnout. HR should ensure that leaders have access to professional development opportunities that enhance their emotional intelligence, stress management capabilities, and resilience.

The Role of Policy and Governance in Supporting Leadership Wellbeing

Sustainable leadership requires organisational governance structures that formally prioritise wellbeing. Boards and leadership teams must take shared responsibility by:

- Including wellbeing metrics in regular reporting cycles
- Integrating wellbeing into leadership succession planning
- Modelling sustainable practices from the top down

Structural Workload Management:
Workload assessments, role audits, and the authority to delegate or restructure tasks are essential tools for preventing overburdened leadership roles (Black Dog Institute, 2023).

Wellbeing Centred Reviews:
Organisations are redefining leadership KPIs to include team wellbeing, resilience practices, and recovery planning alongside traditional outcomes (Deloitte, 2024).

Policy Implementation Tip:
Effective policies must include clear accountability, system-level support structures, and regular evaluation mechanisms (Australian HR Institute, 2023).

Practical Application: Initiating Organisational Change

To begin addressing organisational factors that contribute to burnout:

1. **Select a specific organisational issue:** Rather than attempting comprehensive organisational change, choose one specific factor to address, such as meeting culture, after hours communication expectations, or workload allocation.
2. **Gather relevant data:** Collect evidence of the issue's impact through:
    - Anonymous team feedback about specific pain points
    - Metrics showing impact on productivity or engagement
    - Comparative benchmarks from similar organisations
    - Research on best practices addressing this issue
3. **Develop a focused proposal:** Create a concise, solution-oriented proposal that includes:
    - Clear description of the current challenge
    - Specific impact on wellbeing and performance
    - Proposed intervention with implementation steps
    - Expected benefits and measurement approach
4. **Identify allies and influence points:** Determine who has the authority to implement change and who might be supportive allies. Focus initial conversations on shared goals and mutual benefits rather than problems.

The **Organisational Burnout Assessment** in the Tools and Templates section helps identify organisational factors contributing to burnout and prioritise areas for intervention based on their impact and feasibility.

Organisation Reform: What Organisations Must Change

While individual action matters, leadership burnout is often a byproduct of systems not designed for human sustainability. No amount of mindfulness or resilience training can compensate for structures that perpetuate overload. To make meaningful change, organisations and sectors must reform at the root.

What Needs to Change

Workload Norms: Shift from valuing availability to valuing impact. Cap meeting hours, audit expectations, and reduce administrative bloat.

Leadership Role Design: Redesign roles to allow recovery, team distribution, and mentoring rather than solo heroics.

Accountability Frameworks: Balance outcome metrics with wellbeing indicators. Include burnout data in regular performance reviews.

Education Sector: Reduce compliance burden, invest in principal wellbeing, and challenge the "martyr myth" of school leadership.

Healthcare Sector: Prioritise leader wellbeing alongside patient safety, with mandated recovery protocols after crisis periods.

Corporate Sector: Move beyond wellness perks. Create psychologically safe cultures that reward vulnerability, recovery, and purpose aligned leadership.

True system change means shifting not just what leaders do but what they're expected to be.

Final Thought

Preventing leadership burnout is not about isolated initiatives or individual effort alone. It requires a comprehensive and organisational approach that integrates wellbeing into the very fabric of organisational culture. Reflecting on my own experience, I can see how essential it is for organisations to prioritise emotional intelligence, introduce wellbeing focused KPIs and create environments where leaders are supported to thrive. These actions are not abstract ideals. Global examples show they are both practical and transformational.

At the same time, organisational change must be matched by personal responsibility. Even with strong support structures in place, I had to choose to engage with them and make conscious decisions to protect my wellbeing. This dual responsibility is at the heart of sustainable change. It highlights the importance of collaboration between HR, leadership teams, and individual leaders.

Leadership success can no longer be measured by performance outcomes alone. It must also reflect resilience, psychological safety and the ability to foster wellbeing across teams. By embracing this shared responsibility, organisations and individuals together can redefine leadership in a way that is sustainable, human, and future focused.

In the Next Chapter

With the organisational context now explored, Chapter 12 turns to the realities of hybrid and remote leadership. We will examine how digital fatigue, blurred boundaries and 24/7 expectations have reshaped leadership, and explore practical strategies for sustaining focus, connection and wellbeing in a constantly connected world.

Reflection Questions

Personal Reflection Questions

1. Which specific organisational policies or cultural norms most significantly contribute to your experience of leadership pressure? How do these manifest in your daily work?
2. How can you advocate for organisational changes that prioritise wellbeing without appearing to undermine performance? What evidence would make the most compelling case?
3. Which strategic initiatives would address the root causes of your burnout rather than merely treating symptoms?
4. How might developing your emotional intelligence transform your leadership approach and influence on organisational culture?
5. What specific influence strategies could you employ to catalyse organisational change from your current position? How might you build alliances to support these efforts?

Team Reflection Questions

1. What metrics or KPIs could we implement to measure and value leadership wellbeing alongside performance outcomes?
2. How can we redesign our meeting structures, communication expectations, and decision making processes to reduce leadership pressure points?
3. What resources or support systems could we implement collectively that would be more effective than individual coping strategies?

4. How might we reimagine our leadership development programs to emphasise sustainable leadership practices and emotional intelligence?
5. What commitments are we willing to make as a leadership team to model healthier ways of working, and how will we hold each other accountable?

Key Takeaways

- **Organisational culture must prioritise wellbeing:** A fundamental shift from performance-only metrics to wellbeing inclusive evaluation creates environments where leaders experience lower burnout rates and teams show higher engagement.
- **Emotional intelligence serves as preventative infrastructure:** Developing EQ throughout organisations enhances self awareness, empathy, and resilience, creating critical capabilities for managing stress in high pressure leadership environments.
- **Wellbeing metrics should be core performance indicators:** Organisations that evaluate leaders on wellbeing measures alongside traditional metrics foster sustainable leadership practices and reduce burnout incidence.
- **Organisational changes require structural implementation:** Flexible work policies, streamlined administrative processes, and comprehensive mental health resources provide essential infrastructure for sustainable leadership.
- **HR departments drive wellbeing culture development:** Through wellness programs, leadership coaching, and regular wellbeing check-ins, HR teams ensure leadership health remains a strategic priority throughout organisations.

12

LEADERSHIP BURNOUT IN HYBRID AND REMOTE WORK ENVIRONMENTS

Overview

As we've explored in the previous chapter, sustainable leadership requires integrated solutions – organisational cultures, policies, and structures that support resilience and wellbeing. But what happens when the very structure of work itself shifts? In the era of hybrid and remote leadership, organisational level challenges take on a new shape. The boundaries between work and life blur, digital overload becomes the norm, and leaders are often left to navigate a complex blend of autonomy, isolation, and expectation.

This chapter builds on the organisational principles introduced earlier and applies them to one of the most transformative shifts in the modern workplace: hybrid and remote work. It explores how leaders can thrive, not just survive, in digital environments that demand new forms of communication, boundary setting, and wellbeing strategies.

While I wasn't working remotely full time during the pandemic, I led in a way that often felt more remote than ever. With staff dispersed and communication filtered through screens, I had to rethink how connection, clarity, and care looked in this context. Surprisingly, I discovered that even in the disconnection, there were moments of clarity and growth. This chapter explores those insights, alongside practical, evidence-based approaches, to help leaders stay grounded, engaged, and well in the evolving world of work.

Blurring of Life Work Boundaries

Key Idea:
In remote and hybrid environments, the line between work and personal life becomes increasingly difficult to define. Without a clear physical boundary between the office and home, leaders often struggle to "switch off," leading to chronic stress, fatigue, and eventual burnout.

Life Work Integration vs. Balance:
The traditional notion of life work integration, where work and personal time are clearly delineated, is harder to achieve in hybrid or fully remote roles. Many leaders now operate in a model of life work integration, where work tasks blend with personal life throughout the day. While flexible working conditions provide many benefits, they also carry the risk of overwork, as leaders may feel pressured to stay connected outside of regular office hours.

Research by Microsoft's Work Trend Index found that employees in hybrid roles spent, on average, 46 minutes more on work each day than their office based counterparts. For leaders, this extended time often results in higher stress levels and emotional exhaustion (Microsoft, 2024). The absence of a structured office routine means that leaders are more likely to respond to emails late into the evening or during weekends, further compounding the risk of burnout (Newman, 2022).

Psychological Disconnection:
Leaders working remotely also struggle with achieving psychological disconnection from work. Detachment from work is critical in preventing burnout. Research from the *Journal of Occupational Health Psychology* shows that individuals who can mentally disengage from work report lower stress levels and higher job satisfaction (Sonnentag & Fritz, 2015). In hybrid environments, where notifications and work related communications are constant, this disconnection is more difficult to achieve.

The challenge of disconnecting in hybrid environments is highlighted by Spill's research (2024), which found that of employees who use their annual leave, almost half (47%) find it "impossible" to properly disconnect from work. The reasons reveal our always-on culture: 1 in 5 employees feel the need to keep up with what's happening at work during leave, while 20% are unable to disconnect because they worry about unfinished tasks. This difficulty in achieving psychological separation from work significantly contributes to leadership burnout in hybrid settings.

The post-pandemic landscape has intensified these issues. Microsoft's 2024 Work Trend Index found that hybrid workers spend an average of 46 minutes more on work per day than office based peers (Microsoft, 2024). For leaders, this translates to increased stress, particularly as digital communication expectations have accelerated. Research shows that the pressure to be constantly available and responsive contributes to decision fatigue and limits recovery time (Deloitte, 2022; Harvard Business Review, 2022c).

Digital Fatigue: The Toll of Constant Connectivity

Key Idea:
With the increased reliance on digital communication tools, such as email, messaging apps, and video conferencing, leaders are facing a new type of burnout: digital fatigue. The pressure to be "always available" leads to emotional and physical exhaustion, reducing productivity and straining relationships with teams.

The Impact of Overconnectivity:
Leaders today are often tethered to digital devices, managing a continual influx of emails, messages, and virtual meetings. The concept of "Zoom fatigue" has become widespread, with prolonged video meetings causing cognitive overload and reducing leaders' ability to concentrate. A Stanford University study on digital fatigue revealed that leaders who spend more than four hours a day in virtual meetings experience significant cognitive strain, with symptoms such as eye strain, headaches, and mental fatigue (Massner, 2021).

Emotional Disconnection in Teams:
Digital communication lacks the emotional richness of face-to-face interactions, leading to feelings of emotional disconnection. Leaders in remote

settings find it harder to maintain team cohesion, as non-verbal cues such as body language and tone of voice are diminished in virtual meetings. This emotional disconnect can result in decreased trust between leaders and their teams, contributing to higher stress and burnout (LaFaber, 2024).

The Evolving Landscape of Digital Expectations

The post-pandemic digital environment has brought a fundamental shift in expectations that intensifies leadership pressure. Recent data from Microsoft's 2024 Work Trend Index reveals concerning trends: hybrid workers spend an average of 46 minutes more on work per day than their office based counterparts (Microsoft, 2024). This extended workday represents nearly an additional half-day of work each week, time often taken from personal recovery and family connection.

Even more troubling is the dramatic acceleration of response expectations. What was once considered a reasonable 24-hour window for thoughtful replies has shrunk dramatically, with LinkedIn's 2024 data showing leaders are now expected to respond within just 4 hours (Microsoft, 2024). This compression of response time creates a constant state of hypervigilance that significantly contributes to decision fatigue and emotional exhaustion.

For leaders, these shifts represent more than mere inconvenience, they signal a structural change in leadership demands that makes intentional boundary setting increasingly essential. Organisations must recognise this evolution by establishing explicit communication protocols that protect leaders' capacity for deep work and recovery. Without structural recognition of these changed expectations, individual leaders will continue to bear the burden of navigating impossible demands, regardless of their personal boundary setting efforts.

Solutions for Hybrid Leadership

Key Idea:
While hybrid and remote work environments present new challenges, leaders can adopt strategies to mitigate burnout. Implementing time management techniques, promoting asynchronous communication, and prioritising mental health breaks can help leaders manage their workload and reduce digital fatigue.

Attention Management:
Attention management provides structure in hybrid environments where traditional time boundaries blur. By designating specific focus modes (collaboration, deep work, communication) rather than just time slots, leaders can maintain productivity while preventing digital overwhelm.

Asynchronous Communication:
Promoting asynchronous communication – where messages are exchanged without the expectation of an immediate response – can significantly reduce the pressure on leaders to be constantly available. This approach enables leaders to respond to emails and messages during designated times, rather than feeling compelled to check communications continuously throughout the day. Studies by *Buffer* on remote work demonstrate that companies embracing asynchronous communication have higher employee engagement and lower burnout rates (Griffis, 2020).

Regular Mental Health Breaks:
Mental health breaks are essential in hybrid and remote environments, where the risk of digital fatigue is high. Leaders should encourage themselves and their teams to take regular breaks from screens, engage in mindfulness exercises, or spend time in nature to restore their mental energy. Research published in the *International Journal of Environmental Research and Public Health* confirms that spending just 20 minutes in nature significantly reduces stress hormone levels and improves cognitive function (Meredith et al., 2020).

Digital Wellbeing: Leveraging Technology for Leadership Sustainability

While technology often contributes to leadership burnout, emerging digital tools specifically designed for wellbeing offer promising approaches to counterbalance these effects. These technologies can transform how leaders monitor, manage, and maintain their mental and physical health in high pressure environments.

Biorhythm Monitoring Tools: Wearable technologies that track heart rate variability, sleep quality, and stress indicators provide objective data about a leader's physical state. These tools help leaders recognise early warning signs of burnout that might otherwise go unnoticed amid busy schedules. For example, WHOOP and Oura rings track recovery metrics that can be used to make informed decisions about workload management on particular days (Headspace, n.d.).

AI-Powered Coaching Platforms: Digital coaching platforms use artificial intelligence to deliver personalised resilience strategies based on a leader's specific challenges and preferences. These tools provide consistent support between formal coaching sessions, making wellbeing practices more accessible during high pressure periods. Platforms like BetterUp and Torch combine human coaching with AI-powered exercises to reinforce sustainable leadership habits (Calm, n.d.).

Boundary Management Applications: Apps specifically designed to protect focus time and personal boundaries are becoming increasingly sophisticated. These tools automatically filter communications, schedule recovery periods, and even suggest alternatives to meetings based on cognitive load analysis. Microsoft's MyAnalytics and Focus Assist features exemplify this approach, providing data-driven insights about work patterns while suggesting specific interventions to improve wellbeing (Microsoft, 2024).

Virtual Reality Recovery Spaces: For leaders working in environments where physical breaks are limited, virtual reality offers brief but effective mental escapes. Research from Stanford University (2022) demonstrates that even short immersions in natural VR environments can reduce cortisol levels and improve cognitive function, providing accessible recovery moments throughout demanding days.

While these tools cannot replace fundamental cultural and organisational changes, they provide practical supports for leaders navigating complex demands. The most effective approaches integrate these technologies into broader wellbeing strategies, using the data they generate to inform both individual practices and organisational policies.

Personal Reflection: Finding Clarity in the Chaos

During the pandemic, while many leaders were navigating remote work from the confines of their homes, I was still heading into school every day. But despite physically being present, my leadership felt more remote than ever. Staff were dispersed across suburbs and living rooms. Students were learning from kitchen tables, often surrounded by pets and siblings. Communication was reduced to emails, Zoom calls, and digital platforms.

Leading through a screen felt disjointed – at times, like navigating in the dark without a compass. I was managing wellbeing, curriculum pivots, family anxieties, and a changing staff dynamic, often without the benefit of a corridor chat or face-to-face reassurance.

And yet, here's what caught me off guard: I didn't just survive that experience – I quietly thrived in it. Not because it was easy. It wasn't. But it demanded clarity. The usual noise of leadership – relentless meetings, constant interruptions, and the pressure to be everywhere – suddenly disappeared. With so much stripped away, I found space to think again. Strategically. Creatively. Intentionally.

I became more deliberate in how I communicated. I found new ways to stay connected that weren't just effective – they were fun. Bombing into online classrooms to surprise students gave me a chance to share a laugh, stay visible, and keep a sense of joy in the air. I also started creating short video updates to share on social media, talking directly to families. These quick, informal videos were incredibly well received – they made people feel seen, informed, and still part of a school community, even from afar. In many ways, those messages achieved more connection than the traditional newsletter ever had.

That's what surprised me most. Even through the disruption, I rediscovered the power of simplicity and intention. I had to trust my team more, empower others, and lean into clarity over complexity. With fewer distractions, I could focus on what mattered most – our people, our purpose, and their wellbeing.

It reminded me that leadership doesn't have to be loud or relentless to be impactful. Sometimes, it's the quiet seasons – the ones that force us to rethink, refocus, and reconnect – that bring the deepest growth. I emerged from that time a more present, people-focused leader. Not in spite of the challenges, but because of them.

AI Integration: The Next Frontier of Leadership Pressure

Beyond the challenges of remote work and digital fatigue, leaders now face a new frontier of pressure: navigating artificial intelligence implementation. The rapid acceleration of AI tools in workplace settings has created what McKinsey & Company terms "transformation stress," the pressure leaders feel to simultaneously upskill themselves, support team anxiety, and manage organisational transformation with technologies they may still be learning themselves (McKinsey & Company, 2023d).

This evolving landscape requires leaders to make high stakes decisions about technology implementation while managing both their own learning curves and their teams' concerns about job security and role changes. *Harvard Business Review* (2023) notes that leaders report spending 16% more time managing technological change than before the pandemic, with much of this additional load taking place during traditional personal time.

To manage this new dimension of pressure, leaders must carve out dedicated learning time, create psychological safety around technology adoption, and establish clear boundaries on "always on" collaborative tools. Organisations can support sustainable leadership in this context by:

- Allocating protected time for leaders to explore and understand new technologies
- Creating realistic implementation timelines that account for learning and adjustment
- Providing mental health support specifically addressing technological change anxiety
- Setting explicit expectations about communication boundaries with new collaborative tools

As these technologies continue to evolve, leadership sustainability will increasingly depend on organisations viewing technology implementation as more than operational change; it requires emotional and cognitive space that must be built into leadership roles.

Technology Leadership: Unique Burnout Challenges and Solutions

The technology sector presents distinctive burnout risks for leaders that warrant specific attention. With its rapid innovation cycles, ambiguous problems, and global competition, tech leadership creates pressure patterns unlike those in more established industries.

Tech Specific Burnout Triggers

Several factors uniquely contribute to technology leadership burnout:

1. **Perpetual Beta Culture:** Technology organisations often operate in "perpetual beta" – a state of continuous improvement with few clear endpoints. Unlike projects with defined completion criteria, tech initiatives frequently evolve into new challenges without offering leaders the psychological closure needed for recovery. Research shows this continuous deployment approach, while driving innovation, creates significant pressure on leaders who rarely experience the satisfaction of full project completion (KPMG, 2024).
2. **Technical Debt Management:** Leaders in technology organisations face the constant challenge of balancing new development with maintenance of existing systems. According to KPMG's 2024 Global Tech Report, 57% of organisational leaders report that "flaws in their foundational IT systems disrupt business-as-usual on a weekly basis," creating a cognitive tension between innovation and stability that significantly contributes to decision fatigue (KPMG Australia, 2024).
3. **24/7 Operational Responsibility:** With global user bases and cloud infrastructures, technology leaders often carry implicit or explicit responsibility for systems that never sleep. This "always-on" accountability creates unique psychological burdens. A 2024 BT study found that 96% of business and technology leaders experience anxiety about technology that disrupts their sleep patterns, with cybersecurity threats (32%) and system reliability being primary concerns (TechRepublic, 2024).
4. **Cognitive Overload from Rapid Change:** Technology leaders must constantly adapt to accelerating technological changes while managing current operations. Research by Kin + Carta found that 94% of executives report tech anxiety amongst senior leaders in their organisations, with the top contributing factors being the speed of technological change (35%), internal skills gaps (29%), and limited access to the right talent (28%) (Kin + Carta, 2023).

Effective Interventions for Technology Leaders

Successful technology organisations have developed specialised approaches to leadership sustainability:

1. **Bounded Innovation Cycles:** Companies like Canva implement "bounded innovation cycles" that deliberately include recovery periods between intensive development sprints. Their "4–1" model (four weeks of focused development followed by one week of learning, reflection, and technical debt management) provides natural boundaries that prevent prolonged stress exposure.
2. **Distributed On Call Rotations:** Rather than placing responsibility on individual leaders, mature technology organisations implement formal on call rotations that distribute operational burden. Australia's NEXTDC employs a "leadership coverage matrix" ensuring no leader carries 24/7 responsibility for more than one week monthly.
3. **Technical/Managerial Partnership Models:** Recognising the dual nature of technology leadership, organisations like Atlassian have moved away from requiring technical leaders to also serve as people managers. Their "dual track" career model allows technical leaders to maintain influence while sharing managerial responsibilities with dedicated people leaders.

By implementing these sector specific approaches, technology organisations can protect their leadership talent from the unique burnout risks inherent to the industry while maintaining innovation and competitive advantage.

Practical Application: Digital Wellness and Attention Management

To maintain focus and prevent digital overwhelm in hybrid environments:

1. **Audit your digital behaviour:** For one week, track the gap between your intended and actual digital habits, noting:
    - When you first check and last check work communications

- How quickly you typically respond to messages
- How often you interrupt focus time for digital interruptions

2. **Establish clear availability indicators:** Create explicit signals that communicate your availability to colleagues:

    - Update calendar working hours and status indicators
    - Create standardised email signature noting response timeframes
    - Use status messages that clearly indicate focus or unavailable periods

3. **Implement technology supports:** Configure your devices to reinforce your boundaries:

    - Set up "do not disturb" modes during focus or personal time
    - Create separate work and personal profiles on devices where possible
    - Use apps that limit access to work platforms outside working hours

4. **Communicate digital norms:** Share your approach with key stakeholders: "To ensure I can deliver high quality work, I am adjusting my digital availability to [specific parameters]. I will be fully responsive during [core hours]."

The **Digital Boundary Protocol** in the Tools and Templates section provides a structured framework for establishing clear digital boundaries, creating appropriate communication expectations, and implementing technology settings that support those boundaries.

Final Thought

Navigating the complexities of hybrid and remote work has highlighted a critical truth: leadership today requires adaptability, intentionality, and a proactive approach to wellbeing. While hybrid work offers valuable flexibility, it also brings unique challenges, such as blurred boundaries between life and work, digital fatigue and the ongoing need to stay connected and present with our teams.

Reflecting on my own experience during the pandemic, I recognise how important it is to embrace both the opportunities and the challenges of hybrid leadership. Although I was not working remotely full time, I still felt the strain of constant digital communication and the need to juggle competing demands while learning new systems and tools. What helped me was not only using technology more effectively, but also setting boundaries, maintaining balance and prioritising meaningful connection, even through a screen.

This chapter has explored practical strategies to reduce burnout in hybrid contexts, including time blocking, asynchronous communication, digital detoxes, and regular mental health breaks. These tools are essential for building resilience and sustaining effective leadership. Yet beyond these techniques lies a deeper shift: thriving in hybrid work is not only about managing time. It is about reclaiming how we lead, how we connect and how we care for both ourselves and others.

Leadership in hybrid environments requires a new mindset. Being constantly available does not mean being effective. It is about valuing depth over volume, prioritising recovery as much as productivity, and creating a culture where wellbeing is central. As we continue to adapt, let us treat hybrid work as an opportunity to lead differently, with clarity, purpose, and balance. Hybrid leadership is not about perfection. It is about progress and learning to thrive together in new ways.

In the Next Chapter

While hybrid leadership highlights the challenges of isolation and overload, it also reminds us that leadership should never be a solo act. In Chapter 13, we explore how peer support, shared leadership models, and intentional team culture can help reduce the burden on individual leaders and foster more resilient, collaborative leadership communities.

Reflection Questions

Personal Reflection Questions

1. How has the shift to hybrid or remote work transformed your experience of stress and your ability to disengage from work? What boundaries have become most difficult to maintain?
2. What specific boundaries have proven most effective in protecting your wellbeing in remote work settings? Which boundaries exist only in theory rather than practice?
3. How has digital fatigue affected your leadership presence, decision making capacity, and ability to connect authentically with your team?

4. Which personal practices would help you maintain balance and authentic connection in a hybrid environment? What prevents you from implementing these consistently?
5. How might you redesign your digital leadership approach to prioritise both effectiveness and wellbeing?

Team Reflection Questions

1. What unspoken expectations about availability, response times, and meeting attendance have emerged in our hybrid work environment?
2. How might we establish team protocols around digital communications that respect personal boundaries while maintaining necessary coordination?
3. What collective agreements could we create about camera use, meeting duration, and scheduled breaks that would reduce digital fatigue?
4. How can we foster genuine connection and psychological safety in hybrid or remote settings without creating additional online obligations?
5. What team practices might help us identify and support colleagues who are struggling with isolation or boundary management in remote settings?

Key Takeaways

- **Digital environments blur professional-personal boundaries:** Remote and hybrid work settings create boundary challenges as leaders struggle with constant connectivity and the absence of physical workplace transitions.
- **Clear communication protocols maintain balance:** Leaders need established guidelines around availability, response times, and meeting schedules to manage digital demands and prevent always on expectations.
- **Regular digital disengagement preserves mental resources:** Scheduled breaks from screens and communication technologies are essential for cognitive recovery and emotional regulation in hybrid leadership roles.

- **Life work integration requires intentional structure:** Leaders must design work patterns around personal wellbeing priorities rather than allowing digital work to dominate all available time and attention.
- **Leadership modelling shapes team wellbeing culture:** By demonstrating healthy boundary setting and balanced digital habits, leaders create psychological permission for team members to adopt similar sustainable practices.

13

BUILDING RESILIENT LEADERSHIP TEAMS

PEER SUPPORT AND SHARED LEADERSHIP MODELS

Overview

Leadership, when concentrated in the hands of a few individuals, often leads to overwhelming stress, decision fatigue, and eventual burnout. A growing response to this challenge is the adoption of shared leadership models and the development of peer support networks. These approaches distribute responsibility, foster collaboration, and build resilience across leadership teams.

In my own leadership journey, I've experienced both the strain of carrying decisions alone and the transformative power of working in partnership. Early in my career, I often felt that every major choice rested squarely on my shoulders. It wasn't until I encountered the benefits of shared leadership and peer support firsthand that I truly appreciated the power of collective wisdom. These frameworks didn't just lighten the load, they deepened the quality of my decision making by bringing in diverse perspectives and shared accountability.

DOI: 10.4324/9781003668626-17

This chapter explores the benefits of shared leadership and peer mentoring, offering real world examples of organisations that have successfully implemented these models to create more sustainable and supportive leadership environments. Drawing from both personal experience and research, we'll examine how these practices foster resilience, strengthen team cohesion, and support healthier, more effective leadership dynamics.

While the Leadership Reset Framework focuses on the personal journey from burnout to breakthrough, this chapter reminds us that no leader resets in isolation. Sustainable change depends on structures, like strong teams and peer support, that share the weight, nurture trust, and build collective resilience.

Shared Leadership Models

Key Idea:
Shared leadership is a model that decentralises authority and distributes leadership responsibilities among a team. This structure helps reduce the burden on individual leaders, promotes collaboration, and prevents burnout by ensuring that no one person is solely responsible for critical decision making.

What Is Shared Leadership?
Shared leadership involves a team based approach, where leadership roles and responsibilities are spread among multiple individuals, rather than being concentrated in a single leader. This model is particularly effective in high pressure environments where the demands of leadership can quickly lead to burnout if carried by a single individual. In a shared leadership structure, multiple leaders contribute their unique skills and perspectives, creating a more dynamic and balanced approach to decision making (Wang et al., 2014).

Key Benefits of Shared Leadership:

- **Reduced Decision Fatigue:** By distributing decision making authority, the mental burden is shared, reducing the risk of burnout for any one leader. Leaders can focus on their areas of expertise without feeling overwhelmed by the entire organisation's challenges (Pearce & Manz, 2005).

- **Enhanced Collaboration:** Shared leadership encourages collective problem solving. Leaders collaborate to develop solutions, drawing on diverse perspectives, which can lead to more innovative and effective outcomes (Wang et al., 2014).
- **Increased Flexibility:** Leaders have more flexibility to step back or take breaks during high stress periods, knowing that their peers can take over responsibilities in their absence. This approach prevents overwork and promotes a healthier work life balance (Kocolowski, 2010).

Practical Strategies for Shared Leadership:

1. **Role Specialisation and Task Delegation:** In a shared leadership model, leaders should focus on areas where they have the most expertise and delegate responsibilities that others are better equipped to handle. This prevents cognitive overload and ensures that tasks are completed by those with the best skills for them. For example, dividing leadership tasks into functional areas (finance, operations, strategy) can help balance the load and reduce stress on any single leader (Kocolowski, 2010).
    - **Practical Tip:** Create a leadership map to clearly define who is responsible for what, and ensure regular communication between team members to avoid overlap or confusion.
2. **Rotational Leadership:** Rotating leadership roles within a team allows different individuals to take charge of specific projects or initiatives at different times. This promotes versatility in leadership skills and reduces the risk of burnout by not placing the full burden on one person over extended periods.
    - **Practical Tip:** Introduce project based leadership where different team members lead on specific projects or during different phases of a project. This rotational approach ensures shared responsibility.
3. **Collaborative Decision Making Frameworks:** Utilise frameworks like RACI (Responsible, Accountable, Consulted, Informed) or Consensus Decision Making to structure decision making in teams. These frameworks make it clear who is responsible for each task and ensure input is gathered from multiple leaders, distributing responsibility and encouraging collaboration (Pearce & Manz, 2005).

- **Practical Tip:** Before making key decisions, consult with all leadership team members to gather input and ensure that diverse perspectives are considered.
4. **Leadership Pods or Squads:** Similar to Spotify's model, where small autonomous squads work on different elements of a larger project, creating leadership "pods" enables teams to work with shared responsibility. In this setup, decisions are made collaboratively within pods, while larger organisational goals are aligned through coordination between different pods (Cruth, n.d.).
   - **Practical Tip:** Create teams or pods that operate semi-independently, with defined roles and goals, encouraging decentralised leadership and autonomy within the group.
5. **Cross-Training for Leadership Agility:** Encourage cross-training among leaders so that individuals can step into different roles when necessary. This builds agility and ensures that if a leader is absent or under pressure, others can temporarily fill in without disrupting team performance (Wang et al., 2014).
   - **Practical Tip:** Implement cross-training programs that give leaders exposure to different functional areas of the organisation, enhancing adaptability and resilience within the leadership structure.
6. **Establish Peer Review Systems:** Peer feedback and review systems allow leaders to provide constructive feedback to one another. This promotes accountability and ensures that leaders are continually refining their skills through the perspectives of their colleagues, while also distributing responsibility for performance monitoring (ThriveSparrow, n.d.).
   - **Practical Tip:** Set up regular peer reviews where leadership teams assess each other's progress, share feedback, and discuss areas of improvement.
7. **Implement a Clear Communication Protocol:** Effective communication is crucial for shared leadership to work. Establish clear protocols, including regular team check-ins, updates, and decision making processes to ensure everyone stays aligned on leadership roles and organisational goals.
   - **Practical Tip:** Use communication tools like Slack or Microsoft Teams to facilitate real time discussions and ensure transparency within leadership decisions and responsibilities.

Contemporary Research:
Research published in the *Journal of Applied Psychology* highlights that organisations adopting shared leadership models experience higher levels of team satisfaction, reduced stress across leadership ranks, and improved team performance. These models are particularly successful in sectors where innovation and collaboration are critical, such as technology, healthcare, and education (Wang et al., 2014).

Peer Support Networks

Key Idea:
Peer support networks offer significant emotional and practical benefits by providing leaders with a platform to share challenges, seek advice, and offer support. These networks, often structured as peer mentoring programs or leadership circles, foster collaboration and reduce the isolation that often contributes to leadership burnout.

The Role of Peer Mentoring:
Peer mentoring programs connect leaders with others in similar roles, creating opportunities for sharing experiences, learning from one another, and offering emotional support. In high stress environments, peer support systems help leaders feel understood, reducing the sense of isolation that can exacerbate burnout (Groysberg & Halperin, 2022).

Benefits of Peer Support Networks:

- **Emotional Resilience:** Leaders who participate in peer support networks report higher levels of emotional resilience. Having a trusted group of peers to discuss personal and professional challenges with provides a critical emotional outlet that reduces the buildup of stress (Chipchase & Miller, 2020).
- **Practical Problem Solving:** Peer mentoring also offers practical support. Leaders can share best practices, seek advice on decision making, and learn new strategies for managing teams. Peer support helps leaders become more effective problem-solvers and improves their leadership skills (Reeves, 2023).

Practical Strategies for Peer Support Networks:

1. **Establish Formal Peer Mentoring Programs:** Developing structured peer mentoring programs provides leaders with a reliable system of support. Pairing individuals in similar roles helps them share experiences, seek advice, and learn from one another. These programs should include regular check-ins, opportunities for feedback, and goal-setting sessions to help leaders navigate high pressure environments and prevent burnout.
   - **Practical Tip:** Create a mentoring schedule where leaders meet monthly, share challenges, and collaborate on strategies for managing stress and improving team performance.
2. **Build Leadership Circles:** Leadership circles are small groups of peers who meet regularly to discuss professional challenges, share insights, and provide mutual support. These circles create a sense of community and psychological safety, enabling leaders to feel supported and understood. The informal nature of these groups helps foster open communication and strengthens relationships within the leadership team (Leadership Circle, n.d.-b).
   - **Practical Tip:** Organise quarterly leadership circles where peers can discuss ongoing leadership issues, share their experiences, and explore solutions collectively.
3. **Implement Cross Departmental Support Networks:** Cross-departmental peer networks allow leaders from different areas of the organisation to come together and offer fresh perspectives. This approach encourages collaboration across silos, providing leaders with broader insights into the challenges they face. It also fosters a more unified organisational culture by connecting leaders from diverse departments.
   - **Practical Tip:** Establish quarterly cross-departmental meetups to encourage peer-to-peer learning and break down communication barriers between different areas of the organisation.
4. **Develop Digital Peer Support Platforms:** With the increase in hybrid and remote working environments, digital platforms for peer support have become essential. Leaders can leverage online communities,

forums, or Slack channels to connect with their peers, share advice, and seek help when needed. These platforms offer flexibility and enable leaders to access peer support in real time, regardless of their location.
   - **Practical Tip:** Create a dedicated Slack channel or forum where leaders can ask questions, share resources, and support each other digitally, ensuring easy access to peer support at all times.
5. **Foster Accountability Partnerships:** Pairing leaders in accountability partnerships allows them to check in regularly with one another on their personal and professional goals. This partnership creates mutual accountability for managing stress, setting life work integration boundaries, and pursuing leadership development. It also helps leaders build long-lasting, trust based relationships within their peer network.
   - **Practical Tip:** Encourage leaders to set personal goals and establish accountability partnerships to monitor progress, share challenges, and keep each other motivated.

The Five Dysfunctions of a Team: Addressing Team Dynamics to Prevent Burnout

Another valuable lens for understanding and preventing leadership burnout is Patrick Lencioni's "Five Dysfunctions of a Team" model (Lencioni, 2024). While often used for improving team performance, this framework also highlights how unhealthy team dynamics can intensify stress and lead to burnout, especially when leaders are left to absorb the consequences of dysfunction alone.

Lencioni's model outlines five core dysfunctions:

- **Absence of Trust** – When team members feel unsafe being vulnerable, leaders often become the emotional buffer for unresolved tension.
- **Fear of Conflict** – Avoiding difficult conversations forces leaders to navigate issues solo, often behind the scenes.
- **Lack of Commitment** – Unclear or hesitant team decisions leave leaders to drive follow through on their own.
- **Avoidance of Accountability** – When peer accountability is lacking, leaders become the sole enforcers of standards.

- **Inattention to Results** – Without shared goals, leaders carry the weight of performance outcomes without genuine team ownership.

Each dysfunction increases leadership strain – amplifying emotional exhaustion, decision fatigue, and feelings of isolation.

Addressing Dysfunction to Reduce Leadership Burden:
When teams overcome these dysfunctions, leadership becomes more sustainable. Leaders no longer have to absorb all the pressure because the team itself becomes more self regulating and accountable.

Practical Applications:

- Build trust through vulnerability: Begin meetings with brief check-ins where leaders model openness.
- Embrace constructive conflict: Encourage disagreement around ideas, making it clear that diverse viewpoints strengthen outcomes.
- Create clarity and commitment: Close meetings with clear next steps and shared ownership of decisions.
- Normalise peer accountability: Encourage team members to follow up with each other, not just rely on positional authority.
- Focus on collective results: Set and track visible team goals that everyone is invested in.

This model pairs naturally with shared leadership. As trust and accountability improve, leadership becomes less about individual performance and more about team collaboration. For any leader working towards a sustainable reset approach, addressing these five dysfunctions is a powerful step towards reducing stress and improving team resilience.

Examples of Success

Key Idea:
Several high profile organisations have successfully implemented shared leadership models and peer support networks to reduce leadership burnout and improve team resilience. These examples demonstrate how distributing leadership responsibilities and fostering a culture of support can lead to improved leadership effectiveness and organisational outcomes.

SPOTIFY

Spotify is renowned for its *squad based leadership model*, where responsibility is distributed across small, autonomous teams known as squads. Each squad operates with a shared leadership structure, meaning decision making is collaborative, and authority is decentralised. This model allows Spotify to maintain a high level of innovation while reducing stress at the leadership level. Leaders rely on their teams to make decisions collectively, rather than shouldering the full burden of leadership alone (Cruth, n.d.).

ZAPPOS

Zappos, the online shoe retailer, adopted a *holacracy* model, which eliminates traditional hierarchical leadership in favour of distributed decision making. Leadership is shared across various roles, with each employee responsible for different aspects of the business. This approach has resulted in a more resilient organisational culture, with leaders experiencing less burnout due to the shared responsibility for strategic decision making (Thai, n.d.).

NATIONAL HEALTH SERVICE (UK)

The National Health Service (NHS) in the UK has implemented peer mentoring programs for senior leaders, particularly in high stress roles such as hospital management. These programs connect leaders with experienced mentors who provide guidance on both emotional resilience and practical leadership strategies. Peer support networks within the NHS have led to reduced turnover rates and improved leader satisfaction, even in the highly demanding healthcare environment (NHS England, 2023).

Creating a Supportive Leadership Culture

Building resilient leadership teams requires more than just distributing tasks; it necessitates a cultural shift within organisations. A supportive leadership culture values shared leadership, emotional resilience, and peer collaboration, helping leaders thrive rather than burn out. This section provides actionable steps for fostering such a culture, ensuring leaders can perform at their best while maintaining wellbeing.

Steps to Foster Shared Leadership and Peer Support:

1. **Encourage Collaborative Decision Making:** Organisations should actively promote leadership structures that enable team based decision making, ensuring that critical responsibilities are shared among multiple leaders rather than concentrated in one person. This reduces pressure and prevents burnout by allowing leaders to pool their expertise, distribute workloads, and provide mutual support. When authority is shared, decisions benefit from a broader range of perspectives, leading to more thoughtful, innovative outcomes. Research shows that shared leadership can enhance team satisfaction, reduce stress, and improve overall performance (Wang et al., 2014).
   - **Practical Tip:** Introduce a rotating decision making model, where different leaders take turns chairing meetings and overseeing strategic initiatives. This distributes responsibility and builds collective ownership over the organisation's direction.
2. **Establish Peer Mentoring Programs:** Formal peer mentoring programs provide a vital structure for supporting leadership development. Connecting leaders across different areas of the organisation enables cross-functional collaboration and learning. Peer mentors offer both emotional and practical support, helping to reduce feelings of isolation, especially for leaders in high pressure roles. This also enhances leaders' resilience and ability to handle complex challenges. Mentoring programs that emphasise trust and confidentiality can significantly reduce stress levels.
   - **Practical Tip:** Develop a peer mentoring initiative where experienced leaders are paired with emerging leaders for monthly one-on-one sessions. Focus on creating a safe space for discussing leadership challenges and sharing best practices for stress management and team collaboration.
3. **Promote Leadership Circles:** Leadership circles are small, informal groups of leaders who meet regularly to discuss challenges, share insights, and provide mutual support. These groups promote emotional resilience by allowing leaders to express concerns, receive feedback, and gain alternative perspectives on their challenges. This peer-driven

support fosters a sense of community and trust within leadership teams. Leadership circles not only reduce the emotional burden on individual leaders but also help in building more cohesive teams.
- **Practical Tip:** Set up leadership circles where 6–8 leaders from across the organisation meet quarterly. Each session can focus on different leadership themes, such as stress management, decision making under pressure, or fostering team creativity.

4. **Integrate Emotional Resilience Training:** Training in emotional resilience equips leaders with the tools needed to manage stress, navigate challenges, and maintain personal wellbeing. Emotional resilience training helps leaders recognise stress triggers and provides strategies to stay calm and focused in difficult situations. Leaders who are emotionally resilient can better manage their teams' emotional states, fostering a work environment that prioritises psychological safety and collaboration (Goleman, 2013a).
   - **Practical Tip:** Implement a training program focused on mindfulness, emotional regulation, and stress-reduction techniques. Combine this with ongoing peer mentoring to encourage the application of these strategies in daily leadership practices.

5. **Foster a Culture of Open Communication:** A supportive leadership culture thrives on open communication, where leaders feel empowered to share their struggles without fear of judgment or repercussions. Transparent communication channels help build trust across leadership teams and prevent the accumulation of stress. Organisations should cultivate an environment where leaders can express vulnerabilities and ask for help when needed. Encouraging such openness not only helps alleviate stress but also strengthens relationships within the team.
   - **Practical Tip:** Schedule regular "open forums" for leaders to candidly discuss challenges they are facing, with a focus on finding collective solutions. These forums can be a platform for peer led discussions on topics like life work integration and stress management.

The Critical Element of Recovery Time

Research increasingly recognises that recovery time, structured periods for leaders to psychologically and physically restore themselves, is as important as resilience building practices. Data from the 2024 Australian Principal Occupational Health, Safety and Wellbeing Survey found that school leaders demonstrated "surprisingly strong levels of resilience" according to the Brief Resilience Scale, showing a continued ability to bounce back after adverse experiences despite facing unprecedented challenges (Australian Catholic University, 2024). However, the research identified one critical difference between school leaders and other high pressure professions like emergency services: school leaders receive very little recovery time by comparison.

This insight highlights a crucial but often overlooked dimension of leadership sustainability: it's not just about developing resilience skills but ensuring sufficient recovery periods to apply them effectively. Without adequate recovery, even the most resilient leaders eventually deplete their adaptive capacity, regardless of their personal practices or organisational support.

Effective recovery requires several elements:

1. **Structural Protection:** Organisations must build recovery periods into leadership roles through formal policies rather than leaving recovery to individual discretion, which often results in it being sacrificed to work demands.
2. **Sequential Load Management:** Work intensity should be sequenced to allow for recovery after high pressure periods. This approach acknowledges that leadership capacity is renewable but not infinite, requiring deliberate cycles of engagement and recovery.
3. **Quality vs. Quantity:** Recovery effectiveness depends on more than duration; it requires psychological detachment from work concerns, relaxation, mastery experiences outside work, and a sense of control over one's time. Organisations should evaluate whether supposed recovery periods actually deliver these elements.

By intentionally designing recovery into leadership roles, organisations protect not just individual wellbeing but their leadership capacity as a strategic resource. This approach represents a shift from viewing leadership as an endless marathon to seeing it as a series of focused sprints with essential recovery between them.

Resilience Despite Unprecedented Challenges

Despite the concerning trends in leadership burnout, recent research highlights a remarkable level of resilience among leaders. The 2024 Australian Principal Occupational Health, Safety and Wellbeing Survey found that school leaders demonstrated "surprisingly strong levels of resilience" according to the Brief Resilience Scale, showing a continued ability to bounce back after adverse experiences despite facing unprecedented challenges (Australian Catholic University, 2024). This resilience is comparable to that of emergency service workers, with one key difference: school leaders receive very little recovery time by comparison (The Educator, 2024). This underscores the importance of not only building resilience but ensuring adequate recovery time and support systems for leaders across all sectors.

Practical Application: Creating Collaboration Leadership Success

To develop leadership structures that distribute responsibility and prevent isolated burnout:

1. **Map leadership capabilities:** Conduct a team capabilities assessment to identify:

    - Each member's core strengths and expertise areas
    - Individual workload capacity and current demands
    - Complementary skill sets that could enable partnership

2. **Design leadership partnerships:** Create formal leadership pairs or trios with:

    - Shared accountability for key deliverables
    - Complementary working styles and strengths
    - Clear role definition while maintaining collective ownership

3. **Establish collective decision frameworks:** Implement structured approaches to decision making:

    - Categorise decisions by impact and urgency
    - Assign clear decision rights for different types of issues
    - Create protocols for when decisions require consultation

4. **Develop rotational leadership practices:** For ongoing responsibilities, consider:
   - Monthly rotation of meeting facilitation duties
   - Quarterly rotation of project oversight responsibilities
   - Alternating representation at external stakeholder meetings

The **Shared Leadership Implementation Plan** in the Tools and Templates section provides a comprehensive framework for distributing leadership responsibilities in ways that enhance both effectiveness and sustainability.

Final Thought

Leadership at its best is a shared journey, yet many leaders still find themselves navigating it in isolation. Reflecting on my own experience, I have come to understand that resilience is not built alone. It is strengthened through connection, collaboration, and mutual support. The moments when I embraced shared leadership and leaned on peers for guidance were not just helpful. They were transformative. These experiences brought clarity, balance, and strength at a time when demands felt overwhelming.

This chapter reinforces an essential truth: sustainable leadership is about more than personal resilience. Shared leadership models distribute responsibility and make space for innovation, while peer support networks offer emotional grounding and practical tools for problem solving. Together, these frameworks redefine leadership by embedding trust and collaboration into the fabric of organisational life.

Adopting these approaches, however, requires a cultural shift. Organisations must invest in structures that enable shared decision making, foster open dialogue and promote emotional wellbeing. At the same time, leaders must actively build and maintain their peer networks, engage in ongoing learning and support their colleagues with the same care they offer to their teams.

What stands out most is how these models serve not only the individual leader but the organisation as a whole. When leaders share responsibility and lean into peer support, they create spaces where creativity, psychological safety, and collective success can thrive. They model a leadership style that is both sustainable and deeply human.

In a complex and rapidly evolving world, the need for resilient leadership teams has never been greater. The principles explored in this chapter — shared leadership, peer mentoring, and a culture of support — are not just antidotes to burnout. They are the foundation for long term, meaningful leadership. By embracing these practices, we can shift the story of leadership from one of burden to one of shared strength and collaborative impact.

In the Next Chapter

Our final chapter brings the full reset journey together. In Chapter 14, we explore how to redefine leadership success by embedding wellbeing into leadership pipelines, succession planning, and strategic development. This is where reinvention becomes sustainable, and where the future of leadership is shaped by clarity, care, and purpose.

Reflection Questions

Personal Reflection Questions

1. How have shared leadership or peer support experiences influenced your resilience during particularly challenging periods? What made these relationships especially valuable?
2. What specific steps could you take to build a stronger peer support network that provides both emotional sustenance and practical leadership guidance?
3. How do you balance your need for control with the benefits of distributed leadership? What beliefs or experiences make delegation particularly challenging?
4. In what ways could structured mentoring or coaching relationships help you navigate burnout? What form would these relationships ideally take?
5. What personal barriers might prevent you from fully engaging with peer support or shared leadership approaches?

Team Reflection Questions

1. How might we evolve from a collection of individual leaders to a genuinely shared leadership team? What structures would support this transition?
2. What peer support mechanisms could we implement that would provide authentic connection without creating additional obligations?
3. How can we distribute leadership responsibilities in ways that leverage individual strengths while preventing isolated decision fatigue?
4. What team learning opportunities might help us develop more collaborative leadership practices and mutual support skills?
5. How might we measure and recognise the effectiveness of shared leadership approaches to reinforce their value in our organisation?

Key Takeaways

- **Distributed leadership reduces individual pressure:** Shared leadership models decentralise authority and responsibilities, lowering individual stress, enhancing collaboration, and preventing isolated decision fatigue.
- **Peer support networks build emotional resilience:** Structured peer relationships provide safe spaces for leaders to share challenges, exchange advice, and develop mutual support systems that strengthen leadership capacity.
- **Collaborative structures enhance decision quality:** Team based frameworks for decision making reduce cognitive burden while improving problem solving through diverse perspective integration.
- **Proven models demonstrate implementation success:** Organisations like Spotify, Zappos, and the NHS show how shared leadership and peer mentoring tangibly reduce burnout while improving organisational performance.
- **Supportive leadership cultures require intentional development:** Peer mentoring programs, leadership circles, and emotional resilience training create the infrastructure needed for sustainable leadership effectiveness.

14

BUILDING A RESILIENT LEADERSHIP PIPELINE

PREVENTING BURNOUT IN FUTURE LEADERS

Overview

Leadership burnout is not an isolated issue – it's embedded in the very systems and cultures in which leaders operate. Solving it requires more than encouraging individual resilience; it demands a redefinition of leadership success that places wellbeing at its core. I've experienced this firsthand. I work in an organisation that offers exceptional support – wellness initiatives, mental health resources, leadership development programs. And while these supports are invaluable, I've also come to understand that no system can fully protect a leader who doesn't take personal accountability. Real change comes when both the individual and the organisation commit to doing things differently.

This chapter explores what that organisational shift looks like. It examines how redefining leadership KPIs to include wellbeing, embedding emotional intelligence into leadership culture, and implementing organisational changes, like flexible work policies and mental health support, can create the conditions where leaders not only survive, but thrive. Drawing on practical tools and global examples, we show how these organisational shifts contribute to long term leadership sustainability.

The final phase of the Leadership Reset Framework – Reinvention – isn't just about one leader adopting a new approach. It's about building a culture where future leaders are set up to succeed. This chapter expands the reset beyond the individual and into the organisation itself, challenging systems to rethink what effective leadership really looks like – and to create the structures that will support the next generation to thrive, not burn out.

Shifting from Performance Driven to Wellbeing Centred Leadership

Traditional leadership models have long prioritised performance driven success, with metrics often focused solely on financial outcomes, productivity, and operational efficiency. However, new research demonstrates the limitations of this approach in the face of rising burnout rates. The gender dimension of this challenge is particularly noteworthy, with recent data showing that women's burnout rates have increased to 42% (from 38% in 2023), while men's rates have decreased to 30% (Infinite Potential, 2024). This underscores the importance of leadership approaches that account for diverse experiences and needs within the workforce. However, as global workplace dynamics evolve, leadership must adapt to embrace a model that places wellbeing at the core of success.

Organisations are recognising that leadership effectiveness is not solely about meeting targets but also about maintaining the emotional, mental, and physical health of both the leader and their teams. Leadership burnout is on the rise, with research showing that chronic stress can lead to disengagement, poor decision making, and high turnover rates (Gallup, 2020). Thus, organisations are beginning to integrate wellbeing centred KPIs into their leadership frameworks.

CASE STUDY

SALESFORCE

Salesforce is an example of an organisation that has successfully redefined leadership success by incorporating wellbeing metrics into its culture. The

> company introduced "wellbeing days" and mental health resources to its leadership teams, integrating these metrics into performance reviews. This approach not only improved leader satisfaction but also fostered a more engaged workforce, reducing leadership burnout (Salesforce, 2021).
>
> By shifting away from purely performance-driven leadership models, organisations can nurture leaders who are more resilient and sustainable, promoting a healthier workplace culture.

Practical Strategies for Shifting from Performance Driven to Wellbeing Centred Leadership:

While organisations like Salesforce have successfully incorporated wellbeing into leadership KPIs, there is room for a deeper integration of personalised wellbeing metrics.

1. **Wellbeing Innovation Labs:**

    - Organisations can develop internal Wellbeing Innovation Labs, allowing leadership teams to experiment with different wellbeing practices, tools, and strategies that suit their personal and team needs.
        - o **Practical Tip:** Encourage leaders to try mindfulness apps or biofeedback tools to monitor stress. Leaders can rotate in testing different methods, such as outdoor walking meetings or "digital detox hours," and review these experiments during wellness check-ins.

2. **Sustainability Scorecards:**

    - Incorporating Sustainability Scorecards to assess how effectively leaders manage stress, life work integration, and emotional wellbeing can track progress alongside performance goals.
        - o **Practical Tip:** Add wellbeing metrics to annual leadership reviews, including stress levels, personal time for reflection, and mental resilience, measured through regular self assessment surveys.

3. **Personalised Wellbeing KPIs:**

    - Instead of one-size-fits-all KPIs, organisations can offer personalised wellbeing metrics for each leader, addressing their unique stressors and needs.

- o **Practical Tip:** Implement a bi-annual leadership wellbeing survey that tracks key indicators such as mental health, life work integration, and personal fulfilment. Integrate these results into performance evaluations and career progression discussions.

Stress Management Strategies for Leaders

Effective stress management is critical to preventing burnout in leadership roles. Chronic stress not only affects leaders' performance but also compromises their decision making abilities and impacts the teams they manage. Stress management strategies must be a fundamental component of leadership development programs to create emotionally resilient leaders.

Mindfulness Based Stress Reduction (MBSR):
MBSR is a powerful tool for reducing stress in high pressure environments. Leaders who practice mindfulness are better equipped to manage stress and maintain emotional balance. According to the University of Massachusetts Medical School (2017), MBSR has been shown to significantly reduce burnout among leaders by promoting present-moment awareness and emotional regulation.

Cognitive Behavioural Techniques (CBT):
CBT is another effective approach, enabling leaders to reframe negative thinking patterns and build emotional resilience. CBT helps leaders identify stress triggers and develop strategies for managing them proactively. A study by The International Coaching Federation (2021) found that leaders trained in CBT reported 40% less stress and demonstrated higher emotional intelligence.

Practical Strategies for Stress Management for Leaders:
Stress management is often approached reactively rather than proactively. Leaders need strategies that *predict* and *prevent* stress build up.

1. **Predictive Stress Tools:**
   - Leverage AI-driven predictive stress tools to forecast when leaders may experience high stress levels. By analysing work schedules, project timelines, and team dynamics, these tools help prevent stress before it builds.
     - o **Practical Tip:** Use stress-prediction software that integrates with leadership calendars, suggesting break times, relaxation

exercises, or even scheduling short leave periods ahead of intense work periods.

2. **Dynamic Recovery Plans:**
   - Create dynamic recovery plans that trigger specific actions when stress thresholds are reached. This ensures leaders can reenergise quickly, based on predetermined strategies.
     - **Practical Tip:** Leaders should create personal recovery plans involving guided meditations, short breaks, or creative activities like journaling. These recovery strategies can be scheduled during known stressful periods, such as quarterly deadlines or major project launches.

3. **Leadership Pause Routine:**
   - Implement a Leadership Pause Routine to encourage leaders to take brief breaks throughout the workday, allowing time to recalibrate and refocus.
     - **Practical Tip:** Set up "pause pods" or quiet areas in the workplace where leaders can step away for a quick mental break. Encourage ten minute mindfulness or relaxation practices between meetings.

Self Care as a Leadership Competence

Self care is often overlooked in leadership but is becoming increasingly recognised as a core leadership skill. Leaders who prioritise their physical, mental, and emotional health are better able to perform under pressure, remain resilient in the face of adversity, and inspire their teams.

The Importance of Self Care:
Self care involves setting boundaries, taking time off to recharge, and engaging in activities that promote overall wellbeing. Leaders who integrate self care into their routines are less likely to experience burnout and are more effective in their roles. Goleman et al. (2019) highlight that leaders who engage in regular self care practices, such as physical exercise, mindfulness meditation, and adequate sleep, are 40% less likely to experience burnout.

Practical Self Care Tips:

1. **Leadership Reflection Rituals:**
   - Introduce regular reflection rituals, where leaders spend 15 minutes every week journaling about their challenges, personal growth, and leadership experiences. This encourages self awareness and prevents burnout by identifying stress patterns early.
     o **Practical Tip:** Create a leadership journal template where leaders track their stress levels, energy, and emotional wellbeing, followed by a brief discussion with a mentor or wellness coach.

2. **Creative Renewal Retreats:**
   - Offer leaders creative renewal retreats, where they engage in activities unrelated to their work (art, music, nature retreats), allowing them to recharge and foster creativity.
     o **Practical Tip:** Organise quarterly "creative retreats" that take leaders away from their work environment, encouraging them to participate in creative outlets like painting, writing, or music to reset their mental energy.

3. **Wellness Days for Leaders:**
   - Implement Wellness Days that give leaders permission to completely disconnect from work to focus on rest, relaxation, and personal wellbeing.
     o **Practical Tip:** Schedule monthly mental health days where leaders are encouraged to avoid work emails, meetings, and stress triggers, fostering long term resilience.

When developing future leaders, incorporating flexible work arrangements should be a priority. According to Spill (2024), allowing hybrid working or flexible hours is one of the most effective ways to help avoid workplace burnout, according to 75% of HR managers. Equally important is encouraging the full use of leave: while 72% of full-time employees cite annual leave as an effective way to deal with burnout, only a third report that their employer actively encourages them to take all their holiday time. Building these practices into leadership development establishes healthy patterns before burnout takes hold.

By making self care a leadership competence, organisations can ensure that their leaders are well-equipped to sustain long term performance and wellbeing.

Developing a Burnout Proof Leadership Pipeline

Building a burnout proof leadership pipeline involves integrating emotional intelligence (EQ), stress management, and self care into leadership development programs. These elements are key to fostering a leadership culture that is not only focused on achieving goals but also on maintaining health and resilience.

Emotional Intelligence as a Core Leadership Skill:

EQ development focuses on helping leaders better understand and manage their own emotions while responding appropriately to others'. Leaders who develop EQ skills often report being more self aware, empathetic, and better able to maintain emotional balance under pressure. A study by TalentSmart (2022) suggests that leaders who score higher on EQ assessments report experiencing fewer burnout symptoms, which may be associated with their approach to relationship building and stress management. However, it's important to note that correlation doesn't necessarily indicate causation in this relationship.

Building Resilience into Leadership Programs:

Leadership programs must include resilience building exercises such as mindfulness, emotional regulation training, and stress management workshops. These programs equip leaders with tools to handle stress, maintain emotional balance, and prevent burnout. Mentorship programs that focus on wellbeing and life work integration also play a critical role in developing a burnout proof leadership pipeline.

Succession Planning and Mentorship:

Succession planning should integrate resilience training, ensuring that future leaders are equipped to manage stress and maintain emotional health. Mentorship programs, where emerging leaders learn from experienced mentors on how to manage stress and self care, are crucial for fostering a wellbeing centred leadership pipeline.

Practical Strategies for Developing a Burnout Proof Leadership Pipeline:

1. **Wellbeing Based Succession Planning:**
   - Implement wellbeing based succession planning where future leaders are chosen based on their ability to maintain a balanced life, manage stress effectively, and demonstrate emotional intelligence.
     o **Practical Tip:** Integrate wellness performance into leadership promotions by tracking metrics like mental and physical health management, as well as team wellbeing.

2. **Transformational Leadership Challenges:**
   - Create transformational leadership challenges that focus on energy management alongside task management. Leaders can be assessed on how well they balance workloads with personal wellbeing, rewarding those who excel in both areas.
     o **Practical Tip:** Introduce "energy management" workshops that teach leaders how to maintain high productivity while managing personal energy levels using techniques like mindfulness, reflection, and physical exercise.

3. **Resilience Building Workshops:**
   - Conduct resilience building workshops that focus on emotional regulation, mindfulness, and stress management, embedding these practices into future leadership programs.
     o **Practical Tip:** Include group reflection sessions, journaling exercises, and stress monitoring in leadership workshops. Mentor future leaders on how to incorporate wellbeing practices into their daily leadership roles.

Preventative Protection for Emerging Leaders

Protecting emerging leaders from burnout before they reach senior positions represents a strategic imperative for organisations committed to long term success. Research indicates that burnout patterns established early in leadership careers often persist and intensify as responsibilities increase, suggesting that prevention efforts must begin with first-time managers and high potential employees (Gallup, 2021a).

Effective pipeline protection requires structured approaches that embed sustainable practices from the outset of leadership journeys:

1. **Progressive Responsibility Models:** Rather than the traditional "sink or swim" approach to leadership development, organisations should implement graduated responsibility increases paired with corresponding support systems. This approach allows emerging leaders to develop sustainable habits as their scope expands.
2. **Experiential Wellbeing Training:** Abstract wellbeing concepts often fail to translate into practice under pressure. Organisations like Google have found success with experiential training that simulates leadership pressure scenarios, allowing emerging leaders to practise sustaining performance under stress before facing real world consequences (American Psychological Association, 2022).
3. **Early Identification Systems:** By monitoring early warning signs, such as increased working hours, changes in communication patterns, or shifts in decision quality, organisations can intervene before burnout takes hold in developing leaders. These systems should prioritise supportive responses rather than punitive measures.
4. **Succession Planning Integration:** Traditional succession planning typically focuses on capabilities and experience while overlooking sustainability practices. Progressive organisations now incorporate wellbeing competencies and sustainable leadership behaviours into their succession criteria, ensuring that future leaders model balanced approaches.

By treating the leadership pipeline as a strategic asset requiring protection rather than a resource to be maximised, organisations create the conditions for sustainable leadership cultures over the long term. This approach recognises that leadership development is not just about building capability but about instilling practices that enable those capabilities to flourish throughout entire careers.

Holistic Approach to Sustainable Leadership Success

A sustainable approach to leadership success involves recognising that a leader's long term effectiveness depends on both their performance and their wellbeing. This requires a holistic framework that integrates emotional intelligence, self care, and stress management into leadership roles. Organisations must adopt a dual approach that focuses equally on achieving results and maintaining the health and resilience of their leaders.

Practical Strategies for Holistic Approach to Sustainable Leadership Success:

1. **Mental Agility Training:**
   - Develop mental agility training programs to help leaders switch between different modes of thinking: analytical, creative, and intuitive. This fosters resilience and prevents burnout by keeping the mind flexible.
     - **Practical Tip:** Organise a "mental agility boot camp" where leaders alternate between creative brainstorming, structured strategic thinking, and hands-on problem solving exercises to enhance mental flexibility and stress management.

2. **Personal Fulfilment Coaching:**
   - Offer personal fulfilment coaching, which helps leaders align their professional responsibilities with personal values. This fosters a sense of purpose and prevents burnout through a deeper connection to their work.
     - **Practical Tip:** Implement "fulfilment coaching" where leaders reflect on their core motivations, identify goals that resonate with their personal values, and align their leadership style with their own sense of purpose.

3. **Wellbeing Audits and KPIs:**
   - Conduct regular wellbeing audits to assess the mental, emotional, and physical health of leadership teams. This ensures that leadership success is not solely based on performance but also on sustainable health and resilience.
     - **Practical Tip:** Implement wellbeing KPIs alongside traditional metrics to track mental health, stress levels, and team engagement. Evaluate leaders based on both their professional achievements and how well they maintain their personal wellbeing.

By embedding these practices into the fabric of leadership development, organisations can create a leadership pipeline that is resilient, sustainable, and burnout proof.

Leadership Development Needs a Reset

Many leadership programs still train people to perform under pressure rather than design for sustainability. They prioritise strategic thinking over emotional regulation and equip leaders to manage others before managing themselves.

This gap persists despite changing leadership development landscapes. *Harvard Business Review*'s analysis of leadership development trends highlights how programs are becoming more personalised and contextualised to address specific leader needs (Moldoveanu & Narayandas, 2019). However, even as delivery methods evolve, content often remains focused on traditional competencies rather than sustainable leadership practices that prevent burnout.

To be fair, some organisations are making progress. Companies like Microsoft have begun integrating wellbeing into their leadership frameworks, but these remain exceptions rather than the norm in mainstream leadership development.

What might reimagined leadership development look like? Imagine a program where leaders first master self awareness and boundary setting before tackling strategic management; where success metrics include team wellbeing alongside performance targets; and where case studies examine sustainable success rather than celebrating heroic burnout stories.

To reduce burnout at its source, leadership development must evolve:

- Embed wellbeing and boundary setting as core competencies, not afterthoughts.
- Include training on emotional labour, identity safety, and performance pressure.
- Reframe resilience from coping better to designing better systems and expectations.

We must stop developing leaders to survive dysfunction. We must develop them to change it.

Practical Application: Embedding in Leadership Development

To ensure future leaders develop sustainable practices from the outset:

1. **Audit current leadership development:** Review your organisation's approach to leadership training:
   - How prominently does wellbeing feature in current programs?
   - Are sustainable leadership practices explicitly taught and valued?
   - Do promotion criteria include wellbeing competencies?

2. **Integrate wellbeing competencies:** Identify specific capabilities to incorporate:
   - Self awareness and personal sustainability practices
   - Boundary setting and workload management
   - Creating psychologically safe team environments

3. Create leadership wellbeing mentoring: Establish structures where:
   - New leaders are paired with mentors who model sustainable practices
   - Regular conversations focus on wellbeing alongside performance
   - Challenges and pressures are openly discussed without judgement

4. Develop succession planning criteria: Ensure succession processes value:
   - Demonstrated commitment to personal wellbeing
   - History of creating balanced team environments
   - Willingness to challenge unsustainable organisational practices

The **Leadership Wellbeing Integration Checklist** in the Tools and Templates section provides a structured approach to embedding wellbeing throughout your leadership development pipeline.

Final Thought

Leadership burnout is an organisational issue, and I've seen both the benefits of organisational support and the gaps where organisational changes could have made an even greater difference. Working in an organisation that prioritised wellbeing gave me access to tools and resources that helped me maintain balance during challenging periods. However, I also learned that these resources alone are not enough – leaders must take personal responsibility for their wellbeing, set boundaries, and actively engage with the support systems available.

Preventing burnout requires more than addressing symptoms; it demands a shift in organisational culture. By integrating wellbeing into leadership metrics, fostering emotional intelligence, and embedding mental health support into everyday practices, organisations can create an environment where leaders not only survive but thrive. Examples like Patagonia and Unilever show us what's possible when wellbeing is at the centre of leadership success.

HR and leadership teams play a pivotal role in driving these changes, creating structures that prioritise resilience and sustainability. But this isn't a one-sided effort. Leaders themselves must embrace the opportunity to take ownership of their wellbeing, leveraging organisational resources and building personal habits that prevent burnout.

Ultimately, leadership wellbeing isn't just an individual responsibility or an organisational initiative – it's a partnership. When leaders and organisations work together, they create a culture where resilience, mental health, and long term success coexist. For me, this realisation transformed the way I lead and has become the foundation for fostering sustainable leadership practices in others.

Reflection Questions

Personal Reflection Questions

1. How does your organisation's current definition of leadership success either support or undermine sustainable wellbeing practices? What metrics reflect this definition?
2. What role should wellbeing play in leadership selection, development, and succession planning? How might this differ from conventional approaches?
3. What specific changes to leadership development programs would ensure that future leaders prioritise wellbeing alongside performance?
4. How can you personally model sustainable leadership for emerging leaders in a way that challenges prevailing narratives about success and sacrifice?

5. What legacy of leadership wellbeing do you hope to establish, and what immediate steps would move you towards this vision?

Team Reflection Questions

1. How do our current leadership recruitment and promotion practices select for sustainable leadership qualities vs. potentially harmful traits?
2. What implicit messages might our succession planning process send about the relationship between wellbeing and leadership success?
3. How might we incorporate wellbeing competencies into our leadership development framework without treating them as secondary to performance metrics?
4. What organisational changes would create a leadership pipeline that develops resilient, emotionally intelligent leaders rather than merely high performers?
5. How can we collectively transform our organisational narrative about what constitutes leadership success to include sustainability and wellbeing?

Key Takeaways

- **Leadership development must incorporate wellbeing:** Organisations need to redefine leadership success criteria to value wellbeing alongside performance metrics from the earliest stages of leadership development.
- **Stress management becomes a core leadership competency:** Techniques like mindfulness based stress reduction and cognitive behavioural approaches should be integrated into leadership training as essential professional skills.
- **Self care represents strategic leadership investment:** Leaders must recognise that wellbeing practices constitute critical professional development rather than optional personal activities separate from leadership effectiveness.
- **Pipeline design should embed preventative approaches:** Incorporating emotional intelligence, stress management, and self care throughout

leadership development creates resilient future leaders equipped for sustainable success.
- **Sustainable leadership balances achievement with wellbeing:** Organisations that evaluate leadership through both performance outcomes and wellbeing indicators create cultures where leadership can thrive long term.

CONCLUSION

EMBRACING A WELLBEING FIRST APPROACH TO LEADERSHIP

Leadership today faces extraordinary challenges. The fast paced nature of modern workplaces, relentless decision making demands and constant uncertainty have created an environment that no longer accommodates traditional performance driven leadership models. These approaches, once heralded as effective, are proving unsustainable in an era that demands both personal resilience and organisational adaptability.

As I reflect on my own leadership journey, the lessons from this book feel deeply personal. I once believed that leadership meant pushing through exhaustion, ignoring the warning signs, and putting the needs of others ahead of my own, no matter the cost. I thought that was what good leaders did. But when I hit my breaking point, I realised that I had it all wrong. Leadership is not about sacrifice to the point of burnout; it is about balance, empathy, and fostering a culture where people, including the leader, can thrive.

Why Wellbeing Must Be Prioritised

Burnout is not just an individual issue, it is an organisational crisis. When ignored, it erodes decision making, team morale, and innovation. But when organisations prioritise mental health, they unlock potential: retention improves, engagement rises, and leaders thrive with energy and purpose.

Addressing burnout is not about reducing ambition, it is about enabling sustainability. Leaders who prioritise their wellbeing are more present, empathetic, and effective.

Wellbeing first leadership models are not indulgent, they are essential.

RESET: A Framework for Sustainable Leadership

Throughout this book, we've explored the RESET approach – Recognise, Explore, Shift, Embed, Thrive – not just as a recovery plan but as a leadership renewal path. You can return to these phases at any point, using them as checkpoints for sustainable leadership, not just during crisis but in everyday rhythm.

RESET is not about perfection. It is about recalibration, shifting from survival mode to a leadership rhythm that is aligned, intentional, and human.

Building Resilience and Emotional Intelligence

Resilience and emotional intelligence have been at the heart of this book because they are at the heart of sustainable leadership. These are not innate traits bestowed on a lucky few; they are skills that can be cultivated.

My own journey taught me the value of these tools. It wasn't until I started working with a psychologist, leaning into reflective practices, and building my EQ that I began to reclaim balance and purpose in my leadership.

Throughout this book, we've explored practical strategies to develop resilience and EQ: coaching, mentorship, journaling, feedback loops, and mindfulness practices. These are not theoretical ideas; they are actionable steps that any leader can take. When organisations invest in these areas, they don't just create stronger leaders; they build cultures of connection, empathy, and trust.

A New Model for Leadership

This book challenges the outdated notion that leadership success is defined by financial results and output alone. The new leadership model prioritises life work integration, emotional health, and team engagement as critical metrics of success.

Organisations like Patagonia and Buffer have shown the power of this approach, reducing burnout, retaining top talent and achieving innovative outcomes. The shift to wellbeing driven leadership is not just possible, it is necessary.

For leaders, it means learning to set boundaries, embrace vulnerability, and create space for rest and reflection. For organisations, it means embedding wellbeing into policies, practices, and performance metrics so that leaders and teams alike have the resources to thrive.

Looking Ahead

The future of leadership belongs to those who embrace a wellbeing first philosophy. But this shift isn't just about the present; it's about preparing the next generation. Emerging leaders must be equipped with the tools to navigate stress, build resilience, and lead with empathy.

Succession planning and leadership development must centre on these values, ensuring that tomorrow's leaders are not only high performing but also emotionally and mentally prepared for the challenges ahead.

As I conclude this book, I'm reminded of a moment during my recovery. My psychologist asked me what kind of leader I wanted to be – not the kind I thought I should be, but the kind I truly aspired to become. That question reshaped my approach to leadership. I realised that thriving leaders are not those who push harder, but those who prioritise smarter. Those who put wellbeing, purpose, and empathy at the forefront.

A Call to Action

Leadership burnout is preventable, but it requires us to act. Leaders must commit to recognising their limits. Organisations must create systems that support balance. And we all must redefine what success looks like.

This is not a one-size-fits-all solution, it is a personalised journey for every leader and every culture. But we cannot afford to ignore it any longer.

If you are only just beginning to face your own burnout, or questioning how sustainable your leadership really is, that's okay. Start small. Pick one phase of RESET. Revisit one chapter. Use one tool. Progress is not perfection, it is movement with intention.

I hope this book reminds you that leadership can be fulfilling, not at the cost of your wellbeing, but because of it. When we prioritise what sustains us, we create the conditions to lead with clarity, courage, and impact.

Let this be your invitation to reset, not just for yourself, but for the culture you help shape every day.

Reflection Questions

Personal Reflection Questions

1. What has been your biggest personal insight from reading this book, and how has it changed your understanding of effective leadership?
2. Which chapter or concept resonated with you the most, and why did it particularly connect with your leadership experience?
3. What specific, practical changes will you implement in your leadership approach as a result of this book? Which will you prioritise first?
4. How will you hold yourself accountable for maintaining a leadership style that prioritises wellbeing alongside performance? What measures would show success?
5. What single piece of advice would you now give to another leader struggling with burnout based on your own journey through this book?

Team Reflection Questions

1. What shared insights have we gained as a leadership team, and how might these transform our collective approach to sustainable leadership?
2. How can we redefine leadership success in our organisation to incorporate wellbeing as a foundational element rather than an optional consideration?

3. What specific organisational practices or cultural norms should we reconsider to better support leadership wellbeing across our team?
4. How can we create mutual accountability for wellbeing practices that prevents us from reverting to unhealthy leadership norms during periods of pressure?
5. What collective commitment are we willing to make today that would signal our dedication to sustainable leadership for ourselves, our teams, and future leaders?

EPILOGUE

I DIDN'T SET OUT TO WRITE A BOOK

This all began as a journal, a simple way of writing: a quiet space to make sense of what I was feeling when the wheels started to fall off. I never imagined those reflections would become a book. To be honest, I was reluctant to share my story at all. Leadership often rewards strength over vulnerability, and for a long time, I didn't have the words to explain what was happening to me.

I didn't know it was burnout. I just knew I wasn't myself. When my GP called it burnout and then later finally named it, major depressive disorder, it hit me hard. It was confronting, but it also gave language to what I had been silently enduring.

Five months after leaving my principal role, I was diagnosed with cancer. My psychologist later helped me separate these two events and deal with them independently, but at the time, it certainly didn't help my reinvention stage or my mental health. I am ok now though and still focused on my health and wellbeing.

Still, the purpose of this book is not to explore mental illness. It is to confront burnout in leadership: to help others recognise it earlier, respond more wisely, and recover more sustainably.

This book isn't a badge of recovery. It's a signpost. A way to say: you're not alone, and there is a way forward.

Today, I'm doing well. I'm still on medication. I'm exercising regularly, eating better, journaling, and doing all the things that help me feel grounded. Most of all, I'm leading differently. More intentionally. More sustainably. And with far greater self awareness than I had before all of this began.

If any part of this story has helped you name something you hadn't yet understood, I'm grateful. Burnout is not weakness. It's not failure. It's a signal that something has to change.

And finally, to my immediate family, Lisa, Jacob, Emma and Luke. Thank you! Your love, patience, and quiet presence carried me through. You saw me at my lowest and stayed. This book exists because I didn't have to walk that part of the journey alone.

RESET changed my life. I hope it offers something meaningful for yours too.

REFERENCES

American Psychological Association (APA). (2020). *Stress in America™ 2020: A national mental health crisis.* www.apa.org/news/press/releases/stress/2020/report-october

American Psychological Association (APA). (2021). *Compounding pressures: The state of mental health and wellbeing in 2021.* www.apa.org/pubs/reports/work-wellbeing/compounding-pressure-2021

American Psychological Association (APA). (2022). Burnout and stress are everywhere. *Monitor on Psychology,* 53(1). www.apa.org/monitor/2022/01/special-burnout-stress

Arnsten, A. F. T. (2009). Stress signalling pathways that impair prefrontal cortex structure and function. *Nature Reviews Neuroscience,* 10(6), 410–422. https://doi.org/10.1038/nrn2648

Atlassian. (2022). *ShipIt Days.* Atlassian. www.atlassian.com/company/shipit

Augnito. (2024). *Physician burnout statistics 2024: Current trends and prevention strategies.* Augnito Healthcare Research. https://augnito.ai/resources/physician-burnout-latest-statistics/#:~:text=Demographic%20Trends%20in%20Physician%20Burnout&text=In%202024%2C%2056%25%20of%20female,of%20women%20physicians%20reported%20burnout

Australian Catholic University. (2024). *The Australian principal occupational health, safety and wellbeing survey: 2023 data.* Institute for Positive Psychology and Education. www.healthandwellbeing.org/reports/AU/The%20ACU%20Australian%20Principal%20Occupational%20Health,%20Safety%20and%20Wellbeing%20Survey%20Final%20Report%202023%20Data.pdf

Australian Catholic University. (2024). *The Australian principal occupational health, safety and wellbeing survey: 2024 data.* Institute for Positive Psychology and Education. www.acu.edu.au/about-acu/news/2024/march/violence-escalates-and-mental-health-suffers-but-principals-remain-resilient

Australian HR Institute. (2023). *Navigating Australia's DEI landscape for impact and sustainable change* [Futures Paper]. www.ahri.com.au/wp-content/uploads/AHRI-Futures-Paper-Oct-2023-3-1.pdf

Australian Public Service Commission. (2023). *APS mental health and suicide prevention strategy.* www.apsc.gov.au/initiatives-and-programs/mental-health-and-suicide-prevention

Barsade, S. G. (2002). The ripple effect: Emotional contagion and its influence on group behaviour. *Administrative Science Quarterly, 47*(4), 644–675.

Bendigo and Adelaide Bank. (2024). *Annual report 2023–24: Leadership and wellbeing.* www.bendigoadelaide.com.au/investor-centre/reports

Black Dog Institute. (2023). *Navigating burnout: Practical strategies to support wellbeing* [Workshop resource]. www.blackdoginstitute.org.au/wp-content/uploads/2024/03/Navigating-Burnout_90mins_Web_2023.pdf

Burke, R. J., & Cooper, C. L. (2021). The role of cognitive overload in leadership burnout: Understanding the effects of highstakes decision making. *Journal of Managerial Psychology, 36*(5), 456–472.

Burnout Nutrition. (2024). *Jobs with highest burnout rates across industries – 2024. Burnout Report.* https://burnoutnutrition.com/blog/jobs-with-highest-burnout-rates-across-industries-2024

Byrne, M. (2024). *Are you in spiritual burnout? Here's how to tell and what to do about it!* www.marybyrne.energy/blog/are-you-in-spiritual-burnout-heres-how-to-tell-and-what-to-do-about-it

Calm. (n.d.). *Mindfulness at work: Cultivating calm and clarity in the workplace.* https://blog.calm.com/blog/mindfulness-at-work

Center for American Progress. (2012). *There are significant business costs to replacing employees.* www.americanprogress.org/article/there-are-significant-business-costs-to-replacing-employees

Chartered Institute of Personnel and Development (CIPD) & Simplyhealth. (2022). *Health and wellbeing at work: Survey report 2022.* www.cipd.org/globalassets/media/comms/news/ahealth-wellbeing-work-report-2022_tcm18-108440.pdf

Chipchase, J., & Miller, J. (2020). *Emotional resilience in leadership report.* Studio D. www.researchgate.net/publication/353235429_Emotional_Resilience_In_Leadership_Report

ClickUp. (2024). *60+ burnout statistics impacting today's workforce: Global economic costs.* ClickUp Research Series. https://clickup.com/blog/burnout-statistics

Corporate Mental Health Alliance Australia. (2023). *Leading mentally healthy workplaces survey report.* https://cmhaa.org.au/wp-content/uploads/CMHAA_Mentally-Healthy-Workplaces-Report_August2023.pdf

CreateAndGrow. (2024). *45 worrying burnout statistics for 2024: Workplace stress analysis.* Mental Health at Work Series. https://createandgrow.com/burnout-statistics

Crum, A. J., Akinola, M., Martin, A., & Fath, S. (2017). The role of stress mindset in shaping cognitive, emotional, and physiological responses to challenging and threatening stress. *Anxiety, Stress & Coping, 30*(4), 379–395. https://doi.org/10.1080/10615806.2016.1275585

Cruth, M. (n.d.). *Discover the Spotify model: What the most popular music technology company can teach us about scaling agile.* Atlassian. www.atlassian.com/agile/agile-at-scale/spotify

Dean, W., Talbot, S., & Dean, A. (2020). Reframing clinician distress: Moral injury not burnout. *Federal Practitioner, 37*(9), 400–402.

Deloitte. (2021a). *2021 Global human capital trends: The social enterprise in a world disrupted.* Deloitte Insights. www2.deloitte.com/us/en/insights/focus/human-capital-trends/2021/human-capital-trends.html

Deloitte. (2021b). *Global human capital trends: Leading with wellbeing.* www.subscribe-hr.com.au/blog/global-human-capital-trends-deloittes-2021-report

Deloitte. (2021c). *The reinvention of leadership: Addressing mental health and promoting wellbeing post-burnout.* www.deloitte.com/global/en/about/story/purpose-values/mental-health.html

Deloitte. (2022). *Employee well-being and engagement.* Deloitte Insights. www.deloitte.com/us/en/insights/topics/talent/employee-wellbeing.html

Deloitte. (2023). *Women @ work: A global outlook.* www2.deloitte.com/content/dam/insights/articles/glob175810_global-women-at-Donwork/Women_at_Work_2023.pdf

Deloitte. (2024). *2024 global human capital trends.* www2.deloitte.com/xe/en/insights/focus/human-capital-trends.html

Diversity Council Australia. (2023). *First Nations facing increased discrimination & cultural load.* www.dca.org.au/news/media-releases/first-nations-facing-increased-discrimination

Fernandez, K., Clerkin, C., & Ruderman, M. (2020). *Building leadership resilience: The CORE framework.* Center for Creative Leadership. https://doi.org/10.35613/ccl.2020.2043

FitSmallBusiness. (2024). *19 employee burnout statistics in 2024: Tech industry focus.* FitSmallBusiness Research Reports. https://fitsmallbusiness.com/employee-burnout-statistics

Forbes. (2021). *Employee stress levels and leadership burnout.* www.forbes.com/councils/forbes-coachescouncil/2022/12/19/employee-burnout-how-leaders-can-tip-the-scale

Ford Health. (n.d.). *About us.* https://fordhealth.com.au/about-us

Foremind. (2024). *Employee burnout statistics.* https://foremind.com.au/employee-burnout-statistics

Fritz, C., Lam, C. F., & Spreitzer, G. M. (2011). It's the little things that matter: An examination of knowledge workers' energy management. *Academy of Management Perspectives, 25*(3), 28–39. Gallup. (2020). *Employee burnout: Causes and cures.* www.gallup.com/workplace/282659/employee-burnout-perspective-paper.aspx

Gallup. (2021a). *The global rise of burnout: What leaders need to know to prevent burnout in themselves and their teams.* www.gallup.com/workplace/313160/preventing-and-dealing-with-employee-burnout.aspx

Gallup. (2021b). *The impact of leadership on employee engagement.* www.gallup.com/topic/employee-engagement.aspx

Gallup. (2022). *K-12 workers have highest burnout rate in US.* https://news.gallup.com/poll/393500/workers-highest-burnout-rate.aspx

Gallup. (2023a). *Employee burnout: The causes and cures.* www.gallup.com/workplace/508898/employee-burnout-causes-cures.aspx

Gallup. (2023b). *State of the global workplace report.* www.gallup.com/workplace/349484/state-of-the-global-workplace-2023.aspx

Gallup. (2024). *Employee wellbeing hinges on management, not work mode.* www.gallup.com/workplace/648500/employee-wellbeing-hinges-management-not-work-mode.aspx

Garcia, R. (2024, March 18). *A strong coaching culture can combat employee burnout.* International Coaching Federation. https://coachingfederation.org/blog/employee-burnout

George, B., & Sims, P. (2007). *True north: Discover your authentic leadership.* Jossey-Bass.

Goleman, D. (2013a). *Emotional intelligence: Why it can matter more than IQ.* Bantam Books.

Goleman, D. (2013b). *Emotional intelligence theory explained. Resilient Educator.* https://resilienteducator.com/classroom-resources/daniel-golemans-emotional-intelligence-theory-explained

Goleman, D. (2018a). *Emotional intelligence: Why it can matter more than IQ* (10th Anniversary Edition). Bantam Books.

Goleman, D. (2018b). The role of emotional intelligence in recognising burnout. *Journal of Organisational Behaviour, 39*(4), 444–457. doi:10.1002/job.2258

Goleman, D., Boyatzis, R., & McKee, A. (2019). *Emotional intelligence: Why it can matter more than IQ.* Harvard Business School Press.

Griffis, H. (2020). *Asynchronous communication and why it matters for remote work.* https://buffer.com/resources/asynchronous-communication

Groth, A. (2015, April 7). Inside Google's insanely popular emotional intelligence course. *Fast Company.* www.fastcompany.com/3044157/inside-googles-insanely-popular-emotional-intelligence-course

Groysberg, B., & Halperin, R. R. (2022). How to get the most out of peer support groups: A guide to the benefits and best practices. *Harvard Business Review, 100*(3), 130–141.

Harvard Business Review. (2021a). *How burnout impacts creativity and innovation.* https://hbr.org/2021/02/beyond-burned-out

Harvard Business Review. (2021b). *Reflection and leadership: Emotional clarity in high pressure roles.* https://hbr.org/2021/08/leaders-dont-be-afraid-to-talk-about-your-fears-and-anxieties

Harvard Business Review. (2022a). *The importance of self reflection in leadership: Gaining clarity to prevent burnout.* https://hbr.org/2022/03/dont-underestimate-the-power-of-self-reflection

Harvard Business Review. (2022b). *What first-time managers can do to address burnout.* https://hbr.org/2022/03/what-first-time-managers-can-do-to-address-burnout

Harvard Business Review. (2022c). *Don't underestimate the power of self-reflection.* https://hbr.org/2022/03/dont-underestimate-the-power-of-self-reflectionHarvard Business Review. (2023). *More than 50% of managers feel burned out.* https://hbr.org/2023/05/more-than-50-of-managers-feel-burned-out

Harvard Medical School. (2022). *Compassion fatigue is real and it may be weighing you down.* https://hbsp.harvard.edu/product/H06YB3-PDF-ENG?itemFindingMethod=IDP+Recommendation

Harvard University. (2021). *The effects of stress on brain function and neuroplasticity.* www.health.harvard.edu/mind-and-mood/protect-your-brain-from-stress

Headspace. (n.d.). *The science behind meditation.* www.headspace.com/articles/the-science-behind-meditation

Healthcare Professionals Association of Australia. (2025). *Reducing staff turnover in healthcare settings: Evidence-based approaches.* www.hcpassociation.com.au/post/reducing-staff-turnover-healthcare-evidence-based-approaches

Helsinki Times. (2024, November 6). Finland leads the world in work life balance: The formula for a happier life. www.helsinkitimes.fi/lifestyle/25754-finland-leads-the-world-in-work-life balance-the-formula-for-a-happier-life.html

Hubstaff. (2024). *Burnout statistics in the workplace.* https://hubstaff.com/blog/burnout-statistics-workplace

HumanSmart. (n.d.). *What role does workplace culture play in promoting employee wellbeing?* https://humansmart.com.mx/en/blogs/blog-what-role-does-workplace-culture-play-in-promoting-employee-wellbeing-and-reducing-fatigue-56895

Infinite Potential. (2024). *The state of burnout 2024.* https://infinite-potential.com.au/the-state-of-burnout-2024

International Coaching Federation (ICF). (2021). *Cognitive behavioural techniques in leadership coaching*. https://researchportal.coachingfederation.org/Document/Pdf/3588.pdf^

Johns Hopkins Carey Business School. (2024). *Wellbeing at work report: Creating cultures of support and acknowledgment*. Johns Hopkins University Press. https://carey.jhu.edu/wellbeing-at-work

Juster, R.-P., McEwen, B. S., & Lupien, S. J. (2010). Allostatic load biomarkers of chronic stress and impact on health and cognition. *Neuroscience & Biobehavioral Reviews*, 35(1), 2–16. https://doi.org/10.1016/j.neubiorev.2009.10.002

Kin + Carta. (2023). AI triggers deep tech anxiety for senior leaders, reveals new research. www.kinandcarta.com/en/news/2023/09/2024-leadership-priorities-in-tech

Kocolowski, M. D. (2010). Shared leadership: Is it time for a change? *Emerging Leadership Journeys*, 3(1), 22–32. www.researchgate.net/publication/267978872_Shared_Leadership_Is_It_Time_for_a_Change

KPMG. (2024). *6 tips for tackling technical debt*. www.cio.com/article/472768/5-tips-for-tackling-technical-debt.html

KPMG Australia. (2024). *Global tech report 2024 – Australian insights*. https://kpmg.com/au/en/home/insights/2024/10/global-tech-report-australia.html

LaFaber, R. (2024). *Emotional intelligence in the digital age: Maintaining human connections in a virtual world*. www.linkedin.com/pulse/emotional-intelligence-digital-age-maintaining-human-virtual-richard-bff3c

Langley, S. (2021). *Positive psychology and wellbeing*. Langley Group Institute.

Leaders Edge Inc. (2024). *Key insights on Gallup's state of the workforce report 2024*. www.leadersedgeinc.com/blog/key-insights-on-gallups-state-of-the-workforce-report-2024

Leadership Circle. (n.d.-a). *Building resilient organisations: The leader's role in crisis management*. https://leadershipcircle.com/blog/resilient-organisations-crisis-management

Leadership Circle. (n.d.-b). *Psychological safety in the workplace: Building trust and innovation*. https://leadershipcircle.com/blog/psychological-safety-in-the-workplace

Lencioni, P. M. (2024). *The five dysfunctions of a team: A leadership fable* (20th anniversary ed.). Jossey-Bass.

Liston, C., McEwen, B. S., & Casey, B. J. (2009). Psychosocial stress reversibly disrupts prefrontal processing and attentional control. *Proceedings of the National Academy of Sciences*, 106(3), 912–917. https://doi.org/10.1073/pnas.0807041106

Maslach, C., & Leiter, M. P. (2016). Understanding the burnout experience: Recent research and its implications for clinical practice. *World Psychiatry*, 15(2), 103–111. doi:10.1002/wps.20311

Massner, C. K. (2021). *Zooming in on Zoom fatigue: A case study of videoconferencing and Zoom fatigue in higher education* (Doctoral dissertation). Liberty University. https://digitalcommons.liberty.edu/doctoral/3030

Mayo Clinic. (2022). *Job burnout: How to spot it and take action*. www.mayoclinic.org/healthy-lifestyle/adult-health/in-depth/burnout/art-20046642

McEwen, B. S., & Akil, H. (2020). Revisiting the stress concept: Implications for affective disorders. *The Journal of Neuroscience*, 40(1), 12–21. doi:10.1523/JNEUROSCI.0733-19.2019

McGonigal, K. (2015). *The upside of stress: Why stress is good for you, and how to get good at it*. Penguin Random House.

McKinsey & Company. (2020a). *Leadership in crisis: How realignment prevents burnout*. McKinsey.
McKinsey & Company. (2020b). *Realignment strategies for sustainable leadership*. McKinsey.
McKinsey & Company. (2021). *Preventing burnout in organisations: A focus on leadership*. www.mckinsey.com/mhi/our-insights/addressing-employee-burnout-are-you-solving-the-right-problem
McKinsey & Company. (2022). *Leadership and burnout: Navigating the stress of high level decision making*. McKinsey.
McKinsey & Company. (2023a). *Leadership burnout in a post-pandemic world: How to recognise and address the signs early*. www.mckinsey.com/featured-insights/mckinsey-explainers/what-is-burnout
McKinsey & Company. (2023b). *What is decision making?* www.mckinsey.com/~/media/mckinsey/featured%20insights/mckinsey%20explainers/what%20is%20decision%20making/what-is-decision making.pdf
McKinsey & Company. (2023c). *Women in the workplace 2023*. www.mckinsey.com/featured-insights/diversity-and-inclusion/women-in-the-workplace-2023
McKinsey & Company. (2023d). *The state of organizations in 2023*. www.mckinsey.com/capabilities/people-and-organizational-performance/our-insights/the-state-of-organizations-2023
Mental Health Australia. (2023). *Annual healthcare professionals survey*. https://mhaustralia.org/general/annual-healthcare-professionals-survey
Meredith, G. R., Rakow, D. A., Eldermire, E. R. B., Madsen, C. G., Shelley, S. P., & Sachs, N. A. (2020). Minimum time dose in nature to positively impact the mental health of college-aged students, and how to measure it: A scoping review. *Frontiers in Psychology, 10*, 2942. https://doi.org/10.3389/fpsyg.2019.02942
Microsoft. (2024, May 8). *AI at work is here: Now comes the hard part*. Work Trend Index. www.microsoft.com/en-us/worklab/work-trend-index/ai-at-work-is-here-now-comes-the-hard-part
Mining Magazine Australia. (2023). *Managing fatigue and reducing risks in mines*. https://miningmagazine.com.au/managing-fatigue-and-reducing-risks-in-mines
MIT Sloan. (2022). *Why every leader needs to worry about toxic culture*. https://sloanreview.mit.edu/article/why-every-leader-needs-to-worry-about-toxic-culture
Moldoveanu, M., & Narayandas, D. (2019). *The future of leadership development*. Harvard Business Review. https://hbr.org/2019/03/the-future-of-leadership-development
Newman, D. (2022, March 23). *Microsoft's 2022 work trends index: Exploring hybrid work and a workforce in transition*. Forbes. www.forbes.com/sites/danielnewman/2022/03/23/microsofts-2022-work-trends-index-exploring-hybrid-work-and-a-workforce-in-transition
NHS England. (2023, September 1). *Supported self management: Peer support guide*. www.england.nhs.uk/long-read/peer-support
Northern Health. (2023). *Digital transformation strategy: Annual outcomes report 2023*. www.nh.org.au/about-us/publications
Pearce, C. L., & Manz, C. C. (2005). The new silver bullets of leadership: The importance of shared leadership and collaboration in teams. *Organizational Dynamics, 34*(2), 130–140. doi:10.1016/j.orgdyn.2005.03.003
Pontefract, D. (2024, April 17). *It's time for leaders to embrace digital wellness*. Forbes. www.forbes.com/sites/danpontefract/2024/04/17/its-time-for-leaders-to-embrace-digital-wellness

Positive Group. (2023). Creating a ripple effect: How leadership behaviours shape psychological safety. *Positive Group Research Insights.* www.positivegroup.org/loop/articles/creating-a-ripple-effect-how-leadership-behaviours-shape-psychological-safety

Principal Health and Wellbeing Survey. (2023). *Occupational health and safety risks for Australian principals.* www.principalhealth.org/au

Psychology Today. (2021a). *Emotional intelligence and leadership resilience.* www.psychologytoday.com/us/basics/emotional-intelligence

Psychology Today. (2021b). *Journaling for leadership: How reflective practices improve emotional intelligence.* www.psychologytoday.com/us/basics/emotional-intelligence

Raymaker, D. M., Teo, A. R., Steckler, N. A., Lentz, B., Scharer, M., Delos Santos, A., Kapp, S. K., Hunter, M., Joyce, A., & Nicolaidis, C. (2020). "Having all of your internal resources exhausted beyond measure and being left with no clean-up crew": Defining autistic burnout. *Autism in Adulthood,* 2(2), 132–143. https://doi.org/10.1089/aut.2019.0079

Reeves, M. (2023). Peer learning benefits: Why peer learning is the future of workplace development. *Together Platform.* www.togetherplatform.com/blog/peer-learning-benefits

Reid, R. (2023). *Next level leadership: Integrating resilience, self compassion and authentic success for enduring impact.* https://richard-reid.com/next-level-leadership-integrating-resilience-self-compassion-and-authentic-success-for-enduring-impact

Research.com. (2025, July 9). *24 leadership training statistics for 2025: Data, insights & predictions.* https://research.com/careers/leadership-training-statistics

Reyes-Guerra, D., Maslin-Ostrowski, P., Barakat, M. Y., & Stefanovic, M. A. (2021). Confronting a compound crisis: The school principal's role during initial phase of the COVID-19 pandemic. *Frontiers in Education.* www.frontiersin.org/articles/10.3389/feduc.2021.617875/full

Robinson, B. (2024). *5 signs of "creative burnout" in 2024 and 5 ways to stop.* www.forbes.com/sites/bryanrobinson/2024/10/02/5-signs-of-creative-burnout-in-2024-and-5-ways-to-stop-it

Rosanes, M. (2024, September 19). The top employee mental health programs in Canada. *Benefits and Pensions Monitor.* www.benefitsandpensionsmonitor.com/benefits/mental-health/the-top-employee-mental-health-programs-in-canada/388614

Ruderman, M. N., Clerkin, C., & Connolly, C. (2014). *Leadership development beyond competencies: Moving to a holistic approach.* Center for Creative Leadership. https://cclinnovation.org/wp-content/uploads/2020/02/leadershipdevelopmentcompetencies.pdf

Ruiz-Palomino, P., Yáñez-Araque, B., Gutiérrez-Broncano, S., & Jiménez Estévez, P. (2025). Unlocking organizational change: Servant leadership, change resistance and the mediating role of emotional intelligence. *Management Decision.* https://doi.org/10.1108/MD-04-2024-0874

Salesforce. (2021). *Wellbeing days and leadership mental health.* www.salesforce.com/resources/future-of-work/employee-health-and-wellbeing/#!page=1

Sapolsky, R. M. (2004). *Why zebras don't get ulcers: The acclaimed guide to stress, stress-related diseases, and coping.* W.H. Freeman and Company.

Schaufeli, W. B., & Taris, T. W. (2014). A critical review of the job demands-resources model: Implications for improving leadership wellbeing. *Work & Stress,* 28(2), 107–123.

Selander, K., Nevanperä, N., Nikunlaakso, R., Korkiakangas, E., & Laitinen, J. (2025). Engaging leadership and work recovery among key personnel of a major health-care and social services reform. *Leadership in Health Services*, 38(5), 35–47. https://doi.org/10.1108/LHS-09-2024-0109

Seligman, M. (2011). *Flourish: A visionary new understanding of happiness and wellbeing*. Free Press.

Sinek, S. (2017). *Leaders eat last: Why some teams pull together and others don't*. Portfolio.

Sonnentag, S., & Fritz, C. (2015). Psychological disconnection from work: A key to reducing burnout and improving brain recovery. *Journal of Occupational Health Psychology*, 20(1), 72–89. doi:10.1037/a0038508.

Spataro, J. (2022a). 5 key trends leaders need to understand to get hybrid right. *Harvard Business Review*. https://hbr.org/2022/03/5-key-trends-leaders-need-to-understand-to-get-hybrid-right

Spataro, J. (2022b, March 18). Microsoft's Jared Spataro on how the pandemic sped up technological change (and moved us closer to the metaverse). *Harvard Business Review*. https://hbr.org/2022/03/microsofts-jared-spataro-on-how-the-pandemic-sped-up-technological-change-and-moved-us-closer-to-the-metaverse

Spill. (2024, February 8). *64 workplace burnout statistics you need to know for 2024*. www.spill.chat/mental-health-statistics/workplace-burnout-statistics

Stanford University. (2022). *Mindfulness and neuroplasticity: Reducing stress in leadership roles*. https://med.stanford.edu/contemplation/resources.html

Steffens, N. K., Haslam, S. A., Schuh, S. C., Jetten, J., & van Dick, R. (2017). A meta-nalytic review of social identification and health in organizational contexts. *Personality and Social Psychology Review*, 21(4), 303–335. https://doi.org/10.1177/1088868316656701

TalentSmart. (2022). *Why focus on emotional intelligence*. www.talentsmarteq.com/emotional-intelligence-can-boost-your-career-and-save-your-life

Tang, Y.-Y., Hölzel, B. K., & Posner, M. I. (2015). The neuroscience of mindfulness meditation: How meditation impacts brain function and stress reduction. *Nature Reviews Neuroscience*, 16(4), 213–225. doi:10.1038/nrn3916.

TechRepublic. (2024). *9 out of 10 UK business leaders suffer from tech anxiety that disrupts their sleep, BT study finds*. www.techrepublic.com/article/uk-business-leaders-tech-anxiety

Thai, J. (n.d.). *Developing a self managed team at Zappos*. Wavelength by Asana. https://wavelength.asana.com/zappos-self-managed-team

The Educator. (2024). *Teachers face higher levels of secondary trauma than paramedics and psychologists – study*. www.theeducatoronline.com/k12/news/teachers-face-higher-levels-of-secondary-trauma-than-paramedics-psychologists--study/287144

Thompson, M., Gallagher, S., & Preece, D. (2022). Burnout and professional grief: Understanding emotional fatigue in service professions. *British Journal of Psychology*, 113(2), 255–271.

ThriveSparrow. (n.d.). *30 peer review examples for 360 performance reviews*. www.thrivesparrow.com/blog/peer-review-examples

Unilever. (n.d.). *Employee health and wellbeing*. www.unilever.com/sustainability/responsible-business/employee-wellbeing

University of Massachusetts Medical School. (2017). *Mindfulness-based stress reduction (MBSR) for leadership*. https://positivepsychology.com/mindfulness-based-stress-reduction-mbsr

University of Melbourne. (2024a). *Leading for wellbeing: Faculty leadership support program.* https://staff.unimelb.edu.au/health-safety-wellbeing/wellbeing

University of Melbourne. (2024b). *Leading for wellbeing initiative: Impact evaluation.* https://about.unimelb.edu.au/leadership

VanderWeele, T. J. (2017). On the promotion of human flourishing. *Proceedings of the National Academy of Sciences*, 114(31), 8148–8156. https://doi.org/10.1073/pnas.1702996114

VicHealth. (2023). *Healthier workplaces and leadership wellbeing toolkit.* www.vichealth.vic.gov.au/programs-and-projects/healthy-workplaces

Wang, D., Waldman, D. A., & Zhang, Z. (2014). A meta-analysis of shared leadership and team effectiveness. *The Journal of Applied Psychology*, 99(2), 181–198. doi:10.1037/a0034531.

Wiens, K. (2024, April 23). How burnout became normal – and how to push back against it. *Harvard Business Review.* https://hbr.org/2024/04/how-burnout-became-normal-and-how-to-push-back-against-it

World Economic Forum. (2021). *Leadership for the future: Emotional intelligence and organisational resilience.* www.weforum.org/reports/leadership-for-the-future-emotional-intelligence-and-organisational-resilience

World Economic Forum. (2022, May 4). *These countries have the best work life balance.* www.weforum.org/agenda/2022/05/countries-with-the-best-work-life-balance

World Health Organization. (2019). *Burn-out an "occupational phenomenon": International classification of diseases.* www.who.int/news/item/28-05-2019-burn-out-an-occupational-phenomenon-international-classification-of-diseases

TOOLS AND TEMPLATES

The tools in this section are designed to help you implement the key concepts from each phase of the Leadership Reset Framework. They provide practical structures to support your journey from burnout to breakthrough. These resources can be photocopied, adapted, or recreated to suit your specific leadership context.

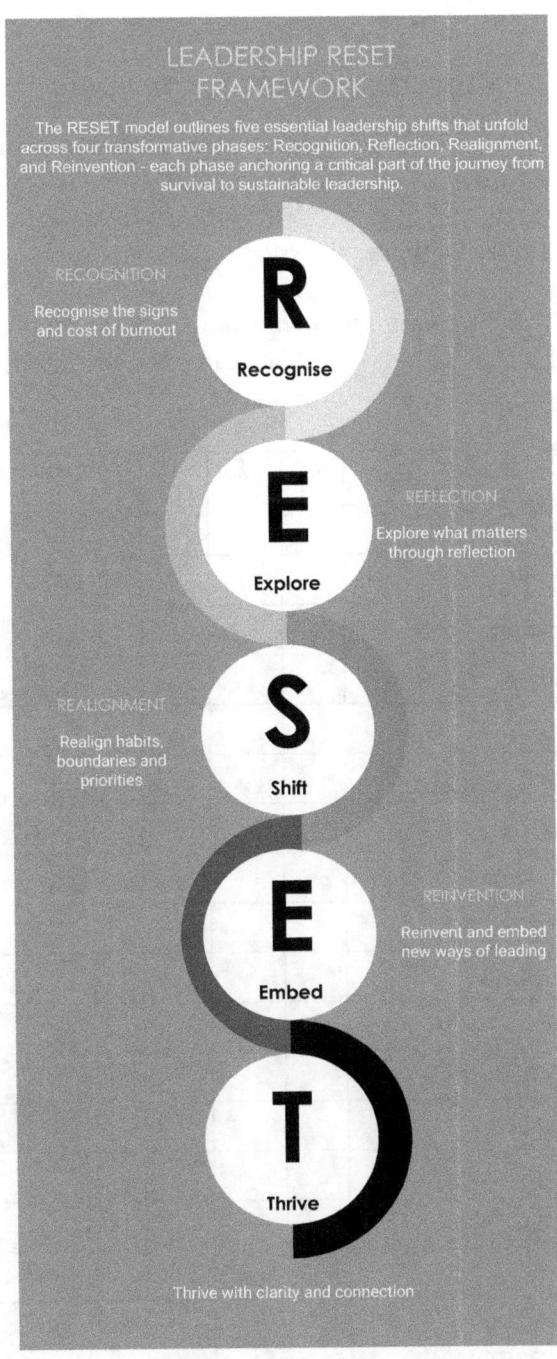

Phase 1: Recognition
BURNOUT SYMPTOM TRACKER

PURPOSE: To help you identify your unique burnout warning signs and track them over time.

ESTIMATED TIME: 5 minutes daily for at least one week

INSTRUCTIONS: Rate each symptom from 1–5 (1 = not present, 5 = severe) daily for at least one week. Note patterns and triggers associated with higher scores.

Date:	Mon	Tue	Wed	Thu	Fri	Sat	Sun	Patterns/Triggers
Physical Symptoms								
Fatigue/exhaustion								
Sleep disturbances								
Headaches/tension								
Emotional Symptoms								
Irritability								
Detachment								
Anxiety								
Cognitive Symptoms								
Decision fatigue								
Concentration issues								
Memory lapses								
Behavioural Symptoms								
Withdrawal from others								
Procrastination								
Increased reliance on coping mechanisms								

INTERPRETATION:

- Scores of 3+ on multiple symptoms: Implement immediate interventions
- Consistent patterns across several days: Address underlying causes
- Specific triggers identified: Develop targeted strategies for these situations

COMMENTS:

LEADERSHIP BURNOUT PREVENTION AND RECOVERY CHEAT SHEET

PURPOSE: To provide a quick reference guide for preventing and addressing burnout symptoms.

ESTIMATED TIME: 2-minute daily check-in

INSTRUCTIONS: Review this cheat sheet regularly and use it to quickly identify warning signs and implement appropriate recovery strategies.

TOP 5 WARNING SIGNS OF BURNOUT:

1. Emotional Exhaustion
    - Feeling mentally drained, overwhelmed, or unable to cope with day-to-day tasks.
2. Detachment from Work
    - Loss of passion or motivation, feeling disconnected from the purpose of your role.
3. Increased Irritability
    - Becoming easily frustrated or impatient with colleagues, family, or minor setbacks.
4. Decreased Productivity
    - Struggling to focus, frequent procrastination, or taking longer than usual to complete tasks.
5. Physical Symptoms
    - Recurring headaches, fatigue, sleep disturbances, or muscle tension.

KEY STRATEGIES FOR BURNOUT RECOVERY:

1. Delegate Tasks
    - Action: Identify tasks that don't require your direct involvement. Train and empower team members to handle these responsibilities.
    - Why: Delegating lowers cognitive load, prevents decision fatigue, and builds team capacity.
2. Use Reflective Practices
    - Action: Set aside 10 minutes at the end of each day to reflect on your emotional state, challenges, and achievements.

- Why: Reflective journaling helps you recognise stressors early, improving emotional regulation and self awareness.
3. Prioritise Wellbeing in Your Calendar
   - Action: Block specific times in your calendar for self care activities. Treat these appointments as non-negotiable meetings.
   - Why: Scheduling wellbeing ensures it remains a priority and creates a life work integration that promotes resilience.

REALIGNMENT CHECKLIST:

- Am I consistently spending time on my top leadership priorities?
- Are my current duties aligned with my core values?
- What tasks or responsibilities can I delegate to focus more on strategic thinking?
- Have I set clear boundaries between work and personal life?
- How often do I engage in activities that recharge my energy?

COMMENTS:

BURNOUT TYPE ASSESSMENT

PURPOSE: To identify which type of burnout is most affecting you and apply targeted interventions.

ESTIMATED TIME: 10–15 minutes

INSTRUCTIONS: Rate each statement from 1–5 (1 = strongly disagree, 5 = strongly agree) based on your experience in the past month.

Emotional Burnout

_____ I feel emotionally drained at the end of the workday
_____ I find it difficult to empathise with colleagues or team members
_____ I feel detached from the purpose of my work
_____ I struggle to maintain enthusiasm about my work
_____ Emotional interactions at work feel particularly taxing

Total: _____

Cognitive Burnout

_____ I struggle to focus on complex tasks
_____ Decision making feels unusually difficult or draining
_____ I find myself forgetting important details
_____ My thinking feels foggy or unclear
_____ I avoid tasks requiring concentrated mental effort

Total: _____

Physical Burnout

_____ I feel physically exhausted regardless of sleep
_____ I experience frequent tension headaches or muscle pain
_____ My sleep is disrupted or non-restorative
_____ I get sick more frequently than usual
_____ I lack energy for physical activity

Total: _____

Relational Burnout

_____ I avoid social interactions at work when possible
_____ I find colleague relationships more draining than energising
_____ I am more irritable or impatient with others
_____ Team dynamics feel more challenging to navigate
_____ I prefer working alone rather than collaboratively

Total: _____

Spiritual Burnout

_____ My work feels disconnected from my values
_____ I question the meaning or purpose of my role
_____ I feel a sense of disillusionment about my work
_____ I struggle to connect with the mission of my organisation
_____ The gap between my ideals and reality feels widening

Total: _____

INTERPRETATION:

- Your highest score indicates your primary burnout type
- Scores above 20 in any category indicate significant burnout in that dimension
- Review the type specific interventions in Chapter 2 for your primary burnout type

COMMENTS:

ENERGY LEVEL TRACKER

PURPOSE: To identify patterns in your daily energy fluctuations and optimise your schedule accordingly.

ESTIMATED TIME: 2 minutes, three times daily for two weeks

INSTRUCTIONS: Track your energy levels across the day for two weeks, noting your energy on a scale from 1 to 10 (1 = completely drained, 10 = highly energised).

Date	Morning (8am–12pm)	Afternoon (12–4pm)	Evening (4–8pm)	Key Activities
Monday				
Tuesday				
Wednesday				
Thursday				
Friday				

IDENTIFY PATTERNS:

- When do you typically experience energy dips?
- Are there specific activities that coincide with low energy points?
- Do your highest energy moments align with your most important tasks?

ADJUST WORKFLOWS TO MATCH ENERGY LEVELS:

Based on your findings, restructure your schedule to align high priority tasks with your peak energy times. For example, if you find that your energy dips in the afternoon, schedule meetings or lower-demand tasks during that time, and reserve your highest-energy hours for creative or strategic work.

COMMENTS:

BURNOUT DIALOGUE TOOLKIT

PURPOSE: To help you prepare for conversations about burnout with peers, team members, or mentors.

ESTIMATED TIME: 15 minutes for preparation, 30–45 minutes for conversation

INSTRUCTIONS: Use this toolkit to structure effective conversations about burnout and wellbeing.

STEP 1: IDENTIFY TRUSTED COLLEAGUES: Write down the names of two trusted colleagues or mentors with whom you feel comfortable discussing your stress levels and burnout risk:

1.

2.

STEP 2: CONVERSATION STARTERS: Choose from these conversation openers:

- "I've noticed I'm feeling overwhelmed lately, and I'm seeing some signs of burnout. I'd value your perspective on how I might manage this better."
- "I'm working on being more proactive about preventing burnout. Could I talk through some of the challenges I'm facing and get your input?"
- "I've observed that you seem to maintain good boundaries at work. Would you be willing to share some strategies that have worked for you?"

STEP 3: GUIDED QUESTIONS: Select 3–4 questions that feel most relevant to your situation:

- "Have you ever experienced burnout, and how did you recognise and manage it?"
- "What do you think contributes most to burnout in our organisation?"

- "I'm considering delegating more tasks to reduce my stress. What's your experience with delegation, and what challenges have you faced?"
- "How do you maintain boundaries between work and personal life?"
- "What sustainable practices have you found most helpful in managing your energy?"

STEP 4: ACTIVE LISTENING REMINDERS: During the conversation, remember to:

- Ask clarifying questions
- Acknowledge insights shared
- Take notes on key strategies mentioned
- Express appreciation for their time and insights

STEP 5: APPLY PEER FEEDBACK: After the conversation, write down one piece of advice or perspective shared by your colleague and how you plan to apply it:

Insight from conversation: _____

How I'll apply this: _____

COMMENTS:

Phase 2: Reflection

REFLECTIVE LEADERSHIP JOURNAL

PURPOSE: To establish a regular reflection practice that builds self awareness and insight.

ESTIMATED TIME: 15–30 minutes weekly

INSTRUCTIONS: Schedule dedicated time weekly to respond to these prompts. Date each entry and track patterns over time.

Date: _____

ENERGY ASSESSMENT:

This week, I felt most energised when:
This week, I felt most depleted when:
On a scale of 1–10, my overall energy level this week was: _____

EMOTIONAL AWARENESS:

The dominant emotions I experienced this week were:
These emotions were triggered by:
How I responded to these emotions:

LEADERSHIP CHALLENGES:

The most significant leadership challenge I faced this week was:
How I handled this challenge:
What I would do differently next time:

VALUE ALIGNMENT:

Moments when my leadership aligned with my values:
Situations where I compromised my values:
One adjustment I could make to better align with my values:

INSIGHTS AND ACTIONS:

Key insight from this week's reflection:
Specific action I will take based on this insight:
Support I need to implement this action:

COMMENTS:

VALUES CLARITY EXERCISE

PURPOSE: To identify your core values and assess how well your leadership aligns with them.

ESTIMATED TIME: 30–45 minutes

INSTRUCTIONS: Complete each section thoughtfully, focusing on what matters most to you as a leader.

1. VALUES IDENTIFICATION: Review the following common values and circle the ten that resonate most strongly with you:

Achievement | Balance | Collaboration | Creativity | Excellence | Family | Growth | Honesty | Impact | Innovation | Integrity | Justice | Kindness | Learning Loyalty | Meaning | Openness | Perseverance | Recognition | Respect | Security Service | Spirituality | Success | Trust | Vision | Wellbeing | Wisdom

Now, narrow your selection to your top five values:

1.

2.

3.

4.

5.

2. VALUES ALIGNMENT ASSESSMENT: For each of your top five values, rate how well your current leadership approach aligns with this value (1 = poor alignment, 10 = perfect alignment):

Value	Alignment (1–10)	Example of Alignment	Example of Misalignment
1.			
2.			
3.			
4.			
5.			

3. VALUES BASED LEADERSHIP VISION: Based on your core values, describe what ideal leadership looks like for you:

When leading in full alignment with my values, I would:

The impact this would have on my team would be:

The impact this would have on me personally would be:

4. ACTION STEPS FOR GREATER ALIGNMENT: For each value with an alignment score below 7, identify one concrete step you can take to bring your leadership into greater alignment:

Value	Action Step	Timeline	Support Needed
1.			
2.			
3.			

COMMENTS:

LEADERSHIP RELATIONSHIP MAP

PURPOSE: To assess how your key relationships impact your leadership energy and effectiveness.

ESTIMATED TIME: 20–30 minutes

INSTRUCTIONS: Identify important relationships in your leadership context and evaluate their current impact on your wellbeing.

STEP 1: RELATIONSHIP IDENTIFICATION: List the 8–10 most significant professional relationships in your leadership role:

Person	Role/Relationship	Frequency of Interaction

STEP 2: RELATIONSHIP ENERGY ASSESSMENT: For each relationship, assess its impact on your energy and wellbeing:

Person	Energy Impact (-5 to +5)	Key Dynamics	Improvement Opportunity

Energy Impact Scale:

- +5: Highly energising, consistently positive impact
- 0: Neutral impact on energy
- −5: Highly draining, consistently negative impact

STEP 3: RELATIONSHIP STRATEGY DEVELOPMENT:

For your most energising relationships (+3 to +5):

- How can I invest more in these relationships?
- What makes these interactions positive?

For your most draining relationships (-3 to -5):

- What boundaries need to be established?
- How might I transform the dynamic?
- What support do I need in managing these relationships?

COMMENTS:

REFLECTIVE LEADERSHIP VISION EXERCISE

PURPOSE: To translate your reflections into a compelling future vision for your leadership.

ESTIMATED TIME: 20–30 minutes

INSTRUCTIONS: Use this structured exercise to visualise and articulate your ideal future leadership state.

STEP 1: IMAGINING FUTURE SUCCESS: Imagine your leadership 12 months from now. You've overcome burnout and are leading in a way that feels fulfilling and sustainable.

What does a typical day look like?
How do you feel at the beginning and end of each day?
How do you interact with your team?
What has changed in how you approach leadership?
What habits or practices have you introduced that are working well?
How has your life work integration improved?

STEP 2: CREATE A VISION STATEMENT: Based on your reflections, write a short "Leadership Vision Statement" that captures your goals for becoming a more balanced, resilient leader:

STEP 3: VISUALISATION AND ACTION: Place this vision statement somewhere visible (e.g., your workspace). Reflect on this statement weekly and identify one small step you can take each week to move towards this vision:

Week 1 Action Step: _____

Week 2 Action Step: _____

Week 3 Action Step: _____

COMMENTS:

Phase 3: Realignment
PRIORITY MATRIX WORKSHEET

PURPOSE: To realign your time and energy with your core priorities and values.

ESTIMATED TIME: 30–45 minutes

INSTRUCTIONS: Categorise your current responsibilities and develop appropriate strategies for each category.

STEP 1: TASK CATEGORISATION: List your key responsibilities and categorise them according to the priority matrix:

Important and Urgent

Tasks: _____

Strategy: Handle immediately, then analyse why these became urgent

Time allocation: _____ hours/week

Important and Not Urgent

Tasks: _____

Strategy: Schedule protected time, invest proactively

Time allocation: _____ hours/week (aim to increase this category)

Not Important and Urgent

Tasks: _____

Strategy: Delegate or develop systems to handle efficiently

Time allocation: _____ hours/week (aim to reduce)

Not Important and Not Urgent

Tasks: _____

Strategy: Eliminate or severely minimise

Time allocation: _____ hours/week (aim to minimise)

STEP 2: TIME ALLOCATION ANALYSIS: Current time allocation:

- Important and Urgent: _____%

- Important and Not Urgent: _____%

- Not Important and Urgent: _____%

- Not Important and Not Urgent: _____%

Target time allocation:

- Important and Urgent: 15–20%

- Important and Not Urgent: 60–70%

- Not Important and Urgent: 10–15%

- Not Important and Not Urgent: <5%

STEP 3: REALIGNMENT ACTIONS: Identify specific actions to shift your time allocation towards your target:

Current Task	Current Category	Target Category	Action to Shift	By When

COMMENTS:

BOUNDARY SETTING PROTOCOL

PURPOSE: To establish and maintain clear boundaries that protect your wellbeing and effectiveness.

ESTIMATED TIME: 30 minutes to create, 10 minutes weekly to review

INSTRUCTIONS: Define specific boundaries for different domains of your leadership role.

STEP 1: BOUNDARY DEFINITION:

Boundary Type	Current State	Desired State	Gap
Time Boundaries			
Working hours			
Email/message response			
Meeting parameters			
Responsibility Boundaries			
Task delegation			
Decision authority			
Problem ownership			
Personal Boundaries			
Work-free zones			
Recovery periods			
Personal priorities			

STEP 2: BOUNDARY COMMUNICATION SCRIPTS: For each boundary type, prepare clear communication to share with relevant stakeholders:

Time Boundary Script: "To ensure I can deliver on our key priorities effectively, I'll be [specific boundary, e.g., 'available for emails between 8am and 6pm weekdays']. For urgent matters outside these hours, please [alternative contact method]. This helps me bring my best focus to our work during core hours."

Responsibility Boundary Script: "I'm working to ensure our team operates at its highest capacity. Going forward, [specific team member] will be handling [specific responsibility]. I'll remain available for guidance on complex issues, but empowering the team in this way allows me to focus on [strategic priorities]."

Personal Boundary Script: "I've found that protecting time for [personal priority] significantly improves my leadership effectiveness. I'll be blocking [specific time] for this purpose. This practice helps me bring renewed energy and perspective to our work together."

STEP 3: BOUNDARY IMPLEMENTATION PLAN:

Boundary	Implementation Date	Potential Challenges	Mitigation Strategies	Support Needed

COMMENTS:

DELEGATION DECISION TREE

PURPOSE: To help you identify which tasks to delegate and to whom.

ESTIMATED TIME: 20–30 minutes

INSTRUCTIONS: Use this decision tree to analyse tasks and determine appropriate delegation.

STEP 1: TASK ANALYSIS: For each task you currently manage, answer these questions:

Is this task critical to my unique role as a leader?

- Yes ' Keep, unless overloaded

- No ' Continue to question 2

Does this task require my specific expertise?

- Yes ' Consider training someone while retaining oversight

- No ' Continue to question 3

Would this task develop someone else's skills?

- Yes ' Delegate as development opportunity

- No ' Continue to question 4

Is this task routine or administrative?

- Yes ' Delegate completely

- No ' Consider partial delegation with oversight

STEP 2: DELEGATION PLANNING:

Task	Decision	Delegate To	Support Required	Check-in Frequency

STEP 3: EFFECTIVE DELEGATION CHECKLIST: For each task being delegated, ensure you:

- Clearly explain the purpose of the task

- Define what success looks like

- Establish authority levels and decision rights

- Agree on check-in schedule and format

- Provide necessary resources and support

- Discuss how problems should be escalated

- Clarify how the task connects to broader goals

COMMENTS:

Phase 4: Reinvention
LEADERSHIP IDENTITY CANVAS

PURPOSE: To craft a new leadership identity aligned with your values and sustainable practices.

ESTIMATED TIME: 45–60 minutes

INSTRUCTIONS: Complete each section thoughtfully to define your reinvented leadership approach.

LEADERSHIP PURPOSE STATEMENT: My purpose as a leader is to:

CORE LEADERSHIP PRINCIPLES: The fundamental principles that guide my leadership decisions and actions:

1.

2.

3.

4.

5.

LEADERSHIP PRACTICES: Daily practices:

Weekly practices:

Monthly practices:

LEADERSHIP BOUNDARIES: What I will no longer do:

How I will protect these boundaries:

LEADERSHIP DEVELOPMENT FOCUS: Areas I am actively developing:

How I will measure growth in these areas:

LEADERSHIP LEGACY: The impact I want my leadership to have:

On my team: _____

On my organisation: _____

On myself: _____

COMMENTS:

DAILY LEADERSHIP PRACTICE PLAN

PURPOSE: To embed sustainable leadership practices into your daily routine.

ESTIMATED TIME: 10 minutes to complete, practices vary in duration

INSTRUCTIONS: Establish consistent practices that reinforce your new leadership identity.

Time	Practice	Purpose	Duration
Morning			
Before checking email	Intention setting	Focus and purpose	3–5 min
Start of workday	Priority review	Strategic focus	5–10 min
Throughout Day			
Between meetings	Recovery breath	Reset and refocus	2–3 min
Before decisions	Values check	Alignment	1–2 min
After challenges	Reflection pause	Learning	3–5 min
End of Day			
Work completion	Closure ritual	Work/life boundary	5 min
Evening	Gratitude practice	Perspective	3–5 min

CUSTOMISE YOUR PLAN:

Time	Practice	Purpose	Duration
Morning			
Throughout Day			
End of Day			

IMPLEMENTATION NOTES:

- Start with just 1 2 practices rather than implementing all at once

- Link new practices to existing habits to improve consistency

- Review effectiveness after two weeks and adjust as needed

COMMENTS:

LEADERSHIP WELLBEING INTEGRATION CHECKLIST

PURPOSE: To ensure wellbeing is embedded in your leadership approach.

ESTIMATED TIME: 15–20 minutes to complete, ongoing implementation.

INSTRUCTIONS: Use this checklist to assess and enhance how wellbeing is integrated into your leadership.

PERSONAL WELLBEING INTEGRATION:

- I have scheduled non-negotiable time for physical activity
- I have clear start and end times to my workday
- I have established technology-free periods
- I have identified and scheduled activities that restore my energy
- I have set up reminders for regular breaks throughout the day
- I have created a restful sleep environment and routine
- I have defined what "emergency" truly means in my context
- I have established support systems for high pressure periods

TEAM WELLBEING INTEGRATION:

- I explicitly discuss wellbeing with my team
- I model healthy boundaries through my actions
- I recognise and reward sustainable work practices
- I check in on team members' energy and capacity regularly

- I adjust expectations during high demand periods

- I encourage use of leave and recovery time

- I provide flexibility where possible

- I create psychological safety for discussing wellbeing concerns

ORGANISATIONAL WELLBEING INTEGRATION:

- I advocate for wellbeing centred policies

- I highlight the connection between wellbeing and performance

- I challenge unsustainable practices or expectations

- I measure success beyond just traditional performance metrics

- I include wellbeing considerations in strategic planning

- I hold other leaders accountable for sustainable practices

- I acknowledge the organisational factors that impact wellbeing

- I celebrate progress in creating a more sustainable culture

COMMENTS:

Organisational Solutions
DIGITAL BOUNDARY PROTOCOL

PURPOSE: To establish healthy boundaries in hybrid and remote work environments.

ESTIMATED TIME: 30 minutes to create, 10 minutes weekly to review

INSTRUCTIONS: Create clear protocols for digital communication and availability.

DIGITAL AVAILABILITY SCHEDULE:

Time Period	Availability Status	Response Expectation
Early Morning		
Core Hours		
Late Afternoon		
Evening		
Weekend		
Leave/Holiday		

COMMUNICATION CHANNEL PROTOCOL:

Channel	Purpose	Response Time	After-Hours Protocol
Email			
Chat/Messaging			
Video Calls			
Phone			
Text Messages			

DIGITAL BOUNDARY IMPLEMENTATION: Technology settings to support boundaries:

- Calendar working hours configured

- Email signature with availability expectations

- Automatic out-of-office responses

- Notification settings customised

- Do Not Disturb modes scheduled

- Separate work/personal profiles on devices

- Email/messaging app time restrictions

DIGITAL BOUNDARY COMMUNICATION:

Email signature example:

"I check emails between [times] on [days]. For urgent matters requiring immediate attention, please [alternative contact method]. This helps me provide focused attention to priorities and respond thoughtfully to communications."

Team communication example:

"To ensure sustainable work practices, I'm implementing clearer digital boundaries. I'll be fully available during [core hours] and will respond to messages during these times. Outside these hours, I'll respond the next working day unless it's genuinely urgent. I encourage everyone to establish boundaries that work for their situation."

COMMENTS:

RECOVERY MICRO-PRACTICES

PURPOSE: Quick interventions to reset your system during the workday.

ESTIMATED TIME: Varies from 1–10 minutes per practice

INSTRUCTIONS: Select practices that resonate with you and implement them during your workday at transition points or when feeling depleted.

Time Required	Practice	Benefit
1 Minute		
	Box breathing (four-count inhale, hold, exhale, hold)	Activates parasympathetic nervous system
	Progressive muscle tensing/releasing	Releases physical tension
	Three gratitude statements	Shifts perspective from stress to appreciation
3–5 Minutes		
	Body scan meditation	Increases body awareness and releases tension
	Perspective journaling (write three sentences)	Creates cognitive distance from stressors
	Sensory grounding (5-4-3-2-1 technique)	Resets attention and reduces rumination
10 Minutes		
	Walking meditation outside	Combines movement with mindfulness
	Guided relaxation audio	Deepens relaxation response
	Creative visualisation	Activates imagination and reduces stress

IMPLEMENTATION TIPS:

- Link these practices to existing habits (e.g., after meetings, before lunch)

- Set reminders or use environmental cues

- Start with 1 2 practices rather than trying all at once

COMMENTS:

COMMUNICATION SCRIPTS FOR HEALTHY BOUNDARIES

PURPOSE: Ready-to-use language for establishing and maintaining boundaries.

ESTIMATED TIME: 5–10 minutes to review before needed conversations

INSTRUCTIONS: Select and adapt these scripts to fit your specific circumstances and communication style.

DECLINING NON-ESSENTIAL MEETINGS:

"Thank you for thinking of me for this meeting. Based on my current priorities and workload, I need to decline. If there are specific items you'd like my input on, I'd be happy to provide feedback via email."

SETTING EMAIL EXPECTATIONS:

"I check emails during [specific times]. For urgent matters requiring immediate attention, please [alternative contact method]. This helps me provide focused attention to priorities and respond thoughtfully to communications."

PROTECTING FOCUS TIME:

"I've scheduled focused work time from [time] to [time] to progress on [project/task]. I'll be unavailable for meetings or immediate responses during this period. I'll check messages at [time] and respond then."

DELEGATING APPROPRIATELY:

"This is a great opportunity for [team member] to take the lead, with my support as needed. This aligns with their development goals while allowing me to focus on [strategic priorities]."

AFTER-HOURS BOUNDARY:

"I've noticed that I'm most effective when I disconnect from work in the evenings. I won't be checking messages after [time] or before [time], except in genuine emergencies. This helps me bring my best self to our work during core hours."

COMMUNICATING CAPACITY LIMITS:

"I currently have several high priority commitments that require my full attention. Taking this on would impact my ability to deliver quality work. Could we discuss timeline flexibility or alternative resources?"

ORGANISATIONAL BURNOUT ASSESSMENT

PURPOSE: To identify organisational factors contributing to burnout within your organisation.

ESTIMATED TIME: 30–45 minutes

INSTRUCTIONS: Rate each factor from 1 to 5 (1 = major contributor to burnout, 5 = effectively prevents burnout).

LEADERSHIP CULTURE:

_____ Leaders model sustainable practices

_____ Wellbeing is discussed openly

_____ Leaders are supported during high pressure periods

_____ Success is defined beyond just performance metrics

_____ Vulnerability is seen as strength, not weakness

Subtotal: _____/25

WORKLOAD MANAGEMENT:

_____ Workloads are realistic and regularly assessed

_____ Resources match expectations

_____ Capacity is considered in planning and deadlines

_____ Priorities are clear and consistently communicated

_____ Unnecessary work is eliminated

Subtotal: _____/25

RECOVERY AND BOUNDARIES:

_____ Leave is encouraged and fully taken

_____ After-hours communication is minimised

_____ Meetings are efficient and purposeful

_____ Breaks are built into the workday

_____ Technology supports rather than erodes boundaries

Subtotal: _____/25

SUPPORT SYSTEMS:

_____ Mental health resources are readily available

_____ Peer support networks exist for leaders

_____ Professional development includes wellbeing

_____ Coaching or mentoring is accessible

_____ Teams are adequately resourced

Subtotal: _____/25

ORGANISATIONAL POLICIES:

_____ Flexible work options are available and supported

_____ Performance reviews include wellbeing dimensions

_____ Promotion criteria include sustainable leadership

_____ Crisis protocols prevent burnout during high demand

_____ Organisational stressors are regularly assessed and addressed

Subtotal: _____/25

Overall Assessment: _____/125

INTERPRETATION:

- 100–125: Excellent burnout prevention culture

- 75–99: Good foundation with room for improvement

- 50–74: Significant burnout risk factors present

- Below 50: Urgent intervention needed to address organisational burnout

PRIORITY AREAS FOR INTERVENTION:

1.

2.

3.

4.

5.

COMMENTS:

LEADERSHIP TEAM RESILIENCE CHECK

PURPOSE: To assess collective burnout risk factors and build proactive strategies for team wellbeing.

ESTIMATED TIME: 30–45 minutes with full leadership team

INSTRUCTIONS: Use these prompts in leadership meetings, retreats, or team development sessions to surface shared stressors, assess team wellbeing, and identify proactive strategies for reducing collective burnout risk.

- What patterns of stress or burnout are emerging across our team right now?

- How often do we check in on each others workload, wellbeing, or mental health?

- Do we reward overwork or model sustainable leadership practices?

- Are our meetings energising or draining? What could we change?

- Where are we duplicating effort or lacking role clarity?

- What conversations are we avoiding that may be fuelling tension?

- How do we collectively recover after periods of peak demand?

Team Activity: Choose two questions to discuss at your next leadership team meeting. Set a time to revisit the full list quarterly as a proactive culture check.

COMMENTS:

SHARED LEADERSHIP IMPLEMENTATION PLAN

PURPOSE: To distribute leadership responsibilities and reduce individual burden.

ESTIMATED TIME: 45–60 minutes

INSTRUCTIONS: Use this tool to design and implement a shared leadership approach.

STEP 1: LEADERSHIP MAPPING:

Team Member	Key Strengths	Areas of Expertise	Development Interests

STEP 2: SHARED LEADERSHIP MODEL SELECTION: Choose the model that best fits your context:

- Domain Based Leadership (divided by expertise areas)

- Rotational Leadership (rotating specific responsibilities)

- Situational Leadership (based on specific challenges)

- Distributed Decision Making (clear decision rights)

STEP 3: RESPONSIBILITY DISTRIBUTION:

Leadership Domain	Primary Leader	Secondary/Support	Decision Authority	Coordination Method

STEP 4: SHARED LEADERSHIP PROTOCOLS:

Decision making process:

- How decisions are made within domains: _____

- How cross-domain decisions are handled: _____

- How conflicts are resolved: _____

Communication structure:

- Regular coordination meetings: _____

- Information sharing protocols: _____

- Handover processes: _____

STEP 5: IMPLEMENTATION TIMELINE:

Phase	Activities	Timeframe	Success Indicators
Preparation			
Initial Implementation			
Refinement			
Full Integration			

COMMENTS:

Quick Reference Guides
WARNING SIGNS QUICK REFERENCE

PURPOSE: A portable reminder of key burnout warning signs to watch for.

ESTIMATED TIME: 2-minute check-in

INSTRUCTIONS: Review this chart regularly to identify early signs of burnout and implement appropriate responses.

Category	Early Warning Signs	Red Flags
Physical	• Persistent tiredness	• Extreme exhaustion
	• Tension headaches	• Frequent illness
	• Minor sleep disturbances	• Insomnia
Emotional	• Irritability	• Emotional numbness
	• Reduced empathy	• Cynicism
	• Decreased enthusiasm	• Feeling trapped
Cognitive	• Difficulty focusing	• Decision paralysis
	• Procrastination	• Persistent brain fog
	• Decreased creativity	• Major memory issues
Behavioural	• Skipping breaks	• Withdrawal from colleagues
	• Working through lunch	• Increased reliance on substances
	• Checking email after hours	• Absenteeism

IMMEDIATE RESPONSE STRATEGIES:

- **Physical:** 10-minute walk outside, stretch break, power nap

- **Emotional:** 5-minute mindfulness practice, connect with supportive colleague

- **Cognitive:** Task batching, postpone non-critical decisions, delegate

- **Behavioural:** Set firm boundary, schedule recovery time, seek support

COMMENTS:

LEADERSHIP RESET WEEKLY CHECK-IN

PURPOSE: To monitor your progress in implementing the Leadership Reset Framework.

ESTIMATED TIME: 5–10 minutes weekly

INSTRUCTIONS: Complete this brief check-in each week to track your progress and make necessary adjustments.

Date: _____

FRAMEWORK PROGRESS: Rate your progress in each phase (1 = not started, 5 = fully implemented):

Phase 1 (Burnout): _____

- Key action taken this week: _____
- Next step: _____

Phase 2 (Reflection): _____

- Key action taken this week: _____
- Next step: _____

Phase 3 (Realignment): _____

- Key action taken this week: _____
- Next step: _____

Phase 4 (Reinvention): _____

- Key action taken this week: _____
- Next step: _____

WELLBEING INDICATORS: Rate each indicator (1 = poor, 10 = excellent):

Energy level: _____

Emotional balance: _____

Quality of relationships: _____

Value alignment: _____

Life work integration: _____

WEEKLY REFLECTION: One success this week:

One challenge I faced:

Adjustment needed for next week:

Support I need to seek:

PRIORITY FOR NEXT WEEK: My top reset priority for next week is:

COMMENTS:

SUSTAINABLE SUCCESS REMINDER

PURPOSE: A pocket-sized reminder of key principles of sustainable leadership.

ESTIMATED TIME: 1-minute periodic review

INSTRUCTIONS: Keep this card accessible and review it regularly, especially before making key decisions.

SUSTAINABLE LEADERSHIP PRINCIPLES:

1. **Effectiveness ≠ Exhaustion:** Success is measured by impact, not hours worked.

2. **Boundaries Create Freedom:** Clear boundaries enable focused, purposeful leadership.

3. **Delegation = Development:** Empower others to grow while freeing your focus.

4. **Wellbeing Drives Performance:** Your energy management directly impacts your leadership quality.

5. **Values Guide Decisions:** Let your core values be your leadership compass.

QUICK RESET TECHNIQUES:

- **60-Second Breath Reset:** Six deep breaths, focus on exhaling completely.

- 2-Minute Mindful Check-In: Body, emotions, thoughts, needs.

- 3-Minute Priority Reset: What actually matters most right now?

- 5-Minute Energy Boost: Quick movement, fresh air, water, protein.

- **10-Minute Boundary Reinforcement:** Say no, delegate, or reschedule one thing.

REMEMBER: Your effectiveness as a leader is directly connected to your wellbeing. Prioritise sustainable practices today for long term impact.

COMMENTS:

INDEX

"always on" culture 22, 45, 48, 54, 105, 173
anxiety 15, 48, 61, 79, 107
artificial intelligence integration 172–173
asynchronous communication 170
Atlassian 50, 175
Australian organisations 153–154
Australian Principal Occupational Health, Safety and Wellbeing Survey 76, 191–192
Australian Public Service Commission 50, 154

Bendigo and Adelaide Bank 154
boundary setting: digital boundaries 55, 176, 259; communication scripts 56, 263; implementation strategies 55
brain function: amygdala 61–65; hippocampus 62, 65, 67; neuroplasticity 48, 61, 64, 68, 72; prefrontal cortex 12, 48, 61, 62, 64, 65, 68, 72, 75; stress effects 43, 61, 71

burnout: costs of 74–78; definition (WHO) 9; early warning signs 25–26; economic impact 35; gender differences 20, 79; generational perspectives 104–105; global trends 17, 33–34; grief 23; identity crisis 10; industry specific patterns 18–20; numbers 10; symptoms 13–15; *vs.* workplace fatigue 12–13
burnout, types of: cognitive 29, 45; compassion 32; creative 32; cultural 36; decision 33; emotional 28; neurodivergent 36; occupational 30; organisational 35; physical 29; relational 31; spiritual 34

case studies: Australian education 75; financial services 80; Google 78, 158; healthcare sector 80; Microsoft 78; NHS 188; Patagonia 155; Salesforce 197; Spotify 188; Unilever 78, 159; Zappos 188
cognitive behavioural therapy (CBT) 61, 67, 199

communication: asynchronous 170; digital protocols 176; scripts for boundaries 56, 71
COVID-19 pandemic impact 2, 28

decision fatigue 33, 106, 174, 180
Delegation: decision tree 251; Matrix 131; task 52, 182
depression: major depressive disorder 15, 89, 107

Eisenhower Matrix 128
emotional intelligence: coaching 28, 211; development 157; emotional regulation 157; in prevention 157; training participants 157

fatigue: digital 168–169; digital wellness 175; overconnectivity 168; Zoom 168
Five Dysfunctions of a Team 186
flourishing: concept 48
Ford Health Program 152
frazzle: neurological state 62–63

healthcare sector burnout 80
human sustainability 155–157
hybrid work environments: challenges 166–169; solutions 169

industry specific burnout: education 18, 34, 80; healthcare 18, 80; technology 174

journaling: Audio Journaling 121; reflective practices 116, 122, 158

key performance indicators (KPIs): wellbeing as KPI 53, 158

leadership: balanced 49; circles 185; coaching 160; identity canvas 144, 253; legacy planning 141, 144; life fist 53; pipeline development 196, 202; pressure cooker 11; shared models 181–183; sustainability 50
Leadership RESET: approach 18, 88–91; overview 88–89; phase 1: recognition 102–114; phase 2: reflection 115–126; phase 3: realignment 127–135; phase 4: reinvention 136–148; phases 88–89
life work integration: vs. work life balance 44–48

major depressive disorder (MDD) 89, 217
meditation: mindfulness-based stress reduction 64
mental health: breaks 170; support systems 160
micro-recovery practices 139–140
Microsoft case studies 78
mindfulness 64
moral injury 34

neuroplasticity: brain adaptation 61; mindfulness 64; recovery potential 68
NHS peer mentoring 188

organisational solutions: culture change 154–155; policy development 162; support systems 160–161

peer support networks: leadership circles 185; mentoring programs 184–185
priority matrix 128

recovery: micro-practices 70, 139–140; neurological aspects 60–72
remote work challenges 166–172

resilience: building strategies 203, 212; challenges 192; emotional resilience 184, 190; team resilience 33

Scandinavian leadership models 49
self-care 200
shared leadership: benefits 181; implementation 181–183; models 181–183
sleep 65
social connectivity 66
Spotify 188
stress management: leaders 199
succession planning 202–204

time blocking: personal priorities 52, for recovery 29

Unilever case study 78, 159

VicHealth initiatives 154

wellbeing: as KPI 158; centred leadership 197; integration checklist 207
WHO burnout definition 9
work life balance: *vs.* life work integration 45–46

Zappos holacracy model 188
Zoom fatigue 168

For Product Safety Concerns and Information please contact our EU representative GPSR@taylorandfrancis.com
Taylor & Francis Verlag GmbH, Kaufingerstraße 24, 80331 München, Germany

www.ingramcontent.com/pod-product-compliance
Lightning Source LLC
Chambersburg PA
CBHW061707300426
44115CB00014B/2592